Basic Concepts of Intercultural Communication

Selected Readings

INTERCULTURAL PRESS

A Nicholas Brealey Publishing Company

BOSTON • LONDON

First published by Intercultural Press, a Nicholas Brealey Publishing Company, in 1998. For information, contact:

Intercultural Press, Inc.,
a division of
Nicholas Brealey Publishing
100 City Hall Plaza, Suite 501
Boston, MA 02108, USA
Tel: (+) 617-523-3801
Fax: (+) 617-523-3708
www.interculturalpress.com

Nicholas Brealey Publishing
3-5 Spafield St., Clerkenwell
London, EC1R 4QB, UK
Tel: 44-207-239-0360
Fax: 44-207-239-0370
www.nbrealey-books.com

© 1998 by Intercultural Press

ISBN-13: 978-1-877864-62-9
ISBN-10: 1-877864-62-5

Printed in the United States of America

10   09   08   07   06   9   10 11 12 13

Library of Congress Cataloging-in-Publication Data

Basic concepts of intercultural communication: a reader/ edited by Milton J. Bennett.
    p.   cm.
    Includes bibliographical references and index.
    ISBN 1-877864-62-5
    1. Intercultural communication.   I. Bennett, Milton.
GN345.6.B37   1998
303.48'2—dc21   98–15278
                                                  CIP

Permissions

Grateful acknowledgment is made to the authors and publishers who granted permission to reprint the following articles:

Adler, Peter S. "Beyond Cultural Identity: Reflections on Multiculturalism." In *Culture Learning: Concepts, Applications, and Research*, edited by Richard W. Brislin, 24-41. Honolulu: University of Hawaii Press, 1977.

Banks, James A. "Multicultural Education: Development, Dimensions, and Challenges." *Phi Delta Kappan* (September 1993): 22-28.

Barna, LaRay M. "Stumbling Blocks in Intercultural Communication." In *Intercultural Communication, A Reader*, edited by Larry A. Samovar and Richard E. Porter, 7th ed., 337-46. Belmont: CA: Wadsworth, 1994.

Barnlund, Dean. "Communication in a Global Village." In *Public and Private Self*, 3-24. Yarmouth, ME: Intercultural Press, 1989.

Bennett, Janet M. "Transition Shock: Putting Culture Shock in Perspective." *International and Intercultural Communication Annual*, vol. 4. Falls Church, VA: Speech Communication Association, December 1977.

Bennett, Milton J. "Overcoming the Golden Rule: Sympathy and Empathy" *Communication Yearbook,* vol. 3. New Brunswick, NJ: Transaction Publishers, March 1966.

Hall, Edward T. "The Power of Hidden Differences." October 1991.

Kochman, Thomas. "Black and White Cultural Styles in Pluralistic Perspective." In *Test Policy and Test Performance: Education, Language, and Culture*, edited by Bernard R. Gifford, 259-95. Norwell, MA: Kluwer Academic Publishers, 1989.

Whorf, Benjamin Lee. "Science and Linguistics." In *Language, Thought, and Reality: The Selected Writings of Benjamin Lee Whorf,* edited by J. B. Carroll, 207-19. Cambridge, MA: MIT Press, 1956.

Table of Contents

Preface

There are two major schools of intercultural communication: the theory-and-research school and the theory-into-practice school. While these two approaches have not been formally defined, they are clearly differentiated by distinct professional organizations, conferences, and journals.

The theory-and-research school tends to be based on traditional sociological and communication perspectives and methods, and it is represented by divisions of the speech communication professional societies and by publications such as the *International and Intercultural Communication Annual*. The theory-into-practice school is more interdisciplinary, drawing on communication theory, psychology, anthropology, sociolinguistics, and other fields. This school is primarily represented by the Society for Intercultural Education, Training and Research (SIETAR) and by The Intercultural Communication Institute. Literature representing this perspective is published by Intercultural Press, Sage Publications, and the *International Journal of Intercultural Relations*, among others.

This book represents the theory-into-practice school. My goal in the book is to present basic concepts from a variety of perspectives which, when taken together, explicate the practical aspects of intercultural relations and present a compelling case for improving intercultural communication skills through education and training. The underlying assumption of this book is that good practice in facilitating intercultural relations must be accompanied by conceptual sophistication, and that good intercultural theory is that which can be applied pragmatically. This volume is not a "how to" book, except in the sense of how to think productively about the topic. It serves as an introduction to the topic of intercultural communication, and it also provides an overview of important concepts for established practitioners.

In addition to its contemporary usefulness, this book is meant to preserve some of the classic statements of what has become known as an intercultural perspective. As the intercultural field matures, more and more of the once-original contributions of its pioneers become the unconsciously accepted assumptions of its third- and fourth-generation practitioners. While this is a healthy sign of the ongoing consensus that defines any discipline, it also begs a reprise. I hope this book will remind us of our conceptual roots.

As a reprise, this book does not pretend to be comprehensive in its treatment of evolving intercultural topics or inclusive of the diversity of contemporary authors in the field. This is particularly true regarding the gender of the contributors, where happily the current crop of scholars is not so overwhelmingly male as the ones represented in this volume. Nor are all the important early contributors to intercultural communication represented here; many compromises were necessary to balance the inclusion of classic authors with coverage of "basic" material. I ask the forgiveness of those who were unfairly excluded from this volume, and I request the patience of readers who must look beyond this book to fully appreciate the variety of topics and authors writing on intercultural subjects today.

Educators will find that the concepts in this book are presented *in developmental sequence*. That is, I have arranged the readings in an order that builds bases for the subsequent material, with the goal of generating in readers a coherent conceptual picture rather than a potpourri of ideas. The rationale for this sequencing can be found in my introductory chapter. Using these readings as a core, educators can build courses that elaborate certain ideas and/or stress particular applications of the perspective.

Trainers will also appreciate the developmental sequence of readings, since, even more than in academic courses, the success of training programs depends on careful attention to the order and type of presentation. Trainers who are aware of underlying theoretical concepts and various sequencing strategies are better able to anticipate resistance, provide early inoculations, and generate with participants significant learning in the compressed format of typical programs. In terms of content, trainers will find that several of the articles provide neat conceptual frameworks that can be used in short programs.

Counselors, mental and physical health care clinicians, international education professionals, and others who work with cultural diversity will find this approach refreshing in its choice of concepts that relate directly to the actual practice of intercultural communication. Such communication demands constant flexibility—more than is provided by any set of techniques. Basic understanding of these core concepts will enable greater creativity of application.

For managers, administrators, and executives of organizations, this book will shed some light on the topic of diversity. With knowledge of the intercultural approach outlined here, people in the position of selecting or using outside consultants can do so with more savvy. They will find in these pages that intercultural communication is not an esoteric skill for overseas travelers, but that it is a constructive approach to managing diversity and providing employee training in domestic settings.

The introductory chapter, "Intercultural Communication: A Current Perspective," lays out a contemporary framework for a theory-into-practice approach to intercultural relations. It is a synthesis of various introductory lectures I have developed over the years for a wide range of audiences. As such, the introduction provides a current context for the concepts explicated in the rest of the book. For instance, the introduction defines culture in a way that includes both international and domestic diversity, an inclusive view of the subject that is relatively recent. It also presents ideas in a developmental sequence that is currently thought to be effective—perception, language, nonverbal behavior, communication style, value differences, and cultural adaptation. So the reader can easily follow up on ideas, I have incorporated references to the other articles in this volume into the introduction as much as possible.

In the first of three articles that provide conceptual overviews, Dean Barnlund's "Communication in a Global Village" establishes the vision that continues to motivate many of us in the field. This is followed by "The Power of Hidden Differences," a selection from the "first interculturalist," Edward T. Hall, which shows how the intercultural focus emerged from earlier studies of language and culture. A more recent addition to the intercultural vision is explored by James A. Banks in "Multicultural Education: Development, Dimensions, and Challenges." His exploration of diversity and domestic cultural pluralism indicates the value of an intercultural perspective in these important arenas.

Five articles illustrate aspects of intercultural communication processes, beginning with the classic statement of linguistic relativity by Benjamin Lee Whorf, "Science and Linguistics," and followed by a more psychologically based treatment of perception by Marshall R. Singer, "Culture: A Perceptual Approach." The effect on interaction of cultural differences in communication style is explored in an international context by Sheila J. Ramsey in "Interactions between North Americans and Japanese" and in a domestic context by Thomas Kochman in "Black and White Cultural Styles in Pluralistic Perspective." At the deep level of cultural values, Edward C. Stewart develops one of the field's most influential systems for analyzing cross-cultural value differences in "Cultural Assumptions and Values" by Stewart, Jack Danielian, and Robert J. Foster.

The last four articles focus on the general topic of cultural adaptation. LaRay M. Barna's venerable and readable article, "Stumbling Blocks in Intercultural Communication," leads off with a clear statement of adaptation problems illustrated by actual quotes from U.S. and foreign students. Her call for greater intercultural empathy is explored next in my article, "Overcoming the Golden Rule: Sympathy and Empathy." Janet M. Bennett's "Transition Shock" brings the somewhat alien notion of culture shock into the more familiar territory of loss and change, and Peter S. Adler presents a slightly revised version of his formative work on becoming a multicultural person, "Beyond Cultural Identity."

It is my hope that everyone who reads these authors will find some conceptually tasty morsels, and that a few will be drawn to the great feast of literature that now exists on this topic. In the several decades of its existence, the field of intercultural communication has generated some extremely effective ways to help people think and behave with more intercultural sensitivity. By providing a synthesis of concepts central to those efforts, this book challenges us to recognize and use what we may already know.

Acknowledgments

Thanks to the patience and perseverance of Toby Frank, Judy Carl-Hendrick, and Karen Hall at Intercultural Press; to the competence and well-modulated nagging of Kathryn Stillings at the Intercultural Institute; to the support of my wife, Janet Bennett, and her incredible mind for detail; and to all the authors whose words speak for themselves, this book could finally be published.

And to those who have passed this way before us, especially Dean Barnlund, thanks for leading the way.

Intercultural Communication: A Current Perspective

Milton J. Bennett

The study of intercultural communication has tried to answer the question, "How do people understand one another when they do not share a common cultural experience?" Just a few decades ago, this question was one faced mainly by diplomats, expatriates, and the occasional international traveler. Today, living in multicultural societies within a global village, we all face the question every day. We now realize that issues of intercultural understanding are embedded in other complex questions: What kind of communication is needed by a pluralistic society to be both culturally diverse and unified in common goals? How does communication contribute to creating a climate of respect, not just tolerance, for diversity? The new vision and innovative competencies we bring to this changing world will determine the answer to another question about the global village posed by Dean Barnlund: "Will its residents be neighbors capable of respecting and utilizing their differences or clusters of strangers living in ghettos and united only in their antipathies for others?"[1]

Dealing with Difference

If we look to our species' primate past and to our more recent history of dealing with cultural difference, there is little reason to be sanguine. Our initial response to difference is usually to avoid it. Imagine, if you will, a group of our primate ancestors gathered around their fire, gnawing on the day's catch. Another group of primates comes into view, heading toward the fire. I wonder how often the first group looked up and said (in effect), "Ah, cultural diversity, how wonderful." More likely it was fight or flight, and things have not changed that much since then. We flee to the suburbs or behind walls to avoid cultural difference, and if we are forced to confront it, there often is a fight.

Historically, if we were unsuccessful in avoiding different people, we tried to convert them. Political, economic, and religious missionaries sought out opportunities to impose their own beliefs on others. The thinking seemed to be, "If only people were more like us, then they would be all right to have around." This assumption can still be seen in the notion of the "melting pot" prevalent this century in the United States. It is difficult for many people to believe that any understanding at all is possible unless people have become similar to one another.

When we could not avoid or convert people who were different from ourselves, we killed them. Examples of genocide are not so very far away from us, either in time or distance, and individual cases of hate crimes are tragically frequent. Of course, one doesn't need to physically terminate the existence of others to effectively eliminate them. When we make their lives miserable in our organizations and neighborhoods, we also "kill" them—they cannot flourish, and often they do not survive.

Given this history of dealing with difference, it is no wonder that the topic of difference—understanding it, appreciating it, respecting it—is central to all practical treatments of intercultural communication. Yet this emphasis on difference departs from the common approaches to communication and relationships based within a single culture.

Monocultural communication is *similarity-based*. Common language, behavior patterns, and values form the base upon which members of the culture exchange meaning with one another in conducting their daily affairs. These similarities generally allow people to predict the responses of others to certain kinds of messages and to take for granted some basic shared assumptions about the nature of reality. In monocultural communication, difference represents the potential for misunderstanding and friction. Thus, social difference of all kinds is discouraged.

Intercultural communication—communication between people of different cultures—cannot allow the easy assumption of similarity. By definition, cultures are different in their languages, behavior patterns, and values. So an attempt to use one's self as a predictor of shared assumptions and responses to messages is unlikely to work.[2] Because cultures embody such variety in patterns of perception and behavior, approaches to communication in cross-cultural situations guard against inappropriate assumptions of similarity and encourage the consideration of difference. In other words, the intercultural communication approach is *difference-based*.[3]

Upper-Case *Culture* and Lower-Case *culture*

When people anticipate doing something *cultural* of an evening, their thoughts turn to art, literature, drama, classical music, or dance. In other words, they plan to participate in one of the *institutions* of culture—behavior that has become routinized into a particular form. I refer to this aspect of culture as "Culture writ large," with a capital "C." The more academic term that is used by most writers is *objective culture*.[4] Other examples of objective culture might include social, economic, political, and linguistic systems—the kinds of things that usually are included in area studies or history courses. The study of these institutions constitutes much of the curriculum in both international and multicultural education. For instance, courses in Japanese culture or African American culture are likely to focus on the history, political structure, and arts of the groups. While this is valuable information, it is limited in its utility to the face-to-face concerns of intercultural communication. One can know a lot about the history of a culture and still not be able to communicate with an actual person from that culture. Understanding objective culture may create knowledge, but it doesn't necessarily generate competence.

The less obvious aspect of culture is its *subjective* side—what we can call "culture writ small." Subjective culture refers to the psychological features that define a group of people—their everyday thinking and behavior—rather than to the institutions they have created. A good working definition of subjective culture is *the learned and shared patterns of beliefs, behaviors, and values of groups of interacting people*. Understanding subjective cultures—one's own and others'—is more likely to lead to intercultural competence.

Of course, social reality is constructed of both large and small "c" aspects of culture; people learn how to behave through socialization into the institutions of the culture, which leads them to behave in ways that perpetuate those same institutions.[5] As

noted above, traditional international and multicultural education tends to focus only on the objective mode of this process; in
contrast, intercultural communication focuses almost exclusively
on the subjective mode. For instance, interculturalists are concerned with *language use* in cross-cultural relationships, rather
than in linguistic structure. They study how language is modified
or supplanted by culturally defined *nonverbal behavior*, how cultural patterns of thinking are expressed in particular *communication styles*, and how reality is defined and judged through cultural *assumptions and values*. In the following pages, examples in
each of these areas will illustrate how understanding subjective
culture can aid in the development of skills in cultural adaptation and intercultural communication.

Levels of Culture

The definition of subjective culture also provides a base for defining "diversity" in a way that includes both international and
domestic cultures at different *levels of abstraction*. National groups
such as Japanese, Mexican, and U.S. American and pan-national
ethnic groups such as Arab and Zulu are cultures at a high level
of abstraction—the qualities that adhere to most (but not all)
members of the culture are very general, and the group includes
a lot of diversity. At this level of abstraction we can only point to
general differences in patterns of thinking and behaving between
cultures. For instance, we might observe that U.S. American culture is more characterized by individualism than is Japanese culture, which is more collectivist.

Analysis at a high level of abstraction provides a view of the
"unifying force" of culture. The very existence of interaction, even
through media, generates a commonality that spans individuals
and ethnicities. For instance, despite their significant individual
and ethnic differences, Mexicans spend more time interacting
with other Mexicans than they do with Japanese. They certainly
spend more time reading Mexican newspapers and watching
Mexican television than they do consuming Japanese media. This
fact generates Mexican "national character"—something that distinguishes Mexicans from Japanese (and from other Latin Americans as well).

U.S. Americans are particularly resistant to recognizing their
national culture. Despite the fact that nearly everyone else in the
world immediately recognizes them as Americans, many of them
still insist on labeling themselves as "just individuals" or "a mixture of cultures." Of course, the very commonality of this ten-

dency is an example of U.S. American national culture; no other people in the world but U.S. Americans are so quick to disavow their cultural affiliation. This is probably a manifestation of the individualism that is generally attibuted to U.S. Americans.[6] Whatever the reason, it is perilous for U.S. Americans to fail to see the cultural force that unifies them. It leads them to see ethnic and other cultural differences as more of a threat to national unity than they are.

While cultural difference at a high level of abstraction provides a rich base for analyzing national cultural behavior, there are significant group and individual differences within each national group that are concealed at this level. These differences provide a diversifying force that balances the unifying force of national culture.

At a lower level of abstraction, more specific groups such as ethnicities can be described in cultural terms.[7] In the United States, some of these groups are African American, Asian American, American Indian, Hispanic/Latino American, and European American. People in these groups may share many of the broad national culture patterns while differing significantly in the more specific patterns of their respective ethnicities.[8] It should be noted that in terms of subjective culture, ethnicity is a cultural rather than a genetic heritage; dark skin and other Negroid features may make one "black," but that person has not necessarily experienced African American enculturation. Most black people in the world are *not* American in any sense. Similarly, "whites" are not necessarily European American, although in the United States it is difficult for them to escape being socialized in the patterns that are currently dominant in U.S. American society.

Other categories of subjective cultural diversity usually include gender, regionality, socioeconomic class, physical ability, sexual orientation, religion, organization, and vocation. The concept can embrace other long-term groupings such as single parents or avid sports fans, as long as the groups maintain the clear patterns of behavior and thinking of an "identity group."[9] By definition, individuals do not have different cultures; the term for patterns of individual behavior is "personality."

Stereotypes and Generalizations

Whenever the topic of cultural difference is discussed, the allegation of stereotyping usually is not far behind. For instance, if cultural patterns of men and women are being compared, someone may well offer that she is a woman and doesn't act that way at all.

Stereotypes arise when we act as if all members of a culture or group share the same characteristics. Stereotypes can be attached to any assumed indicator of group membership, such as race, religion, ethnicity, age, or gender, as well as national culture. The characteristics that are assumedly shared by members of the group may be respected by the observer, in which case it is a *positive stereotype*. In the more likely case that the characteristics are disrespected, it is a *negative stereotype*. Stereotypes of both kinds are problematic in intercultural communication for several obvious reasons. One is that they may give us a false sense of understanding our communication partners. Whether the stereotype is positive or negative, it is usually only partially correct. Additionally, stereotypes may become self-fulfilling prophecies, where we observe others in selective ways that confirm our prejudice.

Despite the problems with stereotypes, it is necessary in intercultural communication to make *cultural generalizations*. Without any kind of supposition or hypothesis about the cultural differences we may encounter in an intercultural situation, we may fall prey to naive individualism, where we assume that every person is acting in some completely unique way. Or we may rely inordinately on "common sense" to direct our communication behavior. Common sense is, of course, common only to a particular culture. Its application outside of one's own culture is usually ethnocentric.

Cultural generalizations can be made while avoiding stereotypes by maintaining the idea of *preponderance of belief*.[10] Nearly all possible beliefs are represented in all cultures at all times, but each different culture has a preference for some beliefs over others.[11] The description of this preference, derived from large-group research, is a cultural generalization. Of course, individuals can be found in any culture who hold beliefs similar to people in a different culture. There just aren't so many of them—they don't represent the preponderance of people who hold beliefs closer to the norm or "central tendency" of the group. As a specific example (see Figure 1), we may note that despite the accurate cultural generalization that U.S. Americans are more individualistic and Japanese are more group-oriented, there are U.S. Americans who are every bit as group-oriented as any Japanese, and there are Japanese who are as individualistic as any U.S. American. However, these relatively few people are closer to the fringe of their respective cultures. They are, in the neutral sociological sense of the term, "deviant."

Figure 1. Generalization Distributions

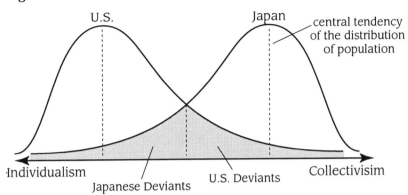

Deductive stereotypes occur when we assume that abstract cultural generalizations apply to every single individual in the culture. While it is appropriate to generalize that U.S. Americans as a group are more individualistic than Japanese, it is stereotyping to assume that every American is strongly individualistic; the person with whom you are communicating may be a deviant. Cultural generalizations should be used tentatively as working hypotheses that need to be tested in each case; sometimes they work very well, sometimes they need to be modified, and sometimes they don't apply to the particular case at all. The idea is to derive the benefit of recognizing cultural patterns without experiencing too much "hardening of the categories."

Generalizing from too small a sample may generate an *inductive stereotype*. For example, we may inappropriately assume some general knowledge about Mexican culture based on having met one or a few Mexicans. This assumption is particularly troublesome, since initial cross-cultural contacts may often be conducted by people who are deviant in their own cultures. ("Typical" members of the culture would more likely associate only with their cultural compatriots—that's how they stay typical.) So generalizing cultural patterns from any one person's behavior (including your own) in cross-cultural contact is likely to be both stereotypical and inaccurate.

Another form of inductive stereotype is derived from what Carlos E. Cortés calls the "social curriculum." He notes that schoolchildren report knowing a lot about Gypsies, even though few of the children have ever met even one member of that culture. According to Cortés' research, the knowledge was gained from old horror movies![12] Through media of all kinds we are besieged with images of "cultural" behavior: African Americans performing hip-hop or bringing warmth to medical practice; Hispanic Americans picking crops or exhibiting savvy in the courtroom; European Americans burning crosses or exercising altruism toward the homeless. When we generalize from any of these images, we are probably creating stereotypes. Media images are chosen not for their typicality, but for their unusualness. So, as with initial cross-cultural contacts, we need to look beyond the immediate image to the cultural patterns that can only be ascertained through research.

Assumptions of an Intercultural Communication Perspective

Beyond its emphasis on cultural difference, intercultural communication is based on some assumptions that both identify it with and distinguish it from other social sciences.

Analysis of Personal Interaction

Like interpersonal communication, intercultural communication focuses on face-to-face (or at least person-to-person) interaction among human beings. For this kind of communication to occur, each participant must perceive him- or herself being perceived by others. That is, all participants must see themselves as potentially engaged in communication and capable of giving and receiving feedback. This assumption allows us to understand why interculturalists are not particularly focused on mass media. Even though the issues of international satellite broadcasting and culture-specific cable productions are fascinating, they are essentially one-way events. However, individual, mediated communication such as faxing, e-mailing, and Internet chat room dialogue does fit the definition of person-to-person communication.

It is surprising to some that intercultural communication does not often generate comprehensive descriptions of culture, or ethnographies. While such descriptions are crucial for any cross-cultural study, they do not in themselves constitute cases of cross-cultural interaction. An intercultural perspective leads researchers to hypothesize, given some difference in the described cultures, how members of the cultures might interact.

Another useful distinction in this context is that between *cultural interaction* and *cultural comparison*. When social science studies deal with culture at all, they frequently compare one aspect of a culture to a similar phenomenon in another. For instance, psychologists might compare how Northern European depth perception differs from that of Amazonian Indians. Or sociolinguists might analyze the differences in ritual greeting between European Americans and African Americans. While interculturalists use these kinds of comparisons for their knowledge base, they focus less on the differences themselves and more on how the differences are likely to affect face-to-face interaction.

This emphasis on interaction does not mean that interculturalists neglect knowledge about specific cultures. On the contrary, it is considered a prerequisite for interculturalists to have expert knowledge of at least their own cultures (an often-neglected skill in other academic fields). Most interculturalists are particularly knowledgeable about one or more cultures in addition to their own.

Culture-Specific and Culture-General Approaches

Interaction analysis and skill development can be undertaken at two levels. At the *culture-specific* level, differences between two particular cultures are assessed for their likely impact on communication between people of those cultures. For instance, the generalization that Hispanic American patterns of cross-status communication differ from the more egalitarian patterns of European Americans[13] could be analyzed for its possible effect on interaction between employees and managers from the two cultures. Training in alternative cross-status communication styles could then help members of both cultures appreciate and deal more effectively with each other in the workplace. This approach, based on specific ethnographies, is an intercultural form of "emic" cultural analysis.[14]

Culture-general approaches to interaction describe general cultural contrasts that are applicable in many cross-cultural situations. For instance, Edward T. Hall's definition of high-context and low-context cultures[15] is a culture-general contrast that suggests a source of miscommunication among many diverse cultures. Similarly, culture-general skills are communication competencies that would be useful in any cross-cultural situation. They usually include cultural self-awareness, nonevaluative perception, cultural adaptation strategies, and cross-cultural empathy. This approach, based on more abstract categories and generalizable skills, is the intercultural equivalent of "etic" cultural analysis.[16]

Emphasis on Process and the Development of Competence

The process of communication can be thought of as the mutual creation of meaning—the verbal and nonverbal behavior of communicating and the interpretations that are made of that behavior. The meaning itself, whatever it is, can be called the *content* of the communication. Everyday communication mainly stresses content, while studies of communication tend to emphasize the process and give less attention to the content. This is particularly true for intercultural communication, where apparently familiar or understandable content may mask radically different cultural processes.

Another implication of this assumption is that knowledge of content does not automatically translate into mastery of process. I have already noted that knowledge about objective cultural institutions does not necessarily yield competence in communicating with the people whose behavior maintains those institutions. Even knowledge about subjective cultural contrasts, while more directly applicable to communication, is still not sufficient in itself for intercultural competence. Specific knowledge of subjective culture needs to be framed in culture-general categories and coupled with an understanding of both the general and specific intercultural processes involved. A knowledge of the differences between U.S. American and Japanese decision-making styles is not, in itself, particularly useful. It needs to be framed in more general value contrasts (e.g., individualism and collectivism), linked with an understanding of how individualists and collectivists generally misconstrue each other's behavior, joined by an awareness of how those misunderstandings manifest themselves in dysfunctional communication patterns (e.g., negative spirals), and finally applied to avoiding negative spirals and other miscommunication in an actual joint decision-making effort.

Focus on Humanistic Phenomena
Most approaches to intercultural communication (and communication in general) treat it as a purely human phenomenon, not, for instance, as an expression of a divine plan. Any assumption of transcendental guidance to communication immediately runs afoul of cultural differences in religious beliefs. And if one believes that his or her communication style is dictated by a divine authority, adapting that style to a different cultural context will be difficult at best. Interculturalists generally leave questions of supernatural order to contexts where improving communication is not the goal.

In a similar vein, interculturalists tend to avoid purely ideological analyses of discourse. When communication behavior is labeled as "Marxist," or "imperialist," or "racist," or "sexist," the human aspects of that behavior are overshadowed by the reifications of principle. Polarization usually supplants any hope of inclusivity, and further exploration of communication differences is drowned out by the political commotion.[17]

I do not mean to say here that the abuse of power is inconsequential to communication. On the contrary, no improvement of intercultural relations is likely to occur in a climate of oppression and disrespect, and interculturalists have a role in changing that climate through their explication and facilitation of interaction. I do, however, mean to suggest that the professional work of interculturalists is not primarily ideological (except insofar as any action taken is inherently political, to some degree). Critical social analysis is an important part of political change. But when the question is how to understand and adapt to another culture more successfully, as it is in intercultural communication, purely ideological analyses yield little light and much heat.

Historical analyses of cultural behavior have some of the same disadvantages as ideological approaches. While it might be accurate to note that U.S. American individualism has Calvinistic roots nurtured in a wild frontier and that Japanese collectivism has grown out of Shintoism and close-knit agricultural communities, such an observation tells us little about how the values of individualism and collectivism are likely to affect the behavior of an American person with a Japanese person today. Similarly, understanding the history of immigration into the United States, while important for other reasons, is not particularly useful in analyzing the cross-cultural aspects of interethnic communication. In both cases, the immediate behavior and its cultural context may be occluded by a preoccupation with historical causes.

The avoidance of history as an analytical frame does not mean that interculturalists neglect the subject altogether. People of most cultures feel respected if the person they encounter knows something about the history of their group, and mutual respect is a major goal of intercultural communication. Also, the acknowledgment of history is particularly important if an oppressor/oppressed relationship existed (or continues to exist) between the communication partners. Any disavowal of that history on the part of a dominant culture member is likely to be interpreted as evidence of continuing (albeit possibly unintentional) oppression. For instance, the failure by European Americans to recognize the history of slavery or of American Indian genocide in the United States is often seen as racist. A knowledge of history is also important for interpreting those aspects of people's behavior that mainly are responses to past and present mistreatment. Scottish people, for instance, take particular umbrage at being confused with the English, their historical oppressors. But, while acknowledging historical context, interculturalists usually focus on patterns of behavior in the here and now. Specifically, they analyze the human interaction that is created each time different cultural patterns are brought into contact through face-to-face communication.

Another aspect of humanism is its assumption of personal and cultural relativity. This means that behavior and values must be understood both in terms of the uniqueness of each person and in terms of the culture of that person. Absolute judgments about the goodness or badness of behavior and values are avoided, as far as communication is concerned. Interculturalists generally consider that evaluations of culturally different behavior are likely to be ethnocentric and that in any case they interfere with the communication necessary to become informed about the worldview context in which the behavior must be interpreted. In the simplest terms, cultural relativity is a commitment to understanding all events in cultural context, including how the event is likely to be evaluated in that context.

It is important to note here that cultural relativity is not the same as ethical relativity. The end result of understanding events in cultural context is not "...whatever." Like most other people, interculturalists are both professionally and personally committed to ethical positions. They may be, however, particularly concerned that their ethical commitments are not based on ethnocentric absolutes.[18]

Intercultural Communication Processes

For the rest of this chapter, processes and skills of intercultural communication will be reviewed. In this section, the review will be restricted to communication process. In the following sections, applications of these concepts to culture-general issues of intercultural adaptation and sensitivity will be considered.

Language and the Relativity of Experience

Many students (and some teachers) view language only as a communication tool—a method humans use to indicate the objects and ideas of their physical and social world. In this view, languages are sets of words tied together by rules, and learning a foreign or second language is the simple (but tedious) process of substituting words and rules to get the same meaning with a different tool.

Language does serve as a tool for communication, but in addition it is a "system of representation" for perception and thinking. This function of language provides us with verbal categories and prototypes that guide our formation of concepts and categorization of objects; it directs how we experience reality.[19] It is this "reality-organizing" aspect of language that engages interculturalists.

A memorable statement of how language organizes and represents cultural experience is now known as the Whorf/Sapir hypothesis:

> We dissect nature along lines laid down by our native languages. The categories and types that we isolate from the world of phenomena we do not find there because they stare every observer in the face; on the contrary, the world is presented in a kaleidoscopic flux of impressions which has to be organized by our minds—and this means largely by the linguistic systems in our minds.[20]

In this statement, Benjamin Lee Whorf advances what has come to be called the "strong form" of the hypothesis: language largely determines the way in which we understand our reality. In other writings, Whorf takes the position that language, thought, and perception are interrelated, a position called the "weak hypothesis." Interculturalists tend to use the weak form of the hypothesis when they discuss language and culture.

An example of how various languages direct different experiences of reality is found in how objects must be represented grammatically. American English has only one way to count things (one, two, three, etc.), while Japanese and Trukese (a Micronesian language) each have many different counting systems. In part, these systems classify the physical appearance of objects. For instance, one (long) thing is counted with different words from one (flat) thing or one (round) thing in Trukese. We could imagine that the experience of objects in general is much richer in cultures where language gives meaning to subtle differences in shape. Indeed, Japanese aesthetic appreciation of objects seems more developed than that of Americans, whose English language has relatively simple linguistic structures to represent shapes.

In addition, both Japanese and Trukese count people with a set of words different from all others used for objects. We might speculate that research on human beings that quantifies behavior "objectively" (i.e., like objects) would not arise as easily in cultures where people were counted distinctly. And indeed, quantitative research on human beings is much more common in Western cultures, particularly U.S. American.

Another example of the relationship of syntax and experience can be found in the grammatical representation of space. In American English, things can be either "here" or "there," with a colloquial attempt to place them further out "over there." In the Trukese language, references to objects and people must be accompanied by a "location marker" that specifies their position relative to both the speaker and listener. A pen, for instance, must be called this (close to me but away from you) pen, this (midway between us) pen, that (far away from both of us but in sight) pen, or that (out of sight of both of us) pen. We may assume that Trukese people, who live on islands, experience "richer" space than do Americans, whose language does not provide so many spatial boundary markers and for whom space is therefore more abstract.

Language syntax also guides our social experience. Perhaps the simplest and best-known examples are linguistic differences in "status markers." Thai, Japanese, and some other Asian languages have elaborate systems of second-person singular (*you*) words that indicate the status of the speaker relative to the listener. In Thai, there are also variable forms of *I* to indicate relative status. Thus, I (relatively lower in status) may be speaking to you (somewhat higher in status) or to you (much higher in status), using a different form of *I* and *you* in each case. It seems apparent that cultures with languages which demand recognition of relative status in every direct address will encourage more acute experience of status difference than does American culture, where English provides only one form of *you*. European cultures, most of whose languages have two forms of *you*, indicating both status distinctions and familiarity, may represent the middle range of this dimension. Europeans are more overtly attentive to status than are Americans, but Europeans are no match for Asians in this regard.

The preceding examples indicate a relationship between language syntax and the experience of physical and social reality. The relationship between language and experience can also be found in the semantic dimension of language. Languages differ in how semantic categories are distinguished and elaborated. For instance, several stages of coconut growth are described with separate words in the Trukese language, while English has only one word to describe the nut. On the other hand, English has an elaborate vocabulary to describe colors, while Trukese describes only a few colors and does not distinguish between blue and green. It is clear that Americans without the extra vocabulary cannot easily distinguish coconuts in their different stages; that is, they do not have the experience of the coconuts as being different. Similarly, it appears that Trukese people without additional color categories do not experience the difference between blue and green.

Other examples abound of how categories are differentiated to greater or lesser degrees. Wine connoisseurs maintain a highly differentiated set of labels for the experience of wine, as opposed to the two or three categories (red, white, and maybe blush) used by casual drinkers. Skiers distinguish more kinds of snow than do nonskiers, and so forth. Of even greater interest are situations where an entire kind of experience seems to disappear when the vocabulary for it is missing. For instance, while English has many words to describe boredom and ennui, Trukese seems to lack any reference to the entire concept. Although we cannot be sure, linguistic relativity would predict that Trukese people do not experience boredom in the same way as English speakers do until they learn to distinguish a category for it.

In summary, categories are constructed differently in different cultures and languages, and with the different constructions go different experiences of physical and social reality. These particular experiences are not *determined* by language, in the sense that other forms of experience are precluded without concomitant linguistic support. Research on color perception[21] and other phenomena indicate that distinctions can be made without a specific "naming strategy." Rather, linguistic relativity suggests that we are predisposed by our languages to make certain distinctions and not others—our language encourages habitual patterns of perception.

This formulation of linguistic and cultural relativity is central to intercultural communication. Without the assumption of relativity at the very root of our experience of reality, naive practitioners of intercultural relations veer toward itemizing different customs and providing tips for minor adjustments of behavior. More sophisticated interculturalists realize that their study is of nothing less than the clash of differing realities and that cultural adaptation demands the apprehension of essentially alien experience.

Perceptual Relativity

The Whorf/Sapir hypothesis alerts us to the likelihood that our experience of reality is a function of cultural worldview categories. At the basic level of perception, language and culture guide us in making *figure/ground distinctions*. From the "kaleidoscopic flux" (ground) of undifferentiated phenomena, we create a boundary that distinguishes some object (figure) from the ground.[22] These figures may literally be objects, or they may be concepts or feelings. Collections of figures are "categories." What we think exists—what is real—depends on whether we have distinguished the phenomenon as figure. And since culture through language guides us in making these distinctions, culture is actually operating directly on perception.

Micronesians, for example, are far more likely than Americans to see wave patterns—interactions of tide and current on the ocean surface that are used for navigation. To a typical American, the ocean is just "ground," and only boats or other objects are figures. But this same American may single out an automobile sound as indicating imminent mechanical failure, while to the Micronesian it is simply part of the background noise. In general, culture provides us with the tendency to perceive phenomena that are relevant to both physical and social survival.

The boundaries of constructed objects are mutable. For instance, as mentioned earlier, speakers of Trukese do not make a blue/green distinction. (One word, *araw*, refers to both colors, and "araw" is the response to either question, "What color is the sea?" or "What color is the grass?") Yet Trukese children are routinely taught to perceive the difference in color as part of their training in English as a second language. The mutability of perceptual boundaries supports the idea that perceivers actively organize stimuli into categories. And evidence from physiological studies of vision indicate that people do indeed see different objects when looking in the same direction.[23] The human eye and brain respond selectively to stimuli, depending on whether the visual system is tuned to the stimulus as figure or as ground.

The observation that perceptual figure/ground distinctions are learned and lead to different experiences of reality contradicts the traditional view of the perceiver who confronts a specific, objective reality. Instead, the perceiver is assumed to respond to culturally influenced categorizations of stimuli. Like the assumption of linguistic relativity, this assumption of perceptual relativity lies at the heart of intercultural communication. If we fail to assume that people of different cultures may sincerely perceive the world differently, then our efforts toward understanding are subverted by a desire to "correct" the one who has it wrong.

Nonverbal Behavior

There is an entire universe of behavior that is unexplored, unexamined, and very much taken for granted. It functions outside conscious awareness and *in juxtaposition to words.*[24]

Verbal language is *digital*, in the sense that words symbolize categories of phenomena in the same arbitrary way that on/off codes symbolize numbers and operations in a computer. Nonverbal behavior, by contrast, is *analogic*. It represents phenomena by creating contexts which can be experienced directly. For instance, it is digital to say "I love you." It is analogic to represent that feeling with a look or a touch. Digital symbolizations are more capable of expressing complexity ("I love you twice as much now as I did last week"), but analogic representations are more credible because they are generally less easily manipulated.[25]

Some languages put more emphasis on the digital quality than others. English, for instance, is strongly digital in the way that it divides continua of human feeling and thought into discrete, abstract categories, providing speakers with many words to name particular affective and cognitive states. In contrast, Japanese is a more analogic language. It demands that its speakers imply and infer meaning from the context of relatively vague statements—the way it's said, by whom, to whom, where, at what time, and just before or after what other statement.[26]

Cultures such as Japanese that stress analogic communication are referred to as "high context."[27] Hall, who coined that term, defines it as a communication "in which *most* of the information is already in the person, while very little is in the coded, explicit, transmitted part of the message."[28] Cultures such as U.S. American that emphasize digital forms of communication are called "low context," defined as communication "where the mass of information is vested in the explicit code."[29]

In both high- and low-context cultures, all verbal messages in face-to-face interpersonal communication are accompanied by nonverbal behavior which provides an analogic background for the digital words.[30] Voice, gestures, eye contact, spacing, and touching all provide direct analogic expressions of emotion that modify (in low context) or supplant (in high context) the verbal message. Even in low-context cultures, only a small percentage of the meaning created in a social communication exchange is based on verbal language,[31] so understanding the more important nonverbal aspects of communication is vital to an overall comprehension of intercultural events.

In low-context cultures such as U.S. American, nonverbal behavior is unconsciously perceived more as a commentary on the verbal message than as a part of the message itself. This tendency is particularly noticeable in the use of voice tone, such as that used in the communication of sarcasm. Words such as "My, what a nice tie" can be modified by a tone of voice that indicates to the listener, "Don't take these words seriously." In other words, the nonverbal cue (tone of voice, in this case) establishes the sarcastic relationship in which the words should be interpreted.

Paralanguage, which also includes the pitch, stress, volume, and speed with which language is spoken, lends itself readily to misinterpretation cross-culturally. The potential for misunderstanding begins with perception. Is the communication stimulus even discriminated as figure from the ground of other behavior? U.S. Americans are likely to miss shadings of tone which in higher-context cultures would scream with meaning. Within the United States, European American males are less likely than some African American males to perceive the use of movement to signal a shift from talking to fighting. And conversely, black males may fail to discriminate the fighting cue of "intensity" in the tone of white male talk.[32]

In cross-cultural situations we may also perceive the appearance of a cue when none was intended. An example of this occurs around the American English use of a pitch drop at the end of sentences. The pitch of our voices goes up on the next to the last syllable and then down on the last syllable in a spoken statement. How quickly the pitch is dropped makes a difference. In even a short utterance such as "Come in," a medium pitch drop signifies normal interaction, while an abrupt drop may signify anger, frustration, anxiety, or impatience. Conversely, an elongated pitch drop usually indicates friendliness and relaxation, but an elongated pitch *increase* at the end of a statement can imply a manipulative or misleading intent. These implications are instantly recognized and reacted to by native speakers.

Nonnative English speakers may not respond to or generate voice tones in the same way. For instance, for native speakers of Cantonese, pitch changes are important within words but are not used to modulate sentences. So a Cantonese speaker of English as a second language may not generate an ending pitch drop. Additionally, Cantonese may sound rather staccato and a little loud to American ears. The combination of these factors leads some native English speakers to evaluate Chinese people as brusque or rude. If a native speaker generated loud, staccato, flat pitch statements, it might indeed indicate rudeness. But when the native Cantonese speaker talks that way in English, it probably means that he or she is using the English language with Cantonese paralanguage. The failure to observe intended cues or the discrimination of nonexistent cues based solely on one's own culture can be termed *ethnocentric perception*.

Finally, we may correctly perceive that a nonverbal cue has been generated but misinterpret its meaning. This is most likely to occur when we assume (perhaps unconsciously) that particular behavior carries the same meaning in every culture. For example, the clipped speech of some British is noticed both by other British and by U.S. Americans. For the British, however, the paralanguage cues are likely to indicate social status, home region, or place of education. For the Americans, the cues may be interpreted simply as haughtiness. This tendency to assign meaning to events solely in the context of one's own culture can be called *ethnocentric interpretation*. Both ethnocentric perception and interpretation are consistent with the idea of cultural relativity—that our experience of reality differs culturally as well as individually.

The form of nonverbal interaction analysis used in the paralanguage examples above is also generally applied to the area of kinesics, or "body language." To illustrate this, we can imagine different degrees of gesturing placed on a continuum extending from the nearly motionless presentation of some Asians and Native Americans to the dramatic sweeps of Greeks and Italians. When they come into contact, people at contrasting positions on the continuum may fall prey to ethnocentric perception and interpretation. For instance, those in the middle of the continuum, such as European Americans, may interpret Native American reserve as "lacking ambition and self-esteem." Native Americans, on the other hand, may interpret European American gesturing as "intrusive and aggressive." African Americans, whose gesturing is a bit further along the continuum, may be interpreted by some Asians (Koreans, for example) as being "violent and unpredictable." The greater reserve of the Koreans might fit into an African American interpretation of "unfriendly (perhaps because of racism)." As should be obvious from these examples, "simple" misinterpretations of nonverbal behavior may contribute to tragic failures in our educational system and terrible social strife.

Another practical consequence of nonverbal ethnocentrism occurs around turn taking in conversation, particularly in group discussion. The European American pattern involves eye contact to cue turns. The speaker ends with his or her eyes in contact with the conversational heir-apparent. If the speaker lowers her eyes at the end of an utterance, a confused babble of fits and starts may ensue. In contrast to this pattern, some Asian cultures routinely require averted eyes and a period of silence between speakers. In groups including more eye-intensive cultures, unacculturated Asians may never get a turn. And on the other end of this continuum, some forms of African American, Middle Eastern, and Mediterranean cultures tend to prefer more of a "relay-race" pattern of turn taking. Whoever wants the turn next just begins talking, and eventually the conversational baton may be passed on to her. Both Asian and European Americans may interpret this last pattern as interrupting. The simple task of facilitating a group discussion increases dramatically in complexity when even this one intercultural dimension is introduced.

Communication Style

Habitual patterns of thought are manifested in communication behavior. Since our habits of thought are largely determined by culture, in cross-cultural situations we should see contrasts in these styles of communication. One of the most striking differences is in how a point is discussed, whether in writing[33] or verbally, as illustrated in the following example.

European Americans, particularly males, tend to use a *linear* style that marches through point *a*, point *b*, and point *c*, establishes links from point to point, and finally states an explicit conclusion. When someone veers off this line, he or she is likely to hear a statement such as "I'm not quite following you," or "Could we cut to the chase," or "What's the bottom line?" In many school systems, this style has been established as the only one indicative of clear critical thinking. It is, however, a culturally rare form of discourse.

An example of a contrasting style occurred in a group of international and U.S. American students. I had asked a question about early dating practices, and the Americans all answered with fairly concise statements that made some explicit connection to the question. When a Nigerian in the group replied, however, he began by describing the path through his village, the tree at the end of the path, the storyteller that performed under the tree, and the beginning of a story the storyteller once told. When, in response to the obvious discomfort of the Americans in the group, I asked the Nigerian what he was doing, he said, "I'm answering the question." The American students protested at that, so I asked, "How are you answering the question?" He replied, "I'm telling you everything you need to know to understand the point." "Good," said one of the Americans. "Then if we're just patient, you will eventually tell us the point." "Oh no," replied the Nigerian. "Once I tell you everything you need to know to understand the point, you will just know what the point is!"

What this student was describing is a circular, or *contextual*, discussion style. It is favored not only by many Africans but also typically by people of Latin, Arab, and Asian cultures. And in the United States, the more circular style is commonly used by African Americans, Asian Americans, Native Americans, Hispanic Americans, and others. Even among European Americans, a contextual approach is more typical of women than of men. The only natural cultural base for the linear style is Northern European and European American males. That doesn't make the style bad, of course, but it does mean that other, more prevalent styles need to be considered as viable alternatives. To some extent, this issue has been addressed in the context of gender differences,[34] and it is getting increasing attention in the context of multicultural classrooms.[35]

When people who favor a contextual approach generate an ethnocentric interpretation of the linear style, they may see it as simple or arrogant: simple because it lacks the richness of detail necessary to establish context, and arrogant because the speaker is deciding what particular points you should hear and then what point you should draw from them! On the other hand, proponents of a linear style are likely to interpret the circular style as vague, evasive, and illogical. Interculturalists sometimes approach this kind of mutual negative evaluation with the idea of *strengths and limits*. In this case, the strength of a linear style may be in efficient, short-term task completion, while its limit is in developing inclusive relationship. Conversely, the strength of a contextual style is its facilitation of team building and consensual creativity, while its limit is that it is slow. The goal of education and training in this area, in addition to developing awareness and respect for alternative styles, may be to develop "bistylistic" competency.

Another area where differences in communication style are particularly obvious is around confrontation. European and African Americans tend to be rather direct in their style of confrontation, compared with the indirectness of many Asians and Hispanics. Adherents of the direct style favor face-to-face discussion of problems, relatively open expression of feeling, and a willingness to say yes or no in answer to questions. People socialized in the more indirect style tend to seek third-person intermediaries for conducting difficult discussions, suggest rather than state feelings, and protect their own and others' "face" by providing the appearance of ambiguity in response to questions.[36]

I was once involved in an incident involving indirect style in Malaysia. The guide had provided our group with a wonderful day of sights and cultural insight, and we were anticipating a trip to the jungle the next day with him. Upon leaving us off at the hotel, he stated somewhat offhandedly, "It will rain tomorrow." I joked back, "Oh, that's all right, we're used to getting wet." But he repeated the statement, this time adding, "It will rain really hard." More seriously this time, I said, "Our schedule is set, so we'll have to make this trip, rain or shine." He said okay and left. The next (sunny) morning, we arrived at our departure point to find a substitute guide who spoke no English. When someone in our party asked me why the original guide hadn't just said he couldn't make it the next day, I found myself ruefully explaining about indirectness and loss of face. Knowledge does not equal intercultural competence.

An elaboration of this basic contrast between direct and indirect styles can be applied to understanding a difficulty in communication between Northern Europeans and U.S. Americans. Northern Europeans (particularly Germans) tend to be direct about intellectual topics but relatively indirect about relational matters. For instance, Northern Europeans are more likely than most U.S. Americans to say, "That idea is the stupidest thing I've ever heard." But those same Northern Europeans are less likely than Americans to discuss their feelings about casual relationships with the people involved. In contrast, U.S. Americans are more likely to be indirect on intellectual topics, making comments such as "Perhaps there is another way to think about that" or simply "Hmmm, interesting." But those same Americans may be quick to state to his or her face how much they like a new acquaintance. So Americans often think that Northern Europeans are relationally haughty, while Northern Europeans may think that Americans are intellectually shallow. Ethnocentric perception leads U.S. Americans to fail to recognize indirectness in relational commentary, while Northern Europeans similarly fail to detect indirectness in intellectual discourse. Additionally, ethnocentric interpretation leads Americans to mistake normal Northern European argument for the intellectual arrogance it would represent in most U.S. con-

texts, and Northern Europeans to mistake normal American relational openness for the boorishness it would represent in many
European contexts.

Values and Assumptions

Cultural values are the patterns of goodness and badness people
assign to ways of being in the world. For instance, Japanese people
typically assign goodness to being interdependent in groups (even
if they often act individually), while U.S. Americans typically assign goodness to being independently self-reliant (even if they
often act interdependently). To shorten this, we would state the
generalization that, relative to the other culture, Japanese value
collectivism and U.S. Americans value individualism. Conversely,
Japanese tend to disvalue many manifestations of individualism
as unnecessarily selfish, while U.S. Americans disvalue many
forms of collectivism as unduly conformist.

Cultural assumptions are interrelated with values but refer to
the existence of phenomena rather than the assignment of value
to them. So, in terms of the above example contrasting Japanese
and U.S. Americans, most Americans assume the existence of
an individual identity, which is necessary for the self-reliance of
individualism to exist. Most Japanese, on the other hand, assume
the existence of a kind of collective consciousness ("we Japanese"), which is necessary for interrelationships of collectivism
to occur. In most intercultural analyses of situations, it is necessary to ascertain both what cultural assumptions are being made
in the situation and what values are being placed on those assumptions.

The system that has been used traditionally by interculturalists for analyzing cultural values is the one developed by Florence R. Kluckhohn and Fred L. Strodtbeck.[37] Based on research
with several cultures, the system defines five dimensions of cultural assumptions: peoples' relationship to the environment, to
each other, to activity, to time, and to the basic nature of human
beings. Constituting each of these dimensions is a continuum of
possible relationships that people might assume with the subject. For instance, people may assume that they can control the
environment, that they can live in harmony with it, or that they
are subjugated by the environment. Kluckhohn and Strodtbeck
state that all positions on the continuum will be represented to
some degree in all cultures, but that one position will be *preferred*. It is this general preference that constitutes a cultural value.
For example, most U.S. Americans prefer to think that nature is

controllable—witness their damming of rivers, their programs to conquer space, and so forth. We could say that, in general, U.S. Americans value being in control of their environment. Other assumptions about an appropriate relationship to nature are present in U.S. society, of course. But with some exceptions, those assumptions are not as yet preferred and so are not now considered general cultural values.[38]

Many modifications of the Kluckhohn and Strodtbeck approach have proved useful for intercultural value analysis. John C. Condon[39] has expanded the original five dimensions into a list that can be applied to a broader range of more specific cultural phenomena, as has L. Robert Kohls.[40] Edward C. Stewart has done the most to develop the theoretical potential of the approach by defining the contrast-American approach to value analysis[41] and by redefining the original dimensions in particularly useful ways.[42]

Another approach to value analysis has been developed by Geert Hofstede.[43] As opposed to the deductive approach of Kluckhohn and Strodtbeck, Hofstede used the inductive technique of surveying a large number of people from various national cultures about their values and preferences in life. Using the statistical technique of factor analysis, he then isolated four dimensions (and later a fifth) that accounted for a large amount of the variation in answers. He named the four dimensions *Power-Distance*, referring to the assumption of status difference; *Masculinity*, referring to (among other things) the assumption of gender difference; *Individualism*, referring to the assumption of self-reliance; and *Uncertainty Avoidance*, referring to the assumption of intolerance of ambiguity. In later studies, he added the dimension of *Confucian Dynamism* or *Long-Term Orientation*, referring to focus on future rewards.[44] Returning to the data from each national culture, he was then able to rank-order the cultures in terms of each dimension. For instance, Japanese ranked 7th out of fifty countries on Uncertainty Avoidance, while the United States ranked 46th; on Individualism the United States scored 1st and Japan 22nd. By statistically combining factors, Hofstede was able to map clusters of cultures in several dimensions. Many contemporary studies of cultural values now use, at least in part, the Hofstede categories.

Cultural Adaptation

In many ways, the crux of intercultural communication is in how people adapt to other cultures. Yet the intercultural concept of adaptation is frequently misunderstood. To clarify the idea, it is useful to distinguish *adaptation* from *assimilation*. Assimilation is the process of resocialization that seeks to replace one's original worldview with that of the host culture. Assimilation is "substitutive." Adaptation, on the other hand, is the process whereby one's worldview is expanded to include behavior and values appropriate to the host culture. It is "additive," not substitutive. The assumed end result of assimilation is becoming a "new person," as Israel Zangwill wrote in his play *The Melting Pot*.[45] The assumed end result of adaptation is becoming a bicultural or multicultural person. Such a person has new aspects, but not at the cost of his or her original socialization. The identity issues around adaptation are quite complex, and understanding them is one of the new frontiers of intercultural communication.

Developmental Approaches to Cultural Adaptation

Cultural adaptation is not an on/off phenomenon. Like many other human abilities, it appears that cultural adaptation develops through stages, in much the same way as does cognition as described by Jean Piaget[46] or ethicality as described by William G. Perry Jr.[47] With descriptions of the stages of development, interculturalists who are responsible for facilitating cross-cultural encounters are able to diagnose learners' levels of development and thus design their interventions more effectively.

A straightforward form of developmental thinking can be illustrated with one of the best-known of all intercultural concepts: *culture shock*. The evolution of this concept began with a relatively simple statement of how disorientation can occur in a different cultural context, along with the implication that culture shock was something like a disease that could be prevented, or caught and cured.[48] From this distinctly nondevelopmental beginning, the concept gained complexity as it was described in terms of *U* or *W* curves extending through time.[49] Then Peter S. Adler[50] suggested that culture shock was a process that went through five stages: the euphoria of Contact, when cultural difference is first encountered; the confusion of Disintegration, when loss of self-esteem intrudes; the anger of Reintegration, when the new culture is rejected and the old self reasserted; the relaxed self-assuredness of Autonomy, when cross-cultural situations can be handled with relative ease; and the creativity of Independence, when choice and responsibility accompany a deep respect for one's own and others' cultures. These ideas were placed in an even broader developmental context by Janet M. Bennett,[51] who defined culture shock as a special case of the typical human response to any transition, loss, or change.

So when even a relatively simple aspect of cultural adaptation—culture shock—is cast in developmental terms, it attains a level of complexity that makes it a richer and more useful descriptor of peoples' experiences. When the broader topic of cultural adaptation in general is described in developmental terms, the result is even more descriptive of complex experience. One example of this attempt is the Developmental Model of Intercultural Sensitivity (DMIS).[52] Based on "meaning-making" models of cognitive psychology and radical constructivism,[53] the DMIS links changes in cognitive structure to an evolution in attitudes and behavior toward cultural difference in general. The DMIS is divided into *Ethnocentric Stages* and *Ethnorelative Stages*.

Figure 2. Development of Intercultural Sensitivity

Experience of Difference

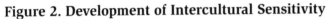

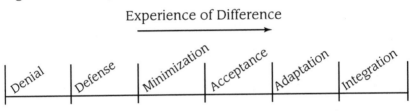

Ethnocentric Stages   Ethnorelative Stages

Ethnocentric is defined as using one's own set of standards and customs to judge all people, often unconsciously. *Ethnorelative* means the opposite; it refers to being comfortable with many standards and customs and to having an ability to adapt behavior and judgments to a variety of interpersonal settings. Following are short descriptions of each of six stages of development.

Denial. People at the denial stage are unable to construe cultural differences in complex ways. They probably live in relative isolation from other cultures, either by happenstance or by choice. Either they do not perceive cultural differences at all, or they can conceive only of broad categories such as "foreigner," "people of color," or "Africans." People at this stage may use stereotypes in their description of others that are not meant to denigrate but are based on knowing only one or two things about the other people. For instance, many U.S. Americans seem to think that all Africans live near jungles and have encounters with wild animals; or many Asians seem to think that all Americans from the Pacific Northwest live on ranches and ride horses.

In contrast to the complexity of our own worldview, the simplicity of these stereotypes makes "their" seemingly sparse experience seem less real than "our" demonstrably rich experience. Consequently, when actually confronted by cultural diversity, people in denial unconsciously attribute less than human status to the outsiders. They may then use power for purposes of exploiting the others, and in extreme cases of threat, they may further dehumanize the outsiders to enable genocide.

Defense. People at the defense stage have more ability to construe cultural difference, but they attach negative evaluations to it. They combat the threat of change to their stable worldview by denigrating others with negative stereotypes and by attaching positive stereotypes to themselves. Consequently, they view their own culture as the acme of "development" and tend to evaluate different cultures as "underdeveloped." A few people may enter a reversed form of defense, wherein they vilify their own culture and become zealous proponents of an adopted culture. For example, some U.S. Americans spurn their European roots while idealizing Native Indian cultures, and some U.S. Americans, when traveling, label most of their compatriots as "the ugly Americans." In all cases, however, defense is characterized by the polarization of a denigrated "them" with a superior "us."

People in defense consider themselves under siege. Members of socially dominant cultures may attempt to protect privilege and deny opportunities to outsiders, while nondominant culture members may aggressively protect their ethnic identity from suppression by the majority. Ironically, while personally directed violence may be more common in defense than in denial, the threat of systematic genocide is reduced by the greater humanity accorded one's enemy.

Minimization. People at the minimization stage try to bury cultural differences within already-familiar categories of physical and philosophical similarity. They recognize and accept superficial cultural differences such as eating customs and other social norms, but they assume that deep down all people are essentially the same—just human. As a consequence of this assumption, certain cultural values may be mistaken for universal desires; for instance, U.S. Americans may believe that people everywhere desire individual freedom, openness, and competition. Religious people may hold that everyone is a child of God, is subject to Allah's will, or acquires karma "whether they know it or not." Political and economic minimizers may suppose that we are all victims of historical Marxist forces or that we are all motivated by the private enterprise of capitalism. While people at the minimization stage are considerably more knowledgeable than those in denial and a lot nicer than those in defense, they are still ethnocentric in their adherence to these culture-bound universalistic assumptions.

In domestic intercultural relations in the United States, minimization is the classic "white liberal" position. It is usually accompanied by strong support for the "melting pot" idea, a distrust of ethnic and other labels for cultural diversity, and an abiding belief in the existence of equal opportunity. While eschewing power exercised through exploitation and denial of opportunity, people in minimization unquestioningly accept the dominant culture privileges built into institutions. People who do not enjoy these privileges—people of color and others who experience oppression in U.S. society—tend not to dwell at this somewhat self-congratulatory stage.

Acceptance. People at the acceptance stage enjoy recognizing and exploring cultural differences. They are aware that they themselves are cultural beings. They are fairly tolerant of ambiguity and are comfortable knowing there is no one right answer (although there are better answers for particular contexts). "Acceptance" does not mean that a person has to agree with or take on a cultural perspective other than his or her own. Rather, people accept the *viability* of different cultural ways of thinking and behaving, even though they might not like them. This is the first stage in which people begin to think about the notion of cultural relativity—that their own behavior and values are not the only good way to be in the world.

People in acceptance tend to avoid the exercise of power in any form. As a consequence, they may at times become paralyzed by the dilemmas posed by conflicting cultural norms. At this stage, people have moved beyond ethnocentric rules for behavior and may not yet have developed ethnorelative principles for taking action.

Adaptation. People at the adaptation stage use knowledge about their own and others' cultures to intentionally shift into a different cultural frame of reference. That is, they can empathize or take another person's perspective in order to understand and be understood across cultural boundaries. Based on their ability to use alternative cultural interpretations, people in this stage can modify their behavior in ways that make it more appropriate to cultures other than their own. Another way to think about this is that people in adaptation have increased their repertoire of behavior—they have maintained the skills of operating in their own cultures while adding the ability to operate effectively in one or more other cultures. This intercultural competence may include the ability to recognize how power is being exercised within a cultural context, and some people may themselves be able to exercise power in ways that are appropriate to the other culture. Advanced forms of adaptation are "bicultural" or "multicultural," wherein people have internalized one or more cultural frames in addition to that in which they were originally socialized. Bicultural people can completely shift their cultural frame of reference without much conscious effort.

Most people at the adaptation stage are generally interculturally sensitive; with varying degrees of sophistication, they can apply skills of empathy and adaptation of behavior to any cultural context. However, in some cases people have become "accidently bicultural," wherein they received primary socialization in two or more cultural frames of reference. (Children of bicultural marriages and of long-term expatriates may fall into this category.) Sometimes these people are very good at shifting between the two cultures they have internalized, but they cannot apply the same adaptation skills to other cultures. In addition, some people in adaptation do not exhibit intercultural sensitivity toward groups that they do not consider cultures. For instance, some people who are otherwise interculturally skilled retain negative stereotypes of gay, lesbian, and bisexual people. When these groups are defined in cultural terms, people in adaptation are more likely to be able to relate to them in interculturally competent ways.

Integration. People at the integration stage of development are attempting to reconcile the sometimes conflicting cultural frames that they have internalized. In the transition to this stage, some people become overwhelmed by the cultures they know and are disturbed that they can no longer identify with any one of them. But as they move into integration, people achieve an identity which allows them to see themselves as "interculturalists" or "multiculturalists" in addition to their national and ethnic backgrounds.[54] They recognize that worldviews are collective constructs and that identity is itself a construction of consciousness. As a consequence, they may seek out roles that allow them to be intercultural mediators and exhibit other qualities of "constructive marginality."[55] They also tend to associate with other cultural marginals rather than people from any one of the cultures they know.

People in integration are inclined to interpret and evaluate behavior from a variety of cultural frames of reference, so that there is never a single right or wrong answer. But, unlike the resulting paralysis of action that may occur in earlier stages, people in integration are capable of engaging in "contextual evaluation." The goodness or ethicality of actions is not given by absolute (and ethnocentric) principles but is constructed by human beings who thereby take responsibility for the realities they are creating. Thus, people in integration face the unending task of guiding their own behavior along the ethical lines that they themselves have created.

Ethnorelative Ethics

Much of the controversy surrounding the development of intercultural sensitivity is about ethics. Some people seem to think that being interculturally sensitive means giving up any set of ethical principles or moral guidelines. They think cultural relativity is the same thing as moral relativism or situational ethics. To understand that criticism, we can turn to yet another developmental model, the Perry Scheme of Cognitive and Ethical Development.[56]

Perry outlines a process whereby people develop ethical thinking and behavior as they learn more about the world. The model describes movement from "dualism" (one simple either/or way of thinking) to "multiplicity" (many ambiguous and equally good ways of thinking), and then on to "contextual relativism" (different actions are judged according to appropriate context) and "commitment in relativism" (people choose the context in which they will act, even though other actions are viable in different contexts).

People who are most critical of multiculturalism seem to be at Perry's stage of dualism. They think of ethics and morality as absolute, universal rules. In this dualistic view, the acceptance of different cultures leads only to multiplicity, where all options are equal and ethical chaos reigns. Therefore, goes the dualistic argument, either you choose the absolutist ethical path that rejects cultural relativism, or you accept cultural relativism and the only alternative it offers to absolutism, moral relativity and situational ethics.

Interculturalists by and large reject this dualistic view in favor of a third alternative, one where ethnorelativism and strong ethical principles coexist. The reconciliation of culture and ethics occurs in parallel to the latter two stages of Perry's model. In contextual relativism, actions must be judged within context. Thus, at this stage, ethical actions must be judged within a cultural context. There is no universal ethical behavior. For instance, it is not universally ethical to be openly honest in dealing with others. That such is the case, however, does not imply that one should be dishonest whenever it is convenient or situationally normative (e.g., "Everyone else is lying to get those payments, so why shouldn't I?"). On the contrary, Perry's last stage suggests that we commit to acting within the context we wish to maintain. If we want a reality in which open honesty is normative, then it is ethical to act in ways that support the viability of that behavior. Perhaps this doesn't mean that someone with such an ethical commitment is openly honest in every situation. But it probably does mean that actions that contradict or undermine a context in which "honesty is the best policy" would be avoided.

Some antagonists of intercultural and multicultural thinking[57] have suggested that interculturalists are the same as any other ethical absolutist in their adherence to the "goodness" of contextual relativity. In so doing, these critics neglect that important aspect of language called "logical type."[58] The statement "It is good to have three wives" is different in logical type from the statement "It is good to know that forms of marriage are evaluated differently in different cultures." The latter statement is actually a "metastatement," a statement about other statements. Interculturalists would certainly think it was good to make that metastatement, but this thought is significantly different in type from thinking that it is good or bad to have one or three wives. Another such metastatement is "absolutists and relativists differ in their belief in the importance of contextual evaluation." It is good to be able to make this distinction, but doing so says nothing about the goodness of either absolutists or relativists. Absolutists might be judged as "bad" in the context of intercultural communication not for any particular beliefs they hold but because they reject seeing their own behavior in cultural context.

Personal Endnote

As you can see, I think an intercultural perspective offers more than an effective way to analyze interaction and facilitate adaptation. In my opinion, intercultural communication envisions a reality which will support the simultaneous existence of unity and diversity, of cooperation and competition in the global village, and of consensus and creative conflict in multicultural societies. In this vision, our different voices can be heard both in their uniqueness and in synergistic harmony. While there are many paths which can converge into this future, the focus brought by interculturalists rests on individuals and relationships. We strive to bring culture into individual consciousness and in so doing bring consciousness to bear on the creation of intercultural relationships.

1   Dean Barnlund, "Communication in a Global Village," this volume.
2   Milton J. Bennett, "Overcoming the Golden Rule," this volume.
3   LaRay M. Barna, "Stumbling Blocks in Intercultural Communication," this volume.
4   For example, see Peter L. Berger and Thomas Luckmann, in *The Analysis of Subjective Culture*, edited by Harry C. Triandis (New York: John Wiley, 1972).
5   Peter L. Berger and Thomas Luckmann, *The Social Construction of Reality: A Treatise in the Sociology of Knowledge* (New York: Doubleday, 1966).
6   Edward C. Stewart and Milton J. Bennett, *American Cultural Patterns: A Cross-Cultural Perspective*, rev. ed. (Yarmouth, ME: Intercultural Press, 1991).
7   Some forms of ethnicity also exist at a higher level of abstraction than does national culture, e.g., Arab ethnicity, which cuts across many national boundaries: the Kurds of Iraq and Turkey, and many other groups in Europe, Asia, and Africa.
8   Each of these ethnic groups is, itself, at a relatively high level of abstraction. For instance, "African American" includes people from many places in Africa and its diaspora, such as the Caribbean, who arrived in America anytime from a dozen generations to only one generation ago. (American Indians, of course, were here earlier.) Appropriately, "European American" and the other categories are at this same level of abstraction.   More specific references, such as to Italian Americans or Mexican Americans, occur at a lower level of abstraction and should not be mixed with the higher-level generalizations. Care with these levels maintains a "conceptually level playing field" for inter-ethnic relations.
9   Marshall R. Singer, "Culture: A Perceptual Approach," this volume.
10 David S. Hoopes, "Intercultural Communication Concepts and the Psychology of Intercultural Experience," in *Multicultural Education: A Cross Cultural Training Approach*, edited by Margaret D. Pusch (LaGrange Park, IL: Intercultural Press, 1980).
11 Florence R. Kluckhohn and Fred L. Strodtbeck, *Variations in Value Orientations* (1961; reprint, Westport, CT: Greenwood Press, 1973); Stewart and Bennett, *American Cultural Patterns*.
12 Carlos E. Cortés, "Pride, Prejudice and Power: The Mass Media as Societal Educator on Diversity," in *Prejudice, Polemic or Progress?*, edited by James Lynch, Celia Modgil, and Sohan Modgil (London: Falmer Press, 1992), 367-81.
13 Stewart and Bennett, *American Cultural Patterns*; Eva S. Kras, *Management in Two Cultures: Bridging the Gap between U.S. and Mexican Managers*, rev. ed. (Yarmouth, ME: Intercultural Press, 1995); John C. Condon, *Good Neighbors: Communicating with the Mexicans*, 2d ed. (Yarmouth, ME: Intercultural Press, 1997).
14 Judith N. Martin and Thomas K. Nakayama, *Intercultural Communication in Contexts* (Mountain View, CA: Mayfield Publishing, 1997).
15 Edward T. Hall, *Beyond Culture* (1976; reprint, New York: Anchor/Doubleday, 1981).

16 Etic analysis as used by interculturalists does not assume the existence of universal categories. Rather, contrastive categories are created to generate cultural distinctions that are useful for the purpose of communication.

17 Deborah Tannen, *Gender and Discourse* (New York: Oxford University Press, 1994).

18 William G. Perry Jr., *Forms of Intellectual and Ethical Development in the College Years: A Scheme* (Fort Worth, TX: Harcourt Brace, 1970).

19 Stewart and Bennett, *American Cultural Patterns.*

20 Benjamin Lee Whorf, "Science and Linguistics," this volume.

21 Brent Berlin and Paul Kay, *Basic Color Terms: Their Universality and Evolution* (Berkeley: University of California Press, 1969); Stewart and Bennett, *American Cultural Patterns.*

22 G. Spencer Brown, *Laws of Form* (Toronto: Bantam Books, 1972); Heinz von Foerster, "On Constructing a Reality," in *The Invented Reality*, edited by Paul Watzlawick (New York: W. W. Norton, 1984): 41-62.

23 von Foerster, "On Constructing a Reality."

24 Edward T. Hall, *The Silent Language* (1959; reprint, New York: Anchor/Doubleday, 1981).

25 Paul Watzlawick, Janet H. Beavin, and Don D. Jackson, *Pragmatics of Human Communication* (New York: Norton, 1967).

26 Kichiro Hayashi, *Intercultural Insights into Japanese Business Methods*, Senior Executive Seminar, Pacific University, Forest Grove, Oregon, Nov. 1990.

27 Hall, *Beyond Culture.*

28 Edward T. Hall, "The Power of Hidden Differences," this volume.

29 Ibid.

30 Watzlawick, Beavin, and Jackson, *Pragmatics*, 53.

31 Lawrence B. Rosenfeld and Jean Civikly, *With Words Unspoken: The Nonverbal Experience* (New York: Holt, Rinehart & Winston, 1976), 5; James A. Banks and Cherry A. McGee Banks, eds., *Handbook of Research on Multicultural Education* (New York: Simon and Schuster, 1995); Christine I. Bennett, *Comprehensive Multicultural Education: Theory and Practice*, 2d ed. (Boston: Allyn and Bacon, 1990).

32 Thomas Kochman, *Black and White Styles in Conflict* (Chicago: University of Chicago Press, 1981), 47.

33 Robert B. Kaplan, "Cultural Thought Patterns" in *Toward Multiculturalism*, edited by Jaime S. Wurzel (Yarmouth, ME: Intercultural Press, 1988), 207-21.

34 Mary Field Belenky et al., *Women's Ways of Knowing: The Development of Self, Voice, and Mind* (New York: HarperCollins, 1997); Nancy Goldberger et al., *Knowledge, Difference, and Power: Essays Inspired by Women's Ways of Knowing* (New York: HarperCollins, 1996).

35 Jaime S. Wurzel and Nancy Fishman, producers, *A Different Place* and *Creating Community: The Intercultural Classroom* (Boston: Intercultural Resource Corporation, 1993), video.

36 Sheila J. Ramsey, "Interactions between North Americans and Japanese: Considerations of Communication Style," this volume; William B. Gudykunst, Stella Ting-Toomey, and Elizabeth Chua, *Culture and Interpersonal Communication*, vol. 8 (Newbury Park, CA: Sage, 1988).

37 Kluckhohn and Strodtbeck, *Variations in Value Orientations.*

38 The Kluckhohn and Strodtbeck system is used by interculturalists to generate convenient and useful contrasts among cultures, and not as the universal etic categories which they were originally assumed to be.

[39] John C. Condon and Fathi Yousef, *An Introduction to Intercultural Communication* (New York: Macmillan, 1975).

[40] L. Robert Kohls, *Values Americans Live By* (Duncanville, TX: Adult Learning Systems, 1988).

[41] Edward C. Stewart, Jack Danielian, and Robert J. Foster, "Cultural Assumptions and Values," this volume.

[42] Stewart and Bennett, *American Cultural Patterns*.

[43] Geert Hofstede, *Culture's Consequences: International Differences in Work-Related Values*, abridged ed., vol. 5, Cross-Cultural Research and Methodology Series (Beverly Hills, CA: Sage, 1984).

[44] Geert Hofstede, *Cultures and Organizations: Software of the Mind* (London: McGraw-Hill, 1991).

[45] Israel Zangwill, *The Melting Pot: Drama in Four Acts* (New York: Macmillan, 1921).

[46] Jean Piaget, *Construction of Reality in the Child* (New York: Ballantine Books, 1954).

[47] Perry, *Forms of Intellectual and Ethical Development*.

[48] Kalvero Oberg, "Cultural Shock: Adjustment to New Cultural Environments," *Practical Anthropology* 7 (1960): 177.

[49] John Gullahorn and Jeanne Gullahorn, "An Extension of the U-Curve Hypothesis," *Journal of Social Issues* 19, no. 3 (1963).

[50] Peter S. Adler, "Culture Shock and the Cross-cultural Learning Experience," in *Readings in Intercultural Communication*, vol. 2, edited by David S. Hoopes (Pittsburgh, PA: Regional Council for International Education, June 1972).

[51] Janet M. Bennett, "Transition Shock: Putting Culture Shock in Perspective," this volume.

[52] Milton J. Bennett, "Towards Ethnorelativism: A Developmental Model of Intercultural Sensitivity," in *Cross-Cultural Orientation: New Conceptualizations and Applications*, edited by R. Michael Paige (New York: University Press of America, 1986).

[53] Paul Watzlawick, ed., *The Invented Reality* (New York: W. W. Norton, 1984).

[54] Peter S. Adler, "Beyond Cultural Identity: Reflections on Multiculturalism," this volume.

[55] Janet M. Bennett, "Cultural Marginality: Identity Issues in Intercultural Training," in *Education for the Intercultural Experience*, 2d ed., edited by R. Michael Paige (Yarmouth, ME: Intercultural Press, 1993).

[56] Perry, *Forms of Intellectual and Ethical Development*.

[57] Dinesh D'Souza, *The End of Racism: Principles for a Multiracial Society* (New York: Free Press, 1995); Arthur M. Schlesinger Jr., *The Disuniting of America: Reflections on a Multicultural Society* (1991; reprint, New York: W. W. Norton, 1998); Dinesh D'Souza, *Illiberal Education: The Politics of Race and Sex on Campus* (New York: Random House, 1998).

[58] Bertrand Russell, *Human Knowledge, Its Scope and Limits* (New York: Simon and Schuster, 1948).

Communication in a Global Village

Dean Barnlund

> *Nearing Autumn's close.*
> *My neighbor—*
> *How does he live, I wonder?*
> —Bashō

These lines, written by one of the most cherished of *haiku* poets, express our timeless and universal curiosity about humankind. When they were written, nearly three hundred years ago, the word *neighbor* referred to people very much like one's self—similar in dress, in diet, in custom, in language—who happened to live next door. Today relatively few people are surrounded by neighbors who are cultural replicas of themselves. Tomorrow we can expect to spend most of our lives in the company of neighbors who will speak in a different tongue, seek different values, move at a different pace, and interact according to a different script. Within no more than a decade or two the probability of spending part of one's life in a foreign culture will exceed the probability a hundred years ago of ever leaving the town in which one was born. As our world is transformed, our neighbors increasingly will be people whose lifestyles contrast sharply with our own.

The technological feasibility of such a global village is no longer in doubt. Only the precise date of its attainment is uncertain. The means already exist: in telecommunication systems linking the world by satellite, in aircraft capable of moving people faster than the speed of sound, in computers which can disgorge facts more rapidly than people can formulate their questions. The methods for bringing people closer physically and electronically are clearly at hand. What is in doubt is whether the erosion of cultural boundaries through technology will bring the realization of a dream or a nightmare. Will a global village be a mere collection of people or a true community? Will its residents be neighbors capable of respecting and utilizing their differences or clusters of strangers living in ghettos and united only in their antipathies for others?

Can we generate the new cultural attitudes required by our technological virtuosity? History is not very reassuring here. It has taken centuries to learn how to live harmoniously in the family, the tribe, the city-state, and the nation. Each new stretching of human sensitivity and loyalty has taken generations to become firmly assimilated in the human psyche. And now we are forced into a quantum leap from the mutual suspicion and hostility that have marked the past relations between peoples into a world in which mutual respect and comprehension are requisite.

Even events of recent decades provide little basis for optimism. Increasing physical proximity has brought no millennium in human relations. If anything, it has appeared to intensify the divisions among people rather than to create a broader intimacy. Every new reduction in physical distance has made us more painfully aware of the psychic distance that divides people and has increased alarm over real or imagined differences. If today people occasionally choke on what seem to be indigestible differences between rich and poor, male and female, specialist and nonspecialist within cultures, what will happen tomorrow when people must assimilate and cope with still greater contrasts in lifestyles? Wider access to more people will be a doubtful victory if human beings find they have nothing to say to one another or cannot stand to listen to each other.

Time and space have long cushioned intercultural encounters, confining them to touristic exchanges. But this insulation is rapidly wearing thin. In the world of tomorrow we can expect to live—not merely vacation—in societies which seek different values and abide by different codes. There we will be surrounded by foreigners for long periods of time, working with others in the closest possible relationships. If people currently show little tolerance or talent for encounters with alien cultures, how can they learn to deal with constant and inescapable coexistence?

The temptation is to retreat to some pious hope or talismanic formula to carry us into the new age. "Meanwhile," as Edwin Reischauer reminds us, "we fail to do what we ourselves must do if 'one world' is ever to be achieved, and that is to develop the education, the skills, and the attitudes that men must have if they are to build and maintain such a world. The time is short, and the needs are great. The task faces all men. But it is on the shoulders of people living in the strong countries of the world, such as Japan and the United States, that this burden falls with special weight and urgency."[1]

Those who have truly struggled to comprehend other people—even those closest to and most like them—will appreciate the immensity of the challenge of intercultural communication. A greater exchange of people between nations, needed as that may be, carries with it no guarantee of increased cultural empathy; experience in other lands often does little but aggravate existing prejudices. Studying guidebooks or memorizing polite phrases similarly fails to explain differences in cultural perspectives. Programs of cultural enrichment, while they contribute to curiosity about other ways of life, do not cultivate the skills to function effectively in the cultures studied. Even concentrated exposure to a foreign language, valuable as it is, provides access to only one of the many codes that regulate daily affairs; human understanding is by no means guaranteed because conversants share the same dictionary. (Within the United States, where people inhabit a common territory and possess a common language, mutuality of meaning among Latino Americans, European Americans, African Americans, Native Americans, to say nothing of old and young, poor and rich, proestablishment and antiestablishment cultures, is a sporadic and unreliable occurrence.) Useful as all these measures are for enlarging appreciation of diverse cultures, they fall short of what is needed for a global village to survive.

What seems most critical is to find ways of gaining entrance into the assumptive world of another culture, to identify the norms that govern face-to-face relations, and to equip people to function within a social system that is foreign but no longer incomprehensible. Without this kind of insight, people are condemned to remain outsiders no matter how long they live in another country. Its institutions and its customs will be interpreted inevitably from the premises and through the medium of their own culture. Whether they notice something or overlook it, respect or ridicule it, express or conceal it, their reaction will be dictated by the logic of their own rather than the alien culture.

There are, of course, shelves and shelves of books on the cultures of the world. They cover the history, religion, political thought, music, sculpture, and industry of many nations. And they make fascinating and provocative reading. But only in the vaguest way do they suggest what it is that really distinguishes the behavior of a Samoan, a Congolese, a Japanese, or an American. Rarely do the descriptions of a political structure or religious faith explain precisely when and why certain topics are avoided or why specific gestures carry such radically different meanings according to the context in which they appear.

When former President Nixon and former Premier Sato met to discuss a growing problem concerning trade in textiles between Japan and the United States, Premier Sato announced that since they were on such good terms with each other the deliberations would be "three parts talk and seven parts *haragei*."[2] Translated literally, *haragei* means to communicate through the belly, that is, to feel out intuitively rather than verbally state the precise position of each person.

Subscribing to this strategy—one that governs many interpersonal exchanges in his culture—Premier Sato conveyed without verbal elaboration his comprehension of the plight of American textile firms threatened by accelerating exports of Japanese fabrics to the United States. President Nixon—similarly abiding by norms that govern interaction within his culture—took this comprehension of the American position to mean that new export quotas would be forthcoming shortly.

During the next few weeks both were shocked at the consequences of their meeting: Nixon was infuriated to learn that the new policies he expected were not forthcoming, and Sato was upset to find that he had unwittingly triggered a new wave of hostility toward his country. If prominent officials, surrounded by foreign advisers, can commit such grievous communicative blunders, the plight of the ordinary citizen may be suggested. Such intercultural collisions, forced upon the public consciousness by the grave consequences they carry and the extensive publicity they receive, only hint at the wider and more frequent confusions and hostilities that disrupt the negotiations of lesser officials, business executives, professionals, and even visitors in foreign countries.

Every culture expresses its purposes and conducts its affairs through the medium of communication. Cultures exist primarily to create and preserve common systems of symbols by which their members can assign and exchange meanings. Unhappily, the distinctive rules that govern these symbol systems are far from obvious. About some of these codes, such as language, we have extensive knowledge. About others, such as gestures and facial codes, we have only rudimentary knowledge. On many others—rules governing topical appropriateness, customs regulating physical contact, time and space codes, strategies for the management of conflict—we have almost no systematic knowledge. To crash another culture with only the vaguest notion of its underlying dynamics reflects not only a provincial naiveté but a dangerous form of cultural arrogance.

It is differences in meaning, far more than mere differences in vocabulary, that isolate cultures and that cause them to regard each other as strange or even barbaric. It is not too surprising that many cultures refer to themselves as "The People," relegating all other human beings to a subhuman form of life. To the person who drinks blood, the eating of meat is repulsive. Someone who conveys respect by standing is upset by someone who conveys it by sitting down; both may regard kneeling as absurd. Burying the dead may prompt tears in one society, smiles in another, and dancing in a third. If spitting on the street makes sense to some, it will appear bizarre that others carry their spit in their pocket; neither may quite appreciate someone who spits to express gratitude. The bullfight that constitutes an almost religious ritual for some seems a cruel and inhumane way of destroying a defenseless animal to others. Although staring is acceptable social behavior in some cultures, in others it is a thoughtless invasion of privacy. Privacy, itself, is without universal meaning.

Note that none of these acts involves an insurmountable linguistic challenge. The words that describe these acts—eating, spitting, showing respect, fighting, burying, and staring—are quite translatable into most languages. The issue is more conceptual than linguistic; each society places events in its own cultural frame, and it is these frames that bestow the unique meaning and differentiated response they produce.

As we move or are driven toward a global village and increasingly frequent cultural contact, we need more than simply greater factual knowledge of each other. We need, more specifically, to identify what might be called the "rule books of meaning" that distinguish one culture from another. For to grasp the way in which other cultures perceive the world, and the assumptions and values that are the foundation of these perceptions, is to gain access to the experience of other human beings. Access to the worldview and the communicative style of other cultures may not only enlarge our own way of experiencing the world but enable us to maintain constructive relationships with societies that operate according to a different logic than our own.

Sources of Meaning

To survive, psychologically as well as physically, human beings must inhabit a world that is relatively free of ambiguity and is reasonably predictable. Some sort of structure must be placed upon the endless profusion of incoming signals. The infant, born into a world of flashing, hissing, moving images, soon learns to adapt by resolving this chaos into toys and tables, dogs and parents. Even adults who have had their vision or hearing restored through surgery describe the world as a frightening and sometimes unbearable experience; only after days of effort are they able to transform blurs and noises into meaningful and therefore manageable experiences.

It is commonplace to talk as if the world "has" meaning, to ask what "is" the meaning of a phrase, a gesture, a painting, a contract. Yet when thought about, it is clear that events are devoid of meaning until someone assigns it to them. There is no appropriate response to a bow or a handshake, a shout or a whisper, until it is interpreted. A drop of water and the color red have no meaning—they simply exist. The aim of human perception is to make the world intelligible so that it can be managed successfully; the attribution of meaning is a prerequisite to and preparation for action.

People are never passive receivers, merely absorbing events of obvious significance, but are active in assigning meaning to sensation. What any event acquires in the way of meaning appears to reflect a transaction between what is there to be seen or heard and what the interpreter brings to it in the way of past experience and prevailing motive. Thus the attribution of meaning is always a creative process by which the raw data of sensation are transformed to fit the aims of the observer.

The diversity of reactions that can be triggered by a single experience—meeting a stranger, negotiating a contract, attending a textile conference—is immense. Observers are forced to see it through their own eyes, interpret it in the light of their own values, fit it to the requirements of their own circumstances. As a consequence, every object and message is seen by every observer from a somewhat different perspective. Each person will note some features and neglect others. Each will accept some relations among the facts and deny others. Each will arrive at some conclusion, tentative or certain, as the sounds and forms resolve into a *temple* or *barn*, a *compliment* or *insult*.

Provide a group of people with a set of photographs, even quite simple and ordinary photographs, and note how diverse are the meanings the photographs provoke. They will recall and forget different pictures; they will also assign quite distinctive meanings to those they do remember. Some will recall the mood of a picture, others the actions; some the appearance and others the attitudes of persons portrayed. Often the observers cannot agree upon even the most "objective" details—the number of people, the precise location and identity of simple objects. A difference in frame of mind—fatigue, hunger, excitement, anger—will change dramatically what they report they have "seen."

It should not be surprising that people raised in different families, exposed to different events, praised and punished for different reasons, should come to view the world so differently. As George A. Kelly has noted, people see the world through templates which force them to construe events in unique ways. These patterns or grids which we fit over the realities of the world are cut from our own experience and values, and they predispose us to certain interpretations. Industrialist and farmer do not see the "same" land; husband and wife do not plan for the "same" child; doctor and patient do not discuss the "same" disease; borrower and creditor do not negotiate the "same" mortgage; daughter and daughter-in-law do not react to the "same" mother.

The worlds people create for themselves are distinctive worlds, not the same worlds others occupy. They fashion from every incident whatever meanings fit their own private biases. These biases, taken together, constitute what has been called the "assumptive world of the individual." The worlds people get inside their heads are the only worlds they know. And these symbolic worlds, not the real world, are what people talk about, argue about, laugh about, fight about.

Interpersonal Encounters

Every communication, interpersonal or intercultural, is a transaction between these private worlds. As people talk, they search for symbols that will enable them to share their experience and converge upon a common meaning. This process, often long and sometimes painful, makes it possible finally to reconcile apparent or real differences between them. Various words are used to describe this moment. When it involves an integration of facts or ideas, it is usually called an *agreement*; when it involves sharing a mood or feeling, it is referred to as *empathy* or *rapport*. But *understanding* is a broad enough term to cover both possibilities; in either case it identifies the achievement of a common meaning.

If understanding is a measure of communicative success, a simple formula—which might be called the *interpersonal equation*—may clarify the major factors that contribute to its achievement:

Interpersonal Understanding = f (Similarity of Perceptual Orientations, Similarity of Belief Systems, Similarity of Communicative Styles)

That is, *Interpersonal Understanding* is a function of or dependent upon the degree of *Similarity of Perceptual Orientations*, *Similarity of Systems of Belief*, and *Similarity in Communicative Styles*. Each of these terms requires some elaboration.

Similarity in Perceptual Orientations refers to people's prevailing approaches to reality and the degree of flexibility they manifest in organizing it. Some people scan the world broadly, searching for diversity of experience, preferring the novel and unpredictable. They may be drawn to new foods, new music, new ways of thinking. Others seem to scan the world more narrowly, searching to confirm past experience, preferring the known and predictable. They secure satisfaction from old friends, traditional art forms, familiar lifestyles. The former have a high tolerance for novelty; the latter a low tolerance for novelty.

It is a balance between these tendencies, of course, that characterizes most people. Within the same person, attraction to the unfamiliar and the familiar coexist. Which prevails at any moment is at least partly a matter of circumstance: when secure, people may widen their perceptual field, accommodate new ideas or actions; when they feel insecure, they may narrow their perceptual field to protect existing assumptions from the threat of new beliefs or lifestyles. The balance may be struck in still other ways: some people like to live in a stable physical setting with everything in its proper place, but welcome new emotional or intellectual challenges; others enjoy living in a chaotic and disordered environment but would rather avoid exposing themselves to novel or challenging ideas.

People differ also in the degree to which their perceptions are flexible or rigid. Some react with curiosity and delight to unpredictable and uncategorizable events. Others are disturbed or uncomfortable in the presence of the confusing and complex.

There are people who show a high degree of tolerance for ambiguity; others manifest a low tolerance for ambiguity. When confronted with the complications and confusions that surround many daily events, the former tend to avoid immediate closure and delay judgment, while the latter seek immediate closure and evaluation. Those with little tolerance for ambiguity tend to respond categorically, that is, by reference to the class names for things (businessmen, radicals, hippies, foreigners) rather than to their unique and differentiating features.

It would be reasonable to expect that individuals who approach reality similarly might understand each other easily, and laboratory research confirms this conclusion: people with similar perceptual styles attract one another, understand each other better, and work more efficiently together and with greater satisfaction than those whose perceptual orientations differ.

Similarity in Systems of Belief refers not to the way people view the world but to the conclusions they draw from their experience. Everyone develops a variety of opinions toward divorce, poverty, religion, television, sex, and social customs. When belief and disbelief systems coincide, people are likely to understand and appreciate each other better. Research done by Donn Byrne and replicated by the author demonstrates how powerfully human beings are drawn to those who hold the same beliefs and how sharply they are repelled by those who do not.[3]

Subjects in these experiments were given questionnaires requesting their opinions on twenty-six topics. After completing the forms, each was asked to rank the thirteen most important and least important topics. Later each person was given four forms, ostensibly filled out by people in another group but actually filled out by the researchers to show varying degrees of agreement with their own answers, and invited to choose among them with regard to their attractiveness as associates. The results were clear: people most preferred to talk with those whose attitudes duplicated their own exactly, next chose those who agreed with them on all important issues, next chose those with similar views on unimportant issues, and finally and reluctantly chose those who disagreed with them completely. It appears that most people most of the time find satisfying relationships easiest to achieve with someone who shares their own hierarchy of beliefs. This, of course, converts many human encounters into rituals of ratification, both people looking to each other only to obtain endorsement and applause for their own beliefs. It is, however, what is often meant by "interpersonal understanding."

Does the same principle hold true for *Similarity of Communicative Styles*? To a large extent, yes. But not completely. By *communicative style* is meant the topics people prefer to discuss, their favorite forms of interaction—ritual, repartee, argument, self-disclosure—and the depth of involvement they demand of each other. It includes the extent to which communicants rely upon the same channels—vocal, verbal, physical—for conveying information and the extent to which they are tuned to the same level of meaning, that is, to the factual or emotional content of messages. The use of a common vocabulary and even preference for similar metaphors may help people to understand each other.

But some complementarity in conversational style may also help. Talkative people may prefer quiet partners, the more aggressive may enjoy the less aggressive, and those who seek affection may be drawn to the more affection-giving, simply because both can find the greatest mutual satisfaction when interpersonal styles mesh. Even this sort of complementarity, however, may reflect a case of similarity in definitions of each other's conversational role.

This hypothesis, too, has drawn the interest of communicologists. One investigator found that people paired to work on common tasks were much more effective if their communicative styles were similar than if they were dissimilar.[4] Another social scientist found that teachers tended to give higher grades on tests to students whose verbal styles matched their own than to students who gave equally valid answers but did not phrase them as their instructors might.[5] To establish common meanings seems to require that conversants share a common vocabulary and compatible ways of expressing ideas and feelings.

It must be emphasized that perceptual orientations, systems of belief, and communicative styles do not exist or operate independently. They overlap and affect each other. They combine in complex ways to determine behavior. What people say is influenced by what they believe and what they believe, in turn, by what they see. Their perceptions and beliefs are themselves partly a product of their manner of communicating with others. The terms that comprise the *interpersonal equation* constitute not three isolated but three interdependent variables. They provide three perspectives to use in the analysis of communicative acts.

The *interpersonal equation* suggests there is an underlying narcissistic bias in human societies that draws similar people together. They seek to find in others a reflection of themselves, those who view the world as they do, who interpret it as they do, and who express themselves in a similar way. It is not surprising, then, that artists should be drawn to artists, radicals to radicals, Jews to Jews—or Japanese to Japanese and Americans to Americans.

The opposite seems equally true: people tend to avoid those who challenge their assumptions, who dismiss their beliefs, and who communicate in strange and unintelligible ways. When one reviews history, whether one examines crises within or between cultures, one finds people have consistently shielded themselves, segregated themselves, even fortified themselves against wide differences in modes of perception or expression (in many cases, indeed, have persecuted and conquered the infidel and afterwards substituted their own cultural ways for the offending ones). Intercultural defensiveness appears to be only a counterpart of interpersonal defensiveness in the face of uncomprehended or incomprehensible differences.

Intercultural Encounters

Every culture attempts to create a "universe of discourse" for its members, a way in which people can interpret their experience and convey it to one another. Without a common system of codifying sensations, life would be absurd and all efforts to share meanings doomed to failure. This universe of discourse—one of the most precious of all cultural legacies—is transmitted to each generation in part consciously and in part unconsciously. Parents and teachers give explicit instruction in it by praising or criticizing certain ways of dressing, of thinking, of gesturing, of responding to the acts of others. But the most significant aspects of any cultural code may be conveyed implicitly, not by rule or lesson but through modelling behavior. The child is surrounded by others who, through the mere consistency of their actions as males and females, mothers and fathers, salesclerks and police officers, display what is appropriate behavior. Thus the grammar of any culture is sent and received largely unconsciously, making one's own cultural assumptions and biases difficult to recognize. They seem so obviously right that they require no explanation.

In *The Open and Closed Mind,* Milton Rokeach poses the problem of cultural understanding in its simplest form, but one that can readily demonstrate the complications of communication between cultures. It is called the "Denny Doodlebug Problem." Readers are given all the rules that govern his culture: Denny is an animal that always faces north and can move only by jumping; he can jump large distances or small distances, but can change direction only after jumping four times in any direction; he can jump north, south, east, or west, but not diagonally. Upon concluding a jump, his master places some food three feet directly west of him. Surveying the situation, Denny concludes he must jump four times to reach the food. No more or less. And he is right. All the reader has to do is to explain the circumstances that make his conclusion correct.[6]

The large majority of people who attempt this problem fail to solve it, despite the fact that they are given all the rules that control behavior in this culture. If there is difficulty in getting inside the simplistic world of Denny Doodlebug—where the cultural code has already been broken and handed to us—imagine the complexity of comprehending behavior in societies where codes have not yet been deciphered—and where even those who obey these codes are only vaguely aware of and can rarely describe the underlying sources of their own actions.

If two people, both of whom spring from a single culture, must often shout to be heard across the void that separates their private worlds, one can begin to appreciate the distance to be overcome when people of different cultural identities attempt to talk. Even with the most patient dedication to seeking a common terminology, it is surprising that people of alien cultures are able to hear each other at all. And the peoples of Japan and the United States would appear to constitute a particularly dramatic test of the ability to cross an intercultural divide. Consider the disparity between them.

Here is Japan, a tiny island nation with a minimum of resources, buffeted by periodic disasters, overcrowded with people, isolated by physical fact and cultural choice, nurtured in Shinto and Buddhist religions, permeated by a deep respect for nature, nonmaterialist in philosophy, intuitive in thought, hierarchical in social structure. Eschewing the explicit, the monumental, the bold and boisterous, it expresses its sensuality in the form of impeccable gardens, simple rural temples, asymmetrical flower arrangements, a theater unparalleled for containment of feeling, an art and literature remarkable for their delicacy, and crafts noted for their honest and earthy character. Its people, among the most homogeneous in the world, are modest and apologetic in manner, communicate in an ambiguous and evocative language, are engrossed in interpersonal rituals, and prefer inner serenity to influencing others. They occupy unpretentious buildings of wood and paper and live in cities laid out as casually as farm villages. Suddenly from these rice paddies emerges an industrial giant, surpassing rival nations with decades of industrial experience, greater resources, and a larger reserve of technicians. Its labor force, working longer, harder, and more frantically than any in the world, builds the earth's largest city, constructs some of its ugliest buildings, promotes the most garish and insistent advertising anywhere, and pollutes its air and water beyond the imagination.

And here is the United States, an immense country, sparsely settled, richly endowed, tied through waves of immigrants to the heritage of Europe, yet forced to subdue nature and find fresh solutions to the problems of survival. Steeped in the Judeo-Christian tradition, schooled in European abstract and analytic thought, it is materialist and experimental in outlook, philosophically pragmatic, politically egalitarian, economically competitive, its raw individualism sometimes tempered by a humanitarian concern for others. Its cities are studies in geometry along whose avenues rise shafts of steel and glass subdivided into separate cubicles for separate activities and separate people. Its popular arts are characterized by the hugeness of cinemascope, the spontaneity of jazz, the earthy loudness of rock; in its fine arts the experimental, striking, and monumental often stifle the more subtle revelation. The people, a smorgasbord of races, religions, dialects, and nationalities, are turned expressively outward, impatient with rituals and rules, casual and flippant, gifted in logic and argument, approachable and direct yet given to flamboyant and exaggerated assertion. They are curious about one another, open and helpful, yet display a missionary zeal for changing one another. Suddenly this nation whose power and confidence have placed it in a dominant position in the world intellectually and politically, whose style of life has permeated the planet, finds itself uncertain of its direction, doubts its own premises and values, questions its motives and materialism, and engages in an orgy of self-criticism.

It is when people nurtured in such different psychological worlds meet that differences in cultural perspectives and communicative codes may sabotage efforts to understand one another. Repeated collisions between a foreigner and the members of a contrasting culture often produce what is called *culture shock*. It is a feeling of helplessness, even of terror or anger, that accompanies working in an alien society. One feels trapped in an absurd and indecipherable nightmare.

It is as if some hostile leprechaun had gotten into the works and as a cosmic caper rewired the connections that hold society together. Not only do the actions of others no longer make sense, but it is impossible even to express one's own intentions clearly. "Yes" comes out meaning "no." A wave of the hand means "come," or it may mean "go." Formality may be regarded as childish or as a devious form of flattery. Statements of fact may be heard as statements of conceit. Arriving early, or arriving late, embarrasses or impresses. "Suggestions" may be treated as "ultimatums," or precisely the opposite. Failure to stand at the proper moment, or failure to sit, may be insulting. The compliment intended to express gratitude instead conveys a sense of distance. A smile signifies disappointment rather than pleasure.

If the crises that follow such intercultural encounters are sufficiently dramatic or the communicants unusually sensitive, they may recognize the source of their trouble. If there is patience and constructive intention, the confusion can sometimes be clarified. But more often foreigners, without knowing it, leave behind them a trail of frustration, mistrust, and even hatred *of which they are totally unaware.* Neither they nor their associates recognize that their difficulty springs from sources deep within the rhetoric of their own societies. All see themselves as acting in ways that are thoroughly sensible, honest, and considerate. And— given the rules governing their own universes of discourse—they all are. Unfortunately, there are few cultural universals, and the degree of overlap in communicative codes is always less than perfect. Experience can be transmitted with fidelity only when the unique properties of each code are recognized and respected, or where the motivation and means exist to bring them into some sort of alignment.

The Collective Unconscious

Among the greatest insights of this modern age are two that bear a curious affinity to each other. The first, evolving from the efforts of psychologists, particularly Sigmund Freud, revealed the existence of an *individual unconscious*. The acts of human beings were found to spring from motives of which they were often vaguely or completely unaware. Their unique perceptions of events arose not from the facts outside their skins but from unrecognized assumptions inside them. When, through intensive analysis, they obtained some insight into these assumptions, they became free to develop other ways of seeing and acting which contributed to their greater flexibility in coping with reality.

The second of these generative ideas, flowing from the work of anthropologists, particularly Margaret Mead and Ruth Benedict, postulated a parallel idea in the existence of a *cultural uncon-scious*. Students of primitive cultures began to see that there was nothing divine or absolute about cultural norms. Every society had its own way of viewing the universe, and each developed from its premises a coherent set of rules of behavior. Each tended to be blindly committed to its own style of life and regarded all others as evil. The fortunate people who were able to master the art of living in foreign cultures often learned that their own modes of life were not universal. With this insight they became free to choose from among cultural values those that seemed to best fit their peculiar circumstances.

Cultural norms so completely surround people, so permeate thought and action, that few ever recognize the assumptions on which their lives and their sanity rest. As one observer put it, if birds were suddenly endowed with scientific curiosity, they might examine many things, but the sky itself would be overlooked as a suitable subject; if fish were to become curious about the world, it would never occur to them to begin by investigating water. For birds and fish would take the sky and sea for granted, unaware of their profound influence, because they comprise the medium for every act. Human beings, in a similar way, occupy a symbolic universe governed by codes that are unconsciously acquired and automatically employed. So much so that they rarely notice that the ways they interpret and talk about events are distinctively different from the ways people conduct their affairs in other cul-tures.

As long as people remain blind to the sources of their mean-ings, they are imprisoned within them. These cultural frames of reference are no less confining simply because they cannot be seen or touched. Whether it is an individual neurosis that keeps an individual out of contact with his or her neighbors, or a col-lective neurosis that separates neighbors of different cultures, both are forms of blindness that limit what can be experienced and what can be learned from others.

It would seem that everywhere people would desire to break out of the boundaries of their own experiential worlds. Their ability to react sensitively to a wider spectrum of events and peoples requires an overcoming of such cultural parochialism. But, in fact, few attain this broader vision. Some, of course, have little oppor-tunity for wider cultural experience, though this condition should change as the movement of people accelerates. Others do not try to widen their experience because they prefer the old and familiar, seek from their affairs only further confirmation of the correctness of their own values. Still others recoil from such experiences because they feel it dangerous to probe too deeply into the personal or cultural unconscious. Exposure may reveal how tenuous and arbitrary many cultural norms are; such exposure might force people to acquire new bases for interpreting events. And even for the many who do seek actively to enlarge the variety of human beings with whom they are capable of communicating, there are still difficulties.

Cultural myopia persists not merely because of inertia and habit but chiefly because it is so difficult to overcome. People acquire personalities and cultures in childhood, long before they are capable of comprehending either of them. To survive, people master the perceptual orientations, cognitive biases, and communicative habits of their own cultures. But once mastered, objective assessment of these same processes is awkward, since the same mechanisms that are being evaluated must be used in making the evaluations. Once children learn Japanese or English or Navajo, the categories and grammar of each language predispose them to perceive and think in certain ways and discourage them from doing so in other ways. When they attempt to discover why they see or think as they do, they use the same techniques they are trying to identify.

Fortunately, there may be a way around this paradox. Or promise of a way around it. It is to expose the culturally distinctive ways various peoples construe events and to seek to identify the conventions that connect what is seen with what is thought with what is said. Once this cultural grammar is assimilated and the rules that govern the exchange of meanings are known, they can be shared and learned by those who choose to work and live in alien cultures.

When people within a culture face an insurmountable problem, they turn to friends, neighbors, and associates for help. To them they explain their predicament, often in distinctive, personal ways. Through talking it out, however, there often emerge new ways of looking at the problem, fresh incentive to attack it, and alternative solutions to it. This sort of interpersonal exploration is often successful within a culture, for people share at least the same communicative style even if they do not agree completely in their perceptions or beliefs.

When people communicate between cultures, where communicative rules as well as the substance of experience differs, the problems multiply. But so, too, do the number of interpretations and alternatives. If it is true that the more people differ the harder it is for them to understand each other, it is equally true that the more they differ the more they have to teach and learn from each other. To do so, of course, there must be mutual respect and sufficient curiosity to overcome the frustrations that occur as they flounder from one misunderstanding to another. Yet the task of coming to grips with differences in communicative styles—between or within cultures—is prerequisite to all other types of mutuality.

---

[1] Edwin Reischauer, *Man and His Shrinking World* (Tokyo: Asahi Press, 1971), 34-35.

[2] Masao Kunihiro, "U.S.-Japan Communications," in *Discord in the Pacific*, edited by Henry Rosovsky (Washington, DC: Columbia Books, 1972), 167.

[3] Donn Byrne, "Interpersonal Attraction and Attitude Similarity," *Journal of Abnormal and Social Psychology* 62 (1961).

[4] Harry C. Triandis, "Cognitive Similarity and Communication in a Dyad," *Human Relations* 13 (1960).

[5] P. Runkel, "Cognitive Similarity in Facilitating Communication," *Sociometry* 19 (1956).

[6] Milton Rokeach, *The Open and Closed Mind* (New York: Basic Books, 1960).

The Power of
Hidden Differences

Edward T. Hall

Culture Is Communication

The galaxies of the universe are controlled by the same laws. This is not true of the cultural worlds created by humans, each of which operates according to its own internal dynamic, its own principles, and its own laws—written and unwritten. Even time and space are unique to each culture.[1] There are, however, some common threads that run through all cultures, for we all share the same basic roots.

In essence, any culture is primarily a system for creating, sending, storing, and processing information. Communication underlies everything.[2] Although we tend to regard language as the main channel of communication, there is general agreement among experts in semiotics that anywhere from 80 to 90 percent of the information we receive is not only communicated nonverbally but occurs outside our awareness.

It is the conflict between the two worlds of verbal and nonverbal culture that does much to explain Bateson's[3] theory of the double bind, Sullivan's[4] theory of disassociation, much of Jung's[5] theory, why Zen[6] (which enhances the acquired) is so difficult for Westerners (who glorify the learned), and why Native Americans like the Tewa of New Mexico (in whose language the words for learning and breathing are the same) have so much trouble making the shift in school from acquisition to learning. One would have to search far and wide to find a facet of life exempt from the pervasive influence of this fundamental difference.

Far removed from the philosophers' lofty ideas, the *tacit-acquired* side of culture includes a broad range of practices and solutions to problems with roots in the common clay of the shared experiences of ordinary people. In spite of this distancing from the academic, I have observed repeatedly that if people fail to attend to these basic, unstated rules of behavior and communication, it is impossible to make the culture work.

"Making the system work" requires attention to everything people do to survive, advance in the world, and gain satisfaction from life. Failure can often be attributed to one of the following:

1. Leaving out crucial steps because one hasn't truly mastered the system.
2. Unconsciously applying one's own rules to another system, which never works.
3. Deliberately rejecting the rules—written or unwritten—and trying to force one's own rules on another system.
4. Changes and/or breakdowns of the system in times of political upheaval, economic collapse, war, and revolution.

Cultural communications are deeper and more complex than spoken or written messages. The essence of cross-cultural communication has more to do with releasing responses than with sending messages. And *it is more important to release the right response than to send the "right message."*

We humans are guided by two forms of information, accessed in two distinctly different ways: type A—manifest culture—which is learned from words and numbers, and type B—tacit-acquired culture—which is *not* verbal but is highly situational and operates according to rules which are not in awareness, not learned in the usual sense but acquired in the process of growing up or simply being in different environments. In humans, tacit-acquired culture is made up of hundreds and possibly thousands of microevents comprising the corpus of the daily cycle of activity, the spaces we occupy, and the way we relate to others, in other words, the bulk of experiences of everyday life. This tacit, taken-for-granted aspect of culture, a natural part of life, is the foundation on which my research of the past forty-five years rests.

My work with acquired culture grew out of the study of transactions at cultural interfaces.[7] The study of an interface between two systems is different from the study of either system alone.

For my purposes, working at the interface has proved fruitful because contrasting and conflicting patterns are revealed. It tells as much about tacit-acquired culture as it does about manifest culture, and it is frequently the only way I know of gathering valid cultural data on the out-of-awareness, virtually automatic, tacit-acquired side of life.

When We Talked but Didn't Know that We Talked

There is always a time when people are doing something without being aware of what they are doing. In fact, the practice of analytic psychiatry is built around this process. Yet, despite the hundreds of thousands of hours devoted by psychoanalysts and anthropologists to the study of change from levels of awareness to awareness of the fact that awareness has changed, *little is known about what happens from the inside when great cultural changes occur, such as when human beings first became aware that language and talking were something special.* Each time this state of awareness is reached, along with it comes a greater appreciation of the self and of the possibilities for the future. This combination seems to be sufficient to motivate people to unusual efforts to solve the massive problems which lie ahead.

Because a great deal is now known about language and so much is taken for granted, it is difficult to imagine what it would be like to stand on the edge of the recognition of language as a system that evolved over many thousands of years. What is even more difficult to imagine are the consequences of this new knowledge and the new analytic and communication skills that are seen only in their incipient form. At times like these everything begins to change. The parts shift around, as does the spotlight of emphasis, which points away from matters which were once thought to be important and toward emergent forms. It is a bit like what occurs in the transition from childhood to young adulthood but on a much grander scale. The world opens up and with it, new responsibilities. It is quite apparent to me that *the world is currently in the midst of one of these big shifts in awareness!* I believe there is something to be gained if we know more about the processes unfolding around us.

To gain perspective on what is going on, I must review a tiny fraction of our past when similar boundaries were being crossed. My purpose is to provide a feeling for the process of discovery as new awareness unfolds in a succession of revolutions in the way we in the West view the world.[8]

Revolution 1: The Evolution of Language

The first of the great revolutions occurred when our ancestors were physiologically and neurologically able to talk, which was about 100,000 years ago.[9] With the beginnings of language established, the base for the distinction between *learned* information (type A) and *acquired* information (type B) was laid down. Up until that time most of what was known in order to survive was obtained through the process of acquisition. Acquisition occurs without awareness and there is no way it can be stopped except by eliminating all sensory input. Young mammals acquire a mastery of the environments into which they are born, and human children, in addition, acquire language as well as the unstated paradigms of their culture on their own. This is true even for deaf children. If these two steps do not occur, the remaining learning process, which is in words, cannot proceed. Acquisition is not restricted to the early part of life but continues throughout life.

Revolution 2: The Discovery of Language as Language (Metalanguages)

My own reconstruction is that after about 90,000 years, during which time language and culture evolved from their primitive state to that of highly complex systems of communication on many levels, some rather bright but not too well adjusted types who were different and who liked to look at things and ask questions, realized that there was something unusual about talking. It was a complete, working system which was discovered, like a jewel lying in the sand of a spring, but it had been there all the time. Talking wasn't like anything else that human beings did. In fact, talking was something quite remarkable. Until that time, talking had been taken for granted as a natural part of life but not particularly special, not worthy of examination or study with a potential far beyond the process itself. It was a tool that could be used. If our ancestors were anything like their more sophisticated—but not necessarily more intelligent—descendants, they asked questions like "Why study this 'noise made by the mouth thing' that happens between people?" As we shall see under "Revolution 5: Words Are Used to Craft Ideas," when this sort of question is asked, strange things happen, such as the crafting of new languages. Indeed, to cope with this insight it was necessary to invent a new language, a *metalanguage*—a language for talking about language, including a vocabulary to distinguish between linguistic events such as words and symbols. All this took a long time—four to seven thousand years—which is not nearly as long as the time that transpired between fully developed speech and prespeech.

Revolution 3: Recording Speech

It was no time at all before the third revolution occurred. There had to be ways of keeping track of all the complexities of language, because otherwise these wise people would have spent too much effort plowing the same ground over and over again. Writing systems were evolved. And what a revolution that was! From that time on, anything was possible. The word transcended time and space.

Revolution 4: Recorded Language as a Tool

In the context of the Greco-Roman past of the West, Solon (the seventh century B.C. Athenian) was an unusually insightful *law giver.* Realizing that the cases which people brought to him fell into categories and that the decisions he made were far from random events, he began classifying his decisions as a way of helping others. The law at that time was like English common law, rooted in the soil of the *acquired* culture of the times. Solon was the first anthropologist. In fact, all of the world's "law givers" from past to present can be viewed as practicing anthropologists.

Revolution 5: Words Are Used to Craft Ideas

Today I am suggesting the outrageous idea that, instead of expanding our horizons, the Greek philosophers—beginning with the elaboration of Socrates and Plato's word-centered paradigm—may have actually built a wall cutting us off from an important part of our selves. In the process, they created an unbridgeable gap between the cultural unconscious (type B) and the manifest culture of words (type A). In so doing, they set in motion the processes attacking the very foundations of identity.

Plato, believing that the result of the dialectic and its logic represented the ultimate and only reality, distinguished between what ordinary people did—events, behaviors, and ways of thinking which seemed an automatic part of life—which he called *doxa,* and the rigid rules of the logic of the dialectic. Only the ideas in philosophers' heads, expressed in "properly constructed" statements, were thought to be relevant to guiding the citizens. This belief set in motion a process ending with the concept that only well-crafted ideas expressed in *words* are real, whereas people and what they do were dismissed as hardly worth noticing.[10]

This split has been with us ever since, even in anthropology, a science which is, with rare exceptions, based on what we have been told in words and much less on what people did and took for granted. Only in the descriptive linguistics of Edward Sapir and later in the field of sociolinguistics do we find a direct examination of cultural data without reference to preconceived ideas or hypotheses. Alfred Korzybski,[11] of course, made a valiant effort with his studies in general semantics. He made the point that there is an unbridgeable gap separating the word or symbol and the event, and that the map is not the terrain.

Revolution 6: The Discovery of the Unconscious

Freud, Jung, Sullivan, and the others are so recent and well known that there is no need to elaborate further on either the content or the structure of the new world they opened up, a world which is still unfolding before our very eyes.

The Discovery of Culture

Like the discovery of the unconscious, the discovery of culture is recent. First described by Louis H. Morgan in 1877 and by Edward B. Tyler[12] in 1881, the concept of culture has only recently begun to be known beyond a small group of practitioners. Culture is *the medium evolved by the human species, the one which characterizes the human species* while at the same time differentiating one social group from another. While the distinction between *overt* and *manifest* culture was popular in the 1930s, the interpretation of the entirety of culture as a system of communication did not appear in print as a systematic theory of culture until 1953.[13] The differentiation between learned and acquired culture is even more recent. I have developed the examination of various facets of acquired culture under the conceptual heading of Nonverbal Communication in some thirteen books.

Up to this point I have reviewed our species' discovery of its extensions—not the material extensions[14] but primarily the extensions of the central nervous system—centered around the process of communication in words and writing, as records of what is going on in the head. I wish to turn now to those nonverbal expressions of culture of which humanity has only recently become aware—the other 80 percent to 90 percent of our commu-

nicative acts. These acts are the ones responsible for the greatest distortions in understanding between peoples—distortions
traceable to the fact that significant, meaningful acts are read as
*projections of one's own culture rather than as expressions of an-
other culture.*

If there is a message I want to convey, it is that humans must
also take into account the existence of "out-of-awareness" features of communication. When interacting with each other, *it
should never be assumed that we ever achieve full awareness of all
the implications of any communication.* This is because there are
not only context factors that are seldom, if ever, pinned down,
but there are additional sources of distortions—cultural and psychological—in meaning as people interact with one another.

Unfortunately, the job of achieving understanding and insight
into other people's mental processes is much more difficult and
the situation more serious than our political leaders care to admit. What makes the current world situation doubly dangerous
is the failure on the part of our leaders to take into account the
deeper levels of cultural differences and their effect on the way
in which different people see the world.

*Culture hides much more than it reveals and, strangely enough,
what it hides, it hides most effectively from its own participants.*
Years of study have convinced me that the ultimate purpose of
the study of culture is not so much the understanding of foreign
cultures as much as the light that study sheds on our own. There
is a feature of culture which, until recently, was unknown and,
as a consequence, unanalyzed. I refer to the *tacit* frames of reference, the rules for living which vary from culture to culture and
which can be traced to *acquired culture.*

It is axiomatic that dissonance in interpersonal and intercultural relations is inevitably traced to perturbations in the percep-
tual-communicative process in one or both of the tacit or explicit
levels of culture. I first became aware of this dimension of culture while working for the Department of State during a trip
through Latin America and the Middle East. Mixing it up with my
compatriots in a wide variety of situations, I became aware that
instead of a simple artifact for planning and scheduling activities, time was being read as a kind of language. Furthermore it
was assumed that this language of time was universal and had
the same significance to South Americans as it did to North Americans. The most critical, observable situations centered around
waiting times in offices when appointments had been made.[15]
Even ambassadors would be kept waiting. It appeared that sta-

tus, the importance of the business, and even insults were all being communicated by the length of the waiting time. It was quite evident that not only were the Latin American diplomats not as prompt as the North Americans expected them to be, but that their entire system of time was different from our own. Further research revealed that the different time systems permeated or influenced virtually every facet of life (a characteristic which was also discovered in their handling of space). What I learned in South America followed patterns I found later in other cultures in other parts of the world. While it is not practical to give a comprehensive view at this time, the two basic types of time are relevant to this discussion.

Monochronic and Polychronic Time

There are many kinds of time systems in the world, but I call the two basic time systems *monochronic* and *polychronic* time. Monochronic time means paying attention to and doing only one thing at a time. Polychronic time means being involved with many things at once. Like oil and water, the two systems do not mix.

In monochronic cultures, beginning in England with the industrial revolution, time is linear—comparable to a road extending from the past into the future. Monochronic time is divided quite naturally into segments; it is scheduled and compartmentalized, making it possible for a person to concentrate on one thing at a time. In a monochronic system, the schedule takes priority above all else and is treated as sacred and unalterable.

In monochronic cultures, time is perceived as being almost *tangible:* people talk about it as though it were money, as something that can be "spent," "saved," "wasted," and "lost." It is also used as a classification system for ordering life and setting priorities: "I don't have time to see him." Because monochronic time concentrates on one thing at a time, people who are governed by it don't like to be interrupted. Monochronic time seals people off from one another and, as a result, intensifies some relationships while shortchanging others. Time becomes a room which some people are allowed to enter, while others are excluded.

Space is closely related to time in some cases and quite different in others. As is the case with time, space falls into a wide variety of slots. Today I will deal with one—personal space.

Personal Space

Personal space as used by North Americans is a sort of mobile territory. Each person has around him or her an invisible bubble of space which expands and contracts depending on a number of things: the relationship to the people nearby, the person's emotional state or cultural background, and the activity being performed. Few people are allowed to penetrate this bit of mobile territory and then only for short periods of time. Changes in the bubble brought about by cramped quarters or crowding cause people to feel uncomfortable or aggressive. In northern Europe the bubbles are quite large, and people keep their distance. In southern France, Italy, Greece, and Spain the bubbles get smaller and smaller so that distance perceived as intimate in the north overlaps normal conversational distance in the south. This means that Mediterranean Europeans get too close to Germans, Scandinavians, English, and those Americans of northern European ancestry. In northern Europe one does not touch others. Even the brushing of the overcoat sleeve elicits an apology.

Context

At an even more abstract level than time and space is the effect of *context* on meaning. Context is a slippery but highly significant subject which has confounded social scientists and linguists for years. Rather than take the traditional road to situationally determined context, I chose another route, based on observations of interpersonal transaction across a wide variety of cultural interfaces that took account of how information was handled. The result was a scale with high-context communication at one end and low-context at the other.

A high-context (HC) communication or message is one in which *most* of the information is already in the person, while very little is in the coded, explicit, transmitted part of the message. A low-context (LC) communication is just the opposite, that is, the mass of the information is vested in the explicit code. A high-context example is twins who have grown up together and can communicate more economically (HC) than two lawyers in a courtroom during a trial (LC), or a mathematician programming a computer (LC), or two politicians drafting legislation (LC), or two administrators writing a regulation (LC). In general, high-context transactions are more on the feeling, intimate side while the low-context ones are much less personal and oriented toward the left brain. It is also relevant that shifts from high- to low-context signal the cooling of a relationship, while a move up the scale signals increased familiarity and usually warming, for example, forms of address from "Professor" or "Doctor" to using first names.

The context generalization, drawn as it is from observations of behavior, has proved to be quickly recognizable as a pattern in a wide range of cultures. Germans and North Europeans in general can be said to operate lower on the context scale than the Japanese or the Tewa of New Mexico, for example.

I should mention that while the ideas expressed here are relatively simple, differences of the sort I have described are far from trivial and can be found in such everyday situations as the differences between words and numbers. An unusually perceptive friend who is bicultural—North American and Latino—solved major conflicts between the New York headquarters of a corporation and its South American subsidiaries. He sorted out these two channels so that when New York wanted information from the field, the numbers people got numbers and those who wanted words got their information in words. Until then, people weren't getting what they needed.

Communication as Information

I would now like to explore further the point about *communication as information.* Information provides the basic patterns for the organization of life. This may mean that life *is* information and vice versa. In cells we know disorganization as cancer. But what happens when people can't reach each other? We call it "getting through" to someone. When we realize that a communicative impasse has been reached, it is a signal that we are at the end of the line, that the only remaining options are force, withdrawal, banishment, or abandonment. In fact, a communications impasse is one of the chief causes of war. Yet war, regardless of who "wins," has never been an answer. While there are plenty of failures to learn from, I think more can be learned from success in overcoming blocks in communication.

Consider the situation of Helen Keller who, because she was both blind and deaf, lacked the generous quantity of acquired knowledge available even to the Deaf;[16] as a result she often behaved like a frustrated, infuriated animal until her teacher, using language as the instrument, found a way to give order to her energy. A colleague of mine, William C. Stokoe, spent years analyzing the communication system of the Deaf. And it wasn't until he was able to produce the first American Sign Language (ASL) dictionary[17] that the Deaf movement took off, leading to the demonstration that Deaf behavior, instead of being chaotic, was a well-organized culture built around its own system of communication. Until Stokoe's breakthrough, Deaf culture was synonymous with the rest of the unknown, tacit sides of culture.

The world is in a situation somewhat similar to that of Helen Keller's when she first made that dramatic connection between water and the word *water*, which provided her the clue she needed to integrate a language that was there waiting for her.

Unconscious Culture

Though there has been a massive amount of research on A type culture—word culture—it is the B type—unconscious culture—that we need to know more about. There is a growing awareness that we are just at the point where humans were when they first became conscious of language. While we do not as yet have a system of notations on which to build a dictionary for the acquired, nonverbal side of culture,[18] there is already a solid beginning.

Little in this world is more frustrating, exasperating, or maddening than confrontations in those situations where one is dependent on others. I am thinking of recognition, advancement, economic survival, skills of any sort, understanding, insights into self, love, and all relations with other human beings. The situation is analogous to that of a middle-aged neophyte confronting for the first time our demanding word-processing software without a guide or tutor. But in real-life situations of relations with other people, the complexity is infinitely greater. The problem is always how to get the other person, or the culture, or the machine to produce for you—to release the desired responses. Consider these situations: making a friend with a foreigner or with someone of the opposite sex, getting a job or an advancement, negotiating an agreement, settling a dispute, selling a product at home or abroad. The "silent language" of equal opportunity involves much more than *legalese.*

Throughout my life, I have been struck by the disparity between A and B types of reality. And because the A type is explicit and highly visible while B is not, I devoted my energies to describing and explaining B. Having observed that it is hard to understand something you have not experienced and since few people have had my experiences, I have come to the realization that there are some things to be said about A which I had, until recently, minimized in my thinking.

In addition to such relatively small differences separating word people from numbers people, as mentioned above, there are the more pervasive ways in which information is processed, stored, and retrieved. For example, those who grew up under the aegis of Western culture live in two worlds: one acquired, the other learned. One is tacit with automatic responses, and the other is explicit and quite technical. One is a synthesis, and the other is linear. One is a whole, the other is fragmented and compartmentalized so that the left hand really does not know what the right hand is doing (and this is a metaphor to be taken quite seriously). One comprises real-life events that are disparaged, the other is largely invented, yet is extolled and treated as real.

What are needed now are bi- and tri-cultural translators—not that there aren't a lot that are not being used—for every significant interface in the world today. In addition to the translators we need knowledge and skills for their selection and use.[19] At this time, what I have referred to as acquired culture—though it is vividly real for those who have been brought up in different cultures—is not seen as culture at all by most people in the world. In fact, it is often perceived only as an aggravating personality trait. An American black woman I once interviewed in Beirut said, "I used to be married to one of these fellows and we had a *lot* of trouble. I thought it was him. But over here they're *all* that way."

Recognition of the acquired side of culture places a heavy burden on each and every one of us. It means relinquishing the special part of ourselves which gives us permission to put other people down. It means extending ourselves to include others in the same envelope of awareness. It means recognizing others as simply different, but not inferior. And most of all, it means being accepting as well as *nonjudgmental.*

None of this is easy because it is an individual matter, one which cannot be legislated. People may not be like us and we may not be like them. But in these very differences lies the future success of the world. I say this because world problems have ballooned to the point where they are unmanageable by any single group. Each person in each group has been endowed with skills— many of them unique—enabling them to cope with the special problems they have faced in the past. As a species, we have evolved ourselves and achieved multiple talents in the process. We need to be able to evolve ways that allow us to make use of them all. But in order to do so it will be necessary to *come to grips with the reality of acquired culture and the associated fact of nonverbal communication.* Unfortunately, we have yet to realize that our most prized possessions are the differences differentiating the people of this earth from each other.

Although the word is bandied about, the people of this earth are now in the early stages of discovering that there is a hidden language of identity—the identity of our true selves, selves which have lain hidden under a cloak of words. It is possible to look ahead and see an age in which the peoples of the world will soon develop new tools for reaching each other's minds and psyches. It is important to remember, however, that insight and understanding are not synonymous with wisdom. Wisdom, while here for some, is unfortunately still over the horizon for most of us.

Nevertheless, it is my conviction that the human world, much like the earth itself, even though desecrated, is still a treasure trove of hidden resources. The surface of discovery has only been barely scratched. I say this because the peoples of the world have endowed me with great riches, taught me much about myself, expanded my horizons, and presented me with a world and a self that had sufficient gnostic reality to make a believer of me. I have the knowledge that the worlds of other people are real, that life itself—although confusing at times—is lawful, and that below or behind surface impressions there is order. Furthermore, there are many others like myself, most of whom have grown up in more than one culture. Most of us remain lonely until we meet someone else who also knows that other people are real and not the paper cutouts that those who do not know make them out to be. This kind of loneliness is impossible to describe but is experienced as a kind of hunger—a hunger for the lost part of the self longing to be reunited.

I will close now with an example of what it can mean to discover the hidden reality in one's self and in others.

The sister of one of my French friends married an American mining engineer. The couple and their young son settled in a medium-sized Colorado mining town. Since the mother didn't want her son to grow up without speaking her native tongue, she spoke to him only in French. One day he approached his mother with a serious expression on his face, wanting to know why it was that the two of them spoke differently from everyone else. She tried explaining to him that they were speaking French and that French was a language and that English was another language. All of this was to no avail. The whole notion of language treated in a vacuum, as it were, was too illusive, too abstract, unreal. Then his mother, being an intelligent woman, understood the problem and at the first opportunity took her son to Montreal. In a flash, he and his mother, whom he had experienced as alien and separated from all others by a process he did not understand, were now members of a new community—speakers of the French language. Everything fell into place and what had been a puzzle was now a door opening to a new world.

My point is that type A—word culture—and type B—unconscious culture—are both languages and that type B is a language of the past, the present, *and* the future that, like the boy who was led through the door to new understanding, is part of culture and of ourselves as well.

---

[1] Einstein said that time is what a clock says and that anything can be a clock: the rotation of the earth, the moon, and other rhythms. It is still possible to use Einstein's definition, as long as it is kept in mind that *each culture has it own clocks.*

[2] The world of communication is divided into three parts: words, material things, and behavior. Words are the medium of business, politics, diplomacy. Material things are usually indicators of status and power. Behavior provides feedback on how others feel and includes techniques for avoiding confrontation.

[3] Gregory Bateson, "The Message: This Is Play," in *Group Processes: Transactions of the Second Conference* (New York, Josiah Macy, Jr. Foundation Publications, 1956); Gregory Bateson, "Minimal Requirements for a Theory of Schizophrenia," in *AMA Archives General Psychiatry* 2, (1960): 477-91.

[4] Harry Stack Sullivan, *Conceptions of Modern Psychiatry*, 2d ed. (Washington, DC: The William Alanson White Psychiatric Foundation, 1947).

[5] Carl G. Jung, *Memories, Dreams, Reflections*, rev. ed. (New York: Pantheon Books, 1973).

[6] Erich Fromm, Daisetz T. Suzuki, et al., *Zen Buddhism and Psychoanalysis* (New York: Harper & Brothers, 1960); Eugen Herrigel, *Zen in the Art of Archery,* translated by Richard Francis Carrington Hull (New York: Vintage Books, 1971).

[7] Interfaces can be interpersonal, intrapersonal, intercultural.

[8] A different set of revolutions in awareness unfolded in other parts of the world. In Japan and China, for example, the world is not sacred as it is with us, with the result that there is an entirely different mindset.

[9] See Philip Lieberman's detailed and original work, *The Biology and Evolution of Language* (Cambridge: Harvard University Press, 1984); Philip Lieberman, "On Human Speech, Syntax, and Language,"*Human Evolution* 3, nos. 1-2 (1988): 3-18.

[10] Isidor F. Stone, *The Trial of Socrates* (Boston: Little Brown, 1988).

[11] Alfred Korzybski, *Science and Sanity: An Introduction to Non-Aristotelian Systems and General Semantics,* 3d ed. (Lakeville, CT: International Non-Aristotelian Library Publishing, 1948).

[12] Edward B. Tyler, *Primitive Culture* (New York: Brentano, 1924).

[13] Edward T. Hall, *The Analysis of Culture* (Washington, DC: American Council of Learned Societies, 1953); Edward T. Hall, *The Hidden Dimension* (1966; reprint, New York: Anchor/Doubleday, 1982); Edward T. Hall, *Beyond Culture* (1976; reprint, New York: Anchor/Doubleday, 1981); Edward T. Hall, *The Dance of Life: The Other Dimension of Time* (New York: Anchor/Doubleday, 1983); Edward T. Hall, *The Silent Language* (1959; reprint, New York: Anchor/Doubleday, 1981).

[14] "Extensions" are just that. When an organism uses something outside of itself to supplement what it once did only with the body, it is extending itself. Examples are a spider's web, a bird's nest, a knife (extending the teeth), a telephone (extending hearing), languages (extending certain aspects of thinking), institutions, and cultures. Once an organism evolves by extension, the rate of its evolution increases.

Rather than being separable, humans and their extensions constitute one interrelated system. The difficulties with man's extensions arise when the extensions are identified with the processes that have been extended and become rigid. For example, when written language is considered primary and spoken language an "adulterated version," the second generation extension (written language) has been confused with what is in reality the primary extension—speaking. In this case, what was once a tool—writing—has supplanted the very function it was supposed to assist—speaking.

[15] Time as expressed by culture is such a vast complex of activities and interpretations of behavior that one or two examples cannot possibly communicate what time as a cultural system is all about. My book *The Dance of Life* is a brief introduction.

[16] *Deaf* is capitalized by those hearing-impaired people who recognize themselves as members of a cultural group.

[17] William C. Stokoe, "Sign Language Structure: An Outline of Visual Communication Systems of the American Deaf," *Studies in Linguistics,* Occasional Papers 8 (Buffalo, NY: University of Buffalo, 1960); William C. Stokoe, Dorothy Casterline, and Carl Croneberg, *A Dictionary of American Sign Language on Linguistic Principles* (Washington, DC: Gallaudet College Press, 1965).

[18] I have developed a notation system for proxemics (human spatial relations), but that is not enough. More is needed in all the other systems of culture.

[19] The rules for the use of translators are the same as those for interpreters, but even more rigorous. The individual who employs either must concentrate on his or her counterpart, choosing an individual who has the greatest likelihood of being able to establish and maintain rapport with the least amount of distortion (noise). See Edward T. Hall, *West of the Thirties: Discoveries among the Navajo and Hopi* (New York: Doubleday, 1994).

Multicultural Education: Development, Dimensions, and Challenges

James A. Banks

�h551515155155155515551555155515551555155515551555155515515551551555

The bitter debate over the literary and historical canon that has been carried on in the popular press and in several widely reviewed books has overshadowed the progress that has been made in multicultural education during the last two decades. The debate has also perpetuated harmful misconceptions about theory and practice in multicultural education. Consequently, it has heightened racial and ethnic tension and trivialized the field's remarkable accomplishments in theory, research, and curriculum development. The truth about the development and attainments of multicultural education needs to be told for the sake of balance, scholarly integrity, and accuracy. But if I am to reveal the truth about multicultural education, I must first identify and debunk some of the widespread myths and misconceptions about it.

Multicultural education is for the others. One misconception about multicultural education is that it is an entitlement program and curriculum movement for African Americans, Hispanics, the poor, women, and other victimized groups.[1] The major theorists and researchers in multicultural education agree that the movement is designed to restructure educational institutions so that all students, including middle-class white males, will acquire the knowledge, skills, and attitudes needed to function effectively in a culturally and ethnically diverse nation and world.[2] Multicultural education, as its major architects have conceived it during the last decade, is not an ethnic- or gender-specific movement. It is a movement designed to empower all students to become knowledgeable, caring, and active citizens in a deeply troubled and ethnically polarized nation and world.

The claim that multicultural education is only for people of color and for the disenfranchised is one of the most pernicious and damaging misconceptions with which the movement has had to cope. It has caused intractable problems and has haunted multicultural education since its inception. Despite all that has been written and spoken about multicultural education being for all students, the image of multicultural education as an entitlement program for the "others" remains strong and vivid in the public imagination as well as in the hearts and minds of many teachers and administrators. Teachers who teach in predominantly white schools and districts often state that they don't have a program or plan for multicultural education because they have few African American, Hispanic, or Asian American students.

When educators view multicultural education as the study of the "others," it is marginalized and held apart from mainstream education reform. Several critics of multicultural education, such as Arthur M. Schlesinger Jr., John Leo, and Paul Gray, have perpetuated the idea that multicultural education is the study of the "other" by defining it as synonymous with Afrocentric education.[3] The history of intergroup education teaches us that only when education reform related to diversity is viewed as essential for all students—and as promoting the broad public interest—will it have a reasonable chance of becoming institutionalized in the nation's schools, colleges, and universities.[4] The intergroup education movement of the 1940s and 1950s failed in large part because intergroup educators were never able to persuade mainstream educators to believe that the approach was needed by and designed for all students. To its bitter but quiet end, intergroup education was viewed by mainstream educators as something for schools with racial problems and as something for "them" and not for "us."

Multicultural education is opposed to the Western tradition. Another harmful misconception about multicultural education has been repeated so often by its critics that many people take it as self-evident. This is the claim that multicultural education is a movement that is opposed to the West and to Western civilization. Multicultural education is not anti-West, because most writers of color—such as Rudolfo Anaya, Paula Gunn Allen, Maxine Hong Kingston, Maya Angelou, and Toni Morrison—are Western writers. Multicultural education itself is a thoroughly Western movement. It grew out of a civil rights movement grounded in such democratic ideals of the West as freedom, justice, and equality. Multicultural education seeks to extend to all people the ideals that were meant only for an elite few at the nation's birth.

Although multicultural education is not opposed to the West, its advocates do demand that the truth about the West be told, that its debt to people of color and women be recognized and included in the curriculum, and that the discrepancies between the ideals of freedom and equality and the realities of racism and sexism be taught to students. Reflective action by citizens is also an integral part of multicultural theory. Multicultural education views citizen action to improve society as an integral part of education in a democracy; it links knowledge, values, empowerment, and action. Multicultural education is also postmodern in its assumptions about knowledge and knowledge construction; it challenges positive assumptions about the relationships among human values, knowledge, and action.

Positivists, who are the intellectual heirs of the Enlightenment, believe that it is possible to structure knowledge that is objective and beyond the influence of human values and interests. Multicultural theorists maintain that knowledge is positional, that it relates to the knower's values and experiences, and that knowledge implies action. Consequently, different concepts, theories, and paradigms imply different kinds of actions. Multiculturalists believe that in order to have valid knowledge, information about the social condition and experiences of the knower is essential.

A few critics of multicultural education, such as John Leo and Dinesh D'Souza, claim that multicultural education has reduced or displaced the study of Western civilization in the nation's schools and colleges. However, as Gerald Graff points out in his welcome book *Beyond the Culture Wars*, this claim is simply not true. Graff cites his own research at the college level and that of Arthur N. Applebee at the high school level to substantiate his conclusion that European and American male authors—such as Shakespeare, Dante, Chaucer, Twain, and Hemingway—still dominate the required reading lists in the nation's high schools and colleges.[5] Graff found that, in the cases he examined, most of the books by authors of color were optional rather than required reading. Applebee found that, of the ten book-length works most frequently required in the high school grades, only one title was by a female author (Harper Lee's *To Kill a Mockingbird*), and not a single work was by a writer of color. Works by Shakespeare, Steinbeck, and Dickens headed the list.

Multicultural education will divide the nation. Many of its critics claim that multicultural education will divide the nation and undercut its unity. Schlesinger underscores this view in the title of his book, *The Disuniting of America: Reflections on a Multicultural Society.* This misconception is based partly on questionable assumptions about the nature of U.S. society and partly on a mistaken understanding of multicultural education. The claim that multicultural education will divide the nation assumes that the nation is already united. While we are one nation politically, sociologically our nation is deeply divided along lines of race, gender, and class. The current debate about admitting gays into the military underscores another deep division in our society.

Multicultural education is designed to help unify a deeply divided nation rather than to divide a highly cohesive one. Multicultural education supports the notion of *e pluribus unum*— out of many, one. The multiculturalists and the Western traditionalists, however, often differ about how the *unum* can best be attained. Traditionally, the larger U.S. society and the schools tried to create unity by assimilating students from diverse racial and ethnic groups into a mythical Anglo-American culture that required them to experience a process of self-alienation. However, even when students of color became culturally assimilated, they were often structurally excluded from mainstream institutions.

The multiculturalists view *e pluribus unum* as an appropriate national goal, but they believe that the *unum* must be negotiated, discussed, and restructured to reflect the nation's ethnic and cultural diversity. The reformulation of what it means to be united must be a process that involves the participation of diverse groups within the nation, such as people of color, women, straights, gays, the powerful, the powerless, the young, and the old. The reformulation must also involve power sharing and participation by people from many different cultures who must reach beyond their cultural and ethnic borders in order to create a common civic culture that reflects and contributes to the well-being of all. This common civic culture will extend beyond the cultural borders of any single group and constitute a civic "borderland" culture.

In *Borderlands*, Gloria Anzaldúa contrasts cultural borders and borderlands and calls for a weakening of the former in order to create a shared borderland culture in which people from many different cultures can interact, relate, and engage in civic talk and action. Anzaldúa states that "borders are set up to define the places that are safe and unsafe, to distinguish us from them. A border is a dividing line, a narrow strip along a steep edge. A borderland is a vague and undetermined place created by the residue of an unnatural boundary. It is in a constant state of transition."[6]

Multicultural Education Has Made Progress

While it is still on the margins rather than in the center of the curriculum in most schools and colleges, multicultural content has made significant inroads into both the school and college curricula within the last two decades. The truth lies somewhere between the claim that no progress has been made in infusing the school and college curricula with multiethnic content and the claim that such content has replaced the European and American classics.

More classroom teachers today have studied the concepts of multicultural education than at any previous point in our history. A significant percentage of today's classroom teachers took a required teacher education course in multicultural education when they were in college. The multicultural education standard adopted by the National Council for Accreditation of Teacher Education in 1977, which became effective in 1979, was a major factor that stimulated the growth of multicultural education in teacher education programs. The standard stated, "The institution gives evidence of planning for multicultural education in its teacher education curricula including both the general and professional studies components."[7]

Some of the nation's leading colleges and universities have either revised their general core curriculum to include ethnic content or have established an ethnic studies course requirement. The list of universities with similar kinds of requirements grows longer each year. However, the transformation of the traditional canon on college and university campuses has often been bitter and divisive. All changes in curriculum come slowly and painfully to university campuses, but curriculum changes that are linked with issues related to race evoke primordial feelings and reflect the racial crisis in American society.

Changes are also coming to elementary and high school textbooks. I believe that the demographic imperative is the major factor driving the changes in school textbooks. The color of the nation's student body is changing rapidly. Nearly half (about 45.5 percent) of the nation's school-age youths will be young people of color by 2020.[8] Black parents and brown parents are demanding that their leaders, their images, their pain, and their dreams be mirrored in the textbooks that their children study in school.

Textbooks have always reflected the myths, hopes, and dreams of people with money and power. As African Americans, Hispanics, Asians, and women become more influential, textbooks will increasingly reflect their hopes, dreams, and disappointments. Textbooks will have to survive in the marketplace of a browner America. Because textbooks still carry the curriculum in the nation's public schools, they will remain an important focus for multicultural curriculum reformers.

The Dimensions of Multicultural Education

One of the problems that continues to plague the multicultural education movement, both from within and without, is the tendency of teachers, administrators, policymakers, and the public to oversimplify the concept. Multicultural education is a complex and multidimensional concept, yet media commentators and educators alike often focus on only one of its many dimensions. Some teachers view it only as the inclusion of content about ethnic groups into the curriculum; others view it as an effort to reduce prejudice; still others view it as the celebration of ethnic holidays and events. After I made a presentation in a school in which I described the major goals of multicultural education, a math teacher told me that what I said was fine and appropriate for language arts and social studies teachers but that it had nothing to do with him. After all, he said, math was math, regardless of the color of the kids.

This reaction on the part of a respected teacher caused me to think more deeply about the images of multicultural education that had been created by the key actors in the field. I wondered whether we were partly responsible for this teacher's narrow conception of multicultural education as merely content integration. It was in response to such statements by classroom teachers that I conceptualized the dimensions of multicultural education. I will use the following five dimensions to describe the field's major components and to highlight important developments within the last two decades: (1) content integration, (2) the knowledge construction process, (3) prejudice reduction, (4) an equity pedagogy, and (5) an empowering school culture and social structure.[9] I will devote most of the rest of this article to the second of these dimensions.

Content Integration

Content integration deals with the extent to which teachers use examples, data, and information from a variety of cultures and groups to illustrate the key concepts, principles, generalizations, and theories in their subject area or discipline. In many school districts as well as in popular writing, multicultural education is viewed almost solely as content integration. This narrow conception of multicultural education is a major reason why many teachers in such subjects as biology, physics, and mathematics reject multicultural education as irrelevant to them and their students.

In fact, this dimension of multicultural education probably has more relevance to social studies and language arts teachers than it does to physics and math teachers. Physics and math teachers can insert multicultural content into their subjects—for example, by using biographies of physicists and mathematicians of color and examples from different cultural groups. However, these kinds of activities are probably not the most important multicultural tasks that can be undertaken by science and math teachers. Activities related to the other dimensions of multicultural education, such as the knowledge construction process, prejudice reduction, and an equity pedagogy, are probably the most fruitful areas for the multicultural involvement of science and math teachers.

Knowledge Construction

The knowledge construction process encompasses the procedures by which social, behavioral, and natural scientists create knowledge in their disciplines. A multicultural focus on knowledge construction includes discussion of the ways in which the implicit cultural assumptions, frames of reference, perspectives, and biases within a discipline influence the construction of knowledge. An examination of the knowledge construction process is an important part of multicultural teaching. Teachers help students to understand how knowledge is created and how it is influenced by factors of race, ethnicity, gender, and social class.

Within the last decade, landmark work related to the construction of knowledge has been done by feminist social scientists and epistemologists as well as by scholars in ethnic studies. Working in philosophy and sociology, Sandra Harding, Lorraine Code, and Patricia Hill Collins have done some of the most important work related to knowledge construction.[10] This ground-breaking work, although influential among scholars and curriculum developers, has been overshadowed in the popular media by the heated debates about the canon. These writers and researchers have seriously challenged the claims made by the positivists that knowledge can be value-free, and they have described the ways in which knowledge claims are influenced by the gender and ethnic characteristics of the knower. These scholars argue that the human interests and value assumptions of those who create knowledge should be identified, discussed, and examined.

Code states that the sex of the knower is epistemologically significant because knowledge is both subjective and objective. She maintains that both aspects should be recognized and discussed. Collins, an African American sociologist, extends and enriches the works of writers such as Code and Harding by describing the ways in which race and gender interact to influence knowledge construction. Collins calls the perspective of African American women the perspective of "the outsider within." She writes, "As outsiders within, Black women have a distinct view of the contradictions between the dominant group's actions and ideologies."[11]

Curriculum theorists and developers in multicultural education are applying to the classroom the work being done by the feminist and ethnic studies epistemologists. In *Transforming Knowledge*, Elizabeth K. Minnich, a professor of philosophy and women's studies, has analyzed the nature of knowledge and described how the dominant tradition, through such logical errors as faulty generalization and circular reasoning, has contributed to the marginalization of women.[12]

I have identified five types of knowledge and described their implications for multicultural teaching.[13] Teachers need to be aware of the various types of knowledge so that they can structure a curriculum that helps students to understand each type. Teachers also need to use their own cultural knowledge and that of their students to enrich teaching and learning. The types of knowledge I have identified and described are (1) personal/cultural, (2) popular, (3) mainstream academic, (4) transformative, and (5) school. (I will not discuss school knowledge in this article).

Personal/cultural knowledge consists of the concepts, explanations, and interpretations that students derive from personal experiences in their homes, families, and community cultures. Cultural conflict occurs in the classroom because much of the personal/cultural knowledge that students from diverse cultural groups bring to the classroom is inconsistent with school knowledge and with the teacher's personal and cultural knowledge. For example, research indicates that many African American and Mexican American students are more likely to experience academic success in cooperative rather than in competitive learning environments.[14] Yet the typical school culture is highly competitive, and children of color may experience failure if they do not figure out the implicit rules of the school culture.[15]

The popular knowledge that is institutionalized by the mass media and other forces that shape the popular culture has a strong influence on the values, perceptions, and behavior of children and young people. The messages and images carried by the media, which Carlos E. Cortés calls the societal curriculum,[16] often reinforce the stereotypes and misconceptions about racial and ethnic groups that are institutionalized within the larger society.

Of course, some films and other popular media forms do make positive contributions to racial understanding. *Dances with Wolves*, *Glory*, and *Malcolm X* are examples. However, there are many ways to view such films, and both positive and negative examples of popular culture need to become a part of classroom discourse and analysis. Like all human creations, even these positive films are imperfect. The multiculturally informed and sensitive teacher needs to help students view these films, as well as other media productions, from diverse cultural, ethnic, and gender perspectives.

The concepts, theories, and explanations that constitute traditional Western-centric knowledge in history and in the social and behavioral sciences constitute mainstream academic knowledge. Traditional interpretations of U.S. history—embodied in such headings as "The European Discovery of America" and "The Westward Movement"—are central concepts in mainstream academic knowledge. Mainstream academic knowledge is established within mainstream professional associations, such as the American Historical Association and the American Psychological Association. It provides the interpretations that are taught in U.S. colleges and universities.

The literary legacy of mainstream academic knowledge includes such writers as Shakespeare, Dante, Chaucer, and Aristotle. Critics of multicultural education, such as Schlesinger, D'Souza, and Leo, believe that mainstream academic knowledge in the curriculum is being displaced by the new knowledge and interpretations that have been created by scholars working in women's studies and in ethnic studies. However, mainstream academic knowledge is not only threatened from without but also from within. Postmodern scholars in organizations such as the American Historical Association, the American Sociological Association, and the American Political Science Association are challenging the dominant positivist interpretations and paradigms within their disciplines and creating alternative explanations and perspectives.

Transformative academic knowledge challenges the facts, concepts, paradigms, themes, and explanations routinely accepted in mainstream academic knowledge. Those who pursue transformative academic knowledge seek to expand and substantially revise established canons, theories, explanations, and research methods. The transformative research methods and theory that have been developed in women's studies and in ethnic studies since the 1970s constitute, in my view, the most important developments in social science theory and research in the last twenty years.

It is important for teachers and students to realize, however, that transformative academic scholarship has a long history in the United States and that the current ethnic studies movement is directly linked to an earlier ethnic studies movement that emerged in the late 1800s.[17] George Washington Williams published volume 1 of the first history of African Americans in 1882 and the second volume in 1883. Other important works published by African American transformative scholars in times past include works by W. E. B. Du Bois, Carter G. Woodson, Horace Mann Bond, and Charles H. Wesley.[18]

The works of these early scholars in African American studies, which formed the academic roots of the current multicultural education movement when it emerged in the 1960s and 1970s, were linked by several important characteristics. Their works were transformative because they created data, interpretations, and perspectives that challenged those that were established by white, mainstream scholarship. The work of the transformative scholars presented positive images of African Americans and refuted stereotypes that were pervasive within the established scholarship of their time.

Although they strove for objectivity in their works and wanted to be considered scientific researchers, these transformative scholars viewed knowledge and action as tightly linked and became involved in social action and administration themselves. Du Bois was active in social protest and for many years was the editor of *Crisis*, an official publication of the National Association for the Advancement of Colored People. Woodson cofounded the Association for the Study of Negro (now Afro-American) Life and History, founded and edited the *Journal of Negro History*, edited the *Negro History Bulletin* for classroom teachers, wrote school and college textbooks on Negro history, and founded Negro History Week (now Afro-American History Month).

Transformative academic knowledge has experienced a renaissance since the 1970s. Only a few of the most important works can be mentioned here because of space. Martin Bernal, in an important two-volume work, *Black Athena*, has created new interpretations about the debt that Greece owes to Egypt and Phoenicia. Before Bernal, Ivan Van Sertima and Cheikh Anta Diop also created novel interpretations of the debt that Europe owes to Africa. In two books, *Indian Givers* and *Native Roots*, Jack Weatherford describes Native American contributions that have enriched the world.

Ronald T. Takaki, in several influential books, such as *Iron Cages: Race and Culture in 19th-Century America* and *Strangers from a Different Shore: A History of Asian Americans*, has given us new ways to think about the ethnic experience in America. The literary contribution to transformative scholarship has also been rich, as shown by *The Signifying Monkey: A Theory of African-American Literary Criticism*, by Henry Louis Gates Jr.; *Long Black Song: Essays in Black American Literature and Culture*, by Houston A. Baker Jr.; and *Breaking Ice: An Anthology of Contemporary African-American Fiction*, edited by Terry McMillan.

A number of important works in the transformative tradition that interrelate race and gender have also been published since the 1970s. Important works in this genre include *Unequal Sisters: A Multicultural Reader in U.S. Women's History*, edited by Carol Ellen DuBois and Vicki L. Ruiz; *Race, Gender, and Work: A Multicultural Economic History of Women in the United States*, by Teresa L. Amott and Julie A. Matthaei; *Labor of Love, Labor of Sorrow: Black Women, Work, and the Family from Slavery to the Present,* by Jacqueline Jones; and *The Forbidden Stitch: An Asian American Women's Anthology*, edited by Shirley Geok-lin Lim, Mayumi Tsutakawa, and Margarita Donnelly.

The Other Dimensions

The "prejudice reduction" dimension of multicultural education focuses on the characteristics of children's racial attitudes and on strategies that can be used to help students develop more positive racial and ethnic attitudes. Since the 1960s, social scientists have learned a great deal about how racial attitudes in children develop and about ways in which educators can design interventions to help children acquire more positive feelings toward other racial groups. I have reviewed that research in two recent publications and refer readers to them for a comprehensive discussion of this topic.[19]

This research tells us that by age four African American, white, and Mexican American children are aware of racial differences and show racial preferences favoring whites. Students can be helped to develop more positive racial attitudes if realistic images of ethnic and racial groups are included in teaching materials in a consistent, natural, and integrated fashion. Involving students in vicarious experiences and in cooperative learning activities with students of other racial groups will also help them to develop more positive racial attitudes and behaviors.

An *equity pedagogy* exists when teachers use techniques and teaching methods that facilitate the academic achievement of students from diverse racial and ethnic groups and from all social classes. Using teaching techniques that cater to the learning and cultural styles of diverse groups and using the techniques of cooperative learning are some of the ways that teachers have found effective with students from diverse racial, ethnic, and language groups.[20]

An *empowering school culture and social structure* will require the restructuring of the culture and organization of the school so that students from diverse racial, ethnic, and social-class groups will experience educational equality and a sense of empowerment. This dimension of multicultural education involves conceptualizing the school as the unit of change and making structural changes within the school environment. Adopting assessment techniques that are fair to all groups, doing away with tracking, and creating the belief among the staff members that all students can learn are important goals for schools that wish to create a school culture and social structure that are empowering and enhancing for a diverse student body.

Multicultural Education and the Future

The achievements of multicultural education since the late sixties and early seventies are noteworthy and should be acknowledged. Those who have shaped the movement during the intervening decades have been able to obtain wide agreement on the goals of and approaches to multicultural education. Most multiculturalists agree that the major goal of multicultural education is to restructure schools so that all students will acquire the knowledge, attitudes, and skills needed to function in an ethnically and racially diverse nation and world. As is the case with other interdisciplinary areas of study, debates within the field continue. These debates are consistent with the philosophy of a field that values democracy and diversity. They are also a source of strength.

Multicultural education is being implemented widely in the nation's schools, colleges, and universities. The large number of national conferences, school district workshops, and teacher education courses in multicultural education are evidence of its success and perceived importance. Although the process of integration of content is slow and often contentious, multicultural content is increasingly becoming a part of core courses in schools and colleges. Textbook publishers are also integrating ethnic and cultural content into their books, and the pace of such integration is increasing.

Despite its impressive successes, however, multicultural education faces serious challenges as we move toward the next century. One of the most serious of these challenges is the highly organized, well-financed attack by the Western traditionalists who fear that multicultural education will transform America in ways that will result in their own disempowerment. Ironically, the successes that multicultural education has experienced during the last decade have played a major role in provoking the attacks.

The debate over the canon and the well-orchestrated attack on multicultural education reflect an identity crisis in American society. The American identity is being reshaped, as groups on the margins of society begin to participate in the mainstream and to demand that their visions be reflected in a transformed America. In the future, the sharing of power and the transformation of identity required to achieve lasting racial peace in America may be valued rather than feared, for only in this way will we achieve national salvation.

---

[1] Nathan Glazer, "In Defense of Multiculturalism," *New Republic*, 2 September 1991, 18-22; Dinesh D'Souza, "Illiberal Education," *Atlantic*, March 1991, 51-79.

[2] James A. Banks, *Multiethnic Education: Theory and Practice*, 3d ed. (Boston: Allyn and Bacon, 1994); James A. Banks and Cherry A. McGee Banks, eds., *Multicultural Education: Issues and Perspectives*, 2d ed. (Boston: Allyn and Bacon, 1993); and Christine E. Sleeter and Carl A. Grant, *Making Choices for Multicultural Education: Five Approaches to Race, Class, and Gender* (Columbus, OH: Merrill, 1988).

3 Arthur M. Schlesinger Jr., *The Disuniting of America: Reflections on a Multicultural Society* (1991; reprint, New York: W. W. Norton, 1998); John Leo, "A Fringe History of the World," *U.S. News & World Report,* 12 November 1990, 25-26; and Paul Gray, "Whose America?" *Time,* 8 July 1991, 13-17.

4 Hilda Taba et al., *Intergroup Education in Public Schools* (Washington, DC: American Council on Education, 1952).

5 Gerald Graff, *Beyond the Culture Wars: How Teaching the Conflicts Can Revitalize American Education* (New York: Norton, 1992); Arthur N. Applebee, "Stability and Change in the High School Canon," *English Journal* (September 1992): 27-32.

6 Gloria Anzaldúa, *Borderlands: La Frontera: The New Mestiza* (San Francisco: Spinsters/Aunt Lute, 1987), 3.

7 *Standards for the Accreditation of Teacher Education* (Washington, DC: National Council for Accreditation of Teacher Education, 1977), 4.

8 Aaron M. Pallas, Gary Natriello, and Edward L. McDill, "The Changing Nature of the Disadvantaged Population: Current Dimensions and Future Trends." *Educational Researcher,* June/July 1989, 16-22.

9 James A. Banks, "Multicultural Education: Historical Development, Dimensions, and Practice," in *Review of Research in Education,* vol. 19, edited by Linda Darling-Hammond (Washington, DC: American Educational Research Association, 1993), 3-49.

10 Sandra Harding. *Whose Science, Whose Knowledge? Thinking from Women's Lives* (Ithaca, NY: Cornell University Press, 1991); Lorraine Code, *What Can She Know? Feminist Theory and the Construction of Knowledge* (Ithaca, NY: Cornell University Press, 1991); Patricia Hill Collins, *Black Feminist Thought: Knowledge, Consciousness, and the Politics of Empowerment* (New York: Routledge, 1990).

11 Collins, *Black Feminist Thought,* 11.

12 Elizabeth K. Minnich. *Transforming Knowledge* (Philadelphia: Temple University Press, 1990).

13 James A. Banks, "The Canon Debate, Knowledge Construction, and Multicultural Education," *Education Researcher,* June/July 1993, 4-14.

14 Robert E. Slavin, *Cooperative Learning* (New York: Longman, 1983).

15 Lisa D. Delpit, "The Silenced Dialogue: Power and Pedagogy in Educating Other People's Children," *Harvard Educational Review* 58 (1988): 280-98.

16 Carlos E. Cortés, "The Societal Curriculum: Implications for Multiethnic Education," in *Education in the 80's: Multiethnic Education,* edited by James A. Banks (Washington, DC: National Education Association, 1981), 24-32.

17 James A. Banks, "African American Scholarship and the Evolution of Multicultural Education," *Journal of Negro Education* (Summer 1992): 273-86.

18 A list of these and other more recent works of transformative scholarship appears at the end of this article.

19 James A. Banks, "Multicultural Education: Its Effects on Students' Racial and Gender Role Attitudes," in *Handbook of Research on Social Studies Teaching and Learning,* edited by James P. Shaver (New York: Macmillan, 1991), 459-69; idem, "Multicultural Education for Young Children: Racial and Ethnic Attitudes and Their Modification," in *Handbook of Research on the Education of Young Children,* edited by Bernard Spodek (New York: Macmillan, 1993), 236-50.

20 Barbara J. R. Shade, ed., *Culture, Style, and the Educative Process* (Springfield, IL: Charles C. Thomas, 1989).

Further Readings

Amott, Teresa L., and Julie A. Matthaei. *Race, Gender, and Work: A Multicultural Economic History of Women in the United States*. Boston: South End Press, 1991.

Baker, Houston A. Jr. *Long Black Song: Essays in Black American Literature and Culture*. Charlottesville: University Press of Virginia, 1990.

Bernal, Martin. *Black Athena: The Afroasiatic Roots of Classical Civilization*. 2 vols. New Brunswick, NJ: Rutgers University Press, 1987, 1991.

Bond, Horace Mann. *Negro Education in Alabama: A Study in Cotton and Steel*. Washington, DC: Associated Publishers, 1939.

DuBois, Carol Ellen, and Vicki L. Ruiz, eds. *Unequal Sisters: A Multicultural Reader in U.S. Women's History*. New York: Routledge, 1990.

Du Bois, W. E. B. *The Suppression of the African Slave Trade to the United States of America, 1638-1870*. Millwood, NY: Kraus-Thomas, 1896.

Gates, Henry Louis Jr. *The Signifying Monkey: A Theory of African-American Literary Criticism*. New York: Oxford University Press, 1988.

Geok-lin Lim, Shirley, Mayumi Tsutakawa, and Margarita Donnelly, eds. *The Forbidden Stitch: An Asian American Women's Anthology*. Corvallis, OR: Calyx Books, 1989.

Jones, Jacqueline. *Labor of Love, Labor of Sorrow: Black Women, Work, and the Family from Slavery to the Present*. New York: Vintage Books, 1985.

McMillan, Terry, ed. *Breaking Ice: An Anthology of Contemporary African-American Fiction*. New York: Penguin Books, 1990.

Takaki, Ronald T., ed. *Iron Cages: Race and Culture in 19th-Century America*. Seattle: University of Washington Press, 1979.

———. *Strangers from a Different Shore: A History of Asian Americans*. Boston: Little, Brown, 1989.

Van Sertima, Ivan, ed. *Great Black Leaders: Ancient and Modern*. New Brunswick, NJ: Africana Studies Department, Rutgers University, 1988.

———, ed. *Great African Thinkers, vol. 1: Cheikh Anta Diop*. New Brunswick, NJ: Transaction Books, 1989.

Weatherford, Jack. *Indian Givers: How the Indians of the Americas Transformed the World*. New York: Fawcett Columbine, 1988.

————. *Native Roots: How the Indians Enriched America*. New York: Fawcett Columbine, 1992.

Wesley, Charles H. *Richard Allen: Apostle of Freedom*. Washington, DC: Associated Publishers, 1935.

Williams, George Washington. *History of the Negro Race in America from 1619 to 1880: Negroes as Slaves, as Soldiers, and as Citizens*. 2 vols. 1882, 1883. Reprint, Salem, NH: Ayer, 1989.

Woodson, Carter G. *The History of the Negro Church*. Washington, DC: Associated Publishers, 1921.

Science and Linguistics

Benjamin Lee Whorf

🔲🔲🔲🔲🔲🔲🔲🔲🔲🔲🔲🔲🔲🔲🔲🔲🔲🔲🔲🔲🔲🔲🔲🔲🔲🔲🔲🔲🔲🔲🔲🔲🔲🔲🔲🔲🔲🔲

Every normal person in the world, past infancy in years, can and does talk. By virtue of that fact, every person—civilized or uncivilized—carries through life certain naive but deeply rooted ideas about talking and its relation to thinking. Because of their firm connection with speech habits that have become unconscious and automatic, these notions tend to be rather intolerant of opposition. They are by no means entirely personal and haphazard; their basis is definitely systematic, so that we are justified in calling them a system of *natural logic*—a term that seems to me preferable to the term *common sense*, often used for the same thing.

According to natural logic, the fact that every person has talked fluently since infancy makes individuals their own authority on the process by which they formulate and communicate. They have merely to consult a common substratum of logic or reason which all people are supposed to possess. Natural logic says that talking is merely an incidental process concerned strictly with communication, not with the formulation of ideas. Talking, or the use of language, is supposed only to "express" what is essentially already formulated nonlinguistically. Formulation is an independent process, called thought or thinking, and is supposed to be largely indifferent to the nature of particular languages. Languages have grammars, which are assumed to be merely norms of conventional and social correctness, but the use of language is supposed to be guided not so much by them as by correct, rational, or intelligent *thinking*.

Thought, in this view, does not depend on grammar but on laws of logic or reason which are supposed to be the same for all observers of the universe—to represent a rationale in the universe that can be "found" independently by all intelligent observers, whether they speak Chinese or Choctaw. In our own culture, the formulations of mathematics and of formal logic have acquired the reputation of dealing with this order of things: that is, with the realm and laws of pure thought. Natural logic holds that different languages are essentially parallel methods for expressing this one-and-the-same rationale of thought and, hence, differ really in but minor ways which may seem important only because they are seen at close range.

Figure 1

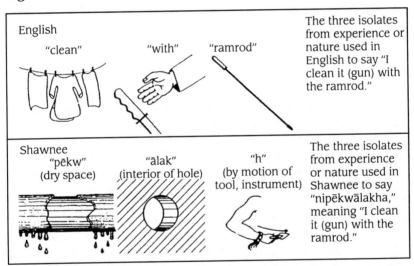

Languages dissect nature differently. The different isolates of meaning (thoughts) used by English and Shawnee in reporting the same experience, that of cleaning a gun by running the ramrod through it. The pronouns *I* and *it* are not shown by symbols, as they have the same meaning in each language. In Shawnee *ni-* equals *I*; *-a* equals *it*.

The familiar saying that the exception proves the rule contains a good deal of wisdom, though from the standpoint of formal logic it became an absurdity as soon as *prove* no longer meant "put on trial." The old saw began to be profound psychology from the time it ceased to have standing in logic. What it might well suggest to us today is that, if a rule has absolutely no exceptions, it is not recognized as a rule or as anything else; it is then part of the background of experience of which we tend to remain unconscious. Never having experienced anything in contrast to it, we cannot isolate it and formulate it as a rule until we so enlarge our experience and expand our base of reference that we encounter an interruption of its regularity. The situation is somewhat analogous to that of not missing the water until the well runs dry, or not realizing that we need air until we are choking.

For instance, if a race of people had the physiological defect of being able to see only the color blue, they would hardly be able to formulate the rule that they saw only blue. The term *blue* would convey no meaning to them, their language would lack color terms, and their words denoting their various sensations of blue would answer to, and translate, our words *light, dark, white, black,* and so on, not our word *blue.* In order to formulate the rule or norm of seeing only blue, they would need exceptional moments in which they saw other colors. The phenomenon of gravitation forms a rule without exceptions; needless to say, the untutored person is utterly unaware of any law of gravitation, for it would never enter his or her head to conceive of a universe in which bodies behaved otherwise than they do at the earth's surface. Like the color blue with our hypothetical race, the law of gravitation is a part of the untutored individual's background, not something he or she isolates from that background. The law could not be formulated until bodies that always fell were seen in terms of a wider astronomical world in which bodies moved in orbits or went this way and that.

Similarly, whenever we turn our heads, the image of the scene passes across our retinas exactly as it would if the scene turned around us. But this effect is background, and we do not recognize it; we do not see a room turn around us but are conscious only of having turned our heads in a stationary room. If we observe critically while turning the head or eyes quickly, we shall see no motion, it is true, yet a blurring of the scene between two clear views. Normally we are quite unconscious of this continual blurring but seem to be looking about in an unblurred world. Whenever we walk past a tree or house, its image on the retina changes just as if the tree or house were turning on an axis; yet we do not see trees or houses turn as we travel about at ordinary speeds. Sometimes ill-fitting glasses will reveal queer movements in the scene as we look about, but normally we do not see the relative motion of the environment when we move; our psychic makeup is somehow adjusted to disregard whole realms of phenomena that are so all-pervasive as to be irrelevant to our daily lives and needs.

Natural logic contains two fallacies. First, it does not see that the phenomena of a language are to its own speakers largely of a background character and so are outside the critical consciousness and control of the speaker who is expounding natural logic. Hence, when people, as natural logicians, are talking about reason, logic, and the laws of correct thinking, they are likely to be simply marching in step with purely grammatical facts that have somewhat of a background character in their own language or family of languages but are by no means universal in all languages and in no sense a common substratum of reason. Second, natural logic confuses agreement about subject matter, attained through use of language, with knowledge of the linguistic process by which agreement is attained: that is, with the province of the despised (and to its notion superfluous) grammarian. Two fluent speakers, of English let us say, quickly reach a point of assent about the subject matter of their speech; they agree about what their language refers to. One of them, A, can give directions that will be carried out by the other, B, to A's complete satisfaction. Because they thus understand each other so perfectly, A and B, as natural logicians, suppose they must of course know how it is all done. They think, for example, that it is simply a matter of choosing words to express thoughts. If you ask A to explain how he got B's agreement so readily, he will simply repeat to you, with more or less elaboration or abbreviation, what he said to B. He has no notion of the process involved. The amazingly complex system of linguistic patterns and classifications, which A and B must have in common before they can adjust to each other at all, is all background to A and B.

These background phenomena are the province of grammarians—or of linguists, to give them a more modern name as scientists. The word *linguist* in common (and especially newspaper) parlance means something entirely different, namely, a person who can quickly attain agreement about subject matter with different people speaking a number of different languages. Such a person is better termed a polyglot or a multilingual. Scientific linguists have long understood that ability to speak a language fluently does not necessarily confer a linguistic knowledge of it, that is, an understanding of its background phenomena and its systematic processes and structure, any more than ability to play a good game of billiards confers or requires any knowledge of the laws of mechanics that operate upon the billiard table.

The situation here is not unlike that in any other field of science. All real scientists have their eyes primarily on background phenomena that cut very little ice, as such, in our daily lives; yet their studies have a way of bringing out a close relation between these unsuspected realms of fact and such decidedly foreground activities as transporting goods, preparing food, treating the sick, or growing potatoes, which in time may become very much modified, simply because of pure scientific investigation in no way concerned with these brute matters themselves. Linguistics presents a quite similar case; the background phenomena with which it deals are involved in all our foreground activities of talking and of reaching agreement, in all reasoning and arguing of cases, in all law, arbitration, conciliation, contracts, treaties, public opinion, weighing of scientific theories, formulation of scientific results. Whenever agreement or assent is arrived at in human affairs, and whether or not mathematics or other specialized symbolisms are made part of the procedure, *this agreement is reached by linguistic processes, or else it is not reached.*

As we have seen, an overt knowledge of the linguistic processes by which agreement is attained is not necessary to reaching some sort of agreement, but it is certainly no bar thereto; the more complicated and difficult the matter, the more such knowledge is a distinct aid, until the point may be reached—I suspect the modern world has about arrived at it—when the knowledge becomes not only an aid but a necessity. The situation may be likened to that of navigation. Every boat that sails is in the lap of planetary forces; yet a child can pilot his or her small craft around a harbor without benefit of geography, astronomy, mathematics, or international politics. To the captain of an ocean liner, however, some knowledge of all these subjects is essential.

When linguists became able to examine critically and scientifically a large number of languages of widely different patterns, their base of reference was expanded; they experienced an interruption of phenomena hitherto held universal, and a whole new order of significances came into their ken. It was found that the background linguistic system (in other words, the grammar) of each language is not merely a reproducing instrument for voicing ideas but rather is itself the shaper of ideas, the program and guide for people's mental activity, for their analysis of impressions, for their synthesis of their mental stock in trade. Formulation of ideas is not an independent process, strictly rational in the old sense, but is part of a particular grammar and differs, from slightly to greatly, among different grammars. We dissect nature along lines laid down by our native languages. The categories and types that we isolate from the world of phenomena we do not find there because they stare every observer in the face; on the contrary, the world is presented in a kaleidoscopic flux of impressions which has to be organized by our minds—and this means largely by the linguistic systems in our minds. We cut nature up, organize it into concepts, and ascribe significances as we do, largely because we are parties to an agreement to organize it in this way—an agreement that holds throughout our speech community and is codified in the patterns of our language. The agreement is, of course, an implicit and unstated one, *but its terms are absolutely obligatory*; we cannot talk at all except by subscribing to the organization and classification of data which the agreement decrees.

This fact is very significant for modern science, for it means that no individuals are free to describe nature with absolute impartiality but are constrained to certain modes of interpretation even while they think themselves most free. The person most nearly free in such respects would be a linguist familiar with very many widely different linguistic systems. As yet no linguist is in any such position. We are thus introduced to a new principle of relativity, which holds that all observers are not led by the same physical evidence to the same picture of the universe, unless their linguistic backgrounds are similar, or can in some way be calibrated.

This rather startling conclusion is not so apparent if we compare only our modern European languages, with perhaps Latin and Greek thrown in for good measure. Among these tongues there is a unanimity of major pattern which at first seems to bear out natural logic. But this unanimity exists only because these tongues are all Indo-European dialects cut to the same basic plan, being historically transmitted from what was long ago one speech community; because the modern dialects have long shared in building up a common culture; and because much of this culture, on the more intellectual side, is derived from the linguistic backgrounds of Latin and Greek. Thus this group of languages satisfies the special case of the clause beginning "unless" in the statement of the linguistic relativity principle at the end of the preceding paragraph. From this condition follows the unanimity of description of the world in the community of modern scientists. But it must be emphasized that "all modern Indo-European-speaking observers" is not the same thing as "all observers." That modern Chinese or Turkish scientists describe the world in the same terms as Western scientists means, of course, only that they have taken over bodily the entire Western system of rationalizations, not that they have corroborated that system from their native posts of observation.

When Semitic, Chinese, Tibetan, or African languages are contrasted with our own, the divergence in analysis of the world becomes more apparent; and, when we bring in the native languages of the Americas, where speech communities for many millenniums have gone their ways independently of each other and of the Old World, the fact that languages dissect nature in many different ways becomes patent. The relativity of all conceptual systems, ours included, and their dependence upon language stand revealed. That American Indians speaking only their native tongues are never called upon to act as scientific observers is in no wise to the point. To exclude the evidence which their languages offer as to what the human mind can do is like expecting botanists to study nothing but food plants and hothouse roses and then tell us what the plant world is like!

Let us consider a few examples. In English we divide most of our words into two classes which have different grammatical and logical properties. Class 1 we call nouns, for example, *house, man*; class 2, verbs, for instance, *hit, run*. Many words of one class can act secondarily as of the other class, for example, "a hit," "a run," or "to man (the boat)," but on the primary level, the division between the classes is absolute. Our language thus gives us a bipolar division of nature. But nature herself is not thus polarized. If it be said that *strike, turn*, and *run* are verbs because they denote temporary or short-lasting events, that is, actions, why then is *fist* a noun? It also is a temporary event. Why are *lightning, spark, wave, eddy, pulsation, flame, storm, phase, cycle, spasm, noise*, and *emotion* nouns? They are temporary events. If *man* and *house* are nouns because they are long-lasting and stable events, that is, things, what then are *keep, adhere, extend, project, continue, persist, grow, dwell*, and so on doing among the verbs? If it be objected that *possess* and *adhere* are verbs because they are stable relationships rather than stable percepts, why then should *equilibrium, pressure, current, peace, group, nation, society, tribe, sister*, or any kinship term be among the nouns? It will be found that an "event" to us means "what our language classes as a verb" or something analogized therefrom. And it will be found that it is not possible to define *event, thing, object, relationship*, and so on from nature, but that to define them always involves a circuitous return to the grammatical categories of the definer's language.

In the Hopi language, *lightning, wave, flame, meteor, puff of smoke*, and *pulsation* are verbs—events of necessarily brief duration cannot be anything but verbs. *Cloud* and *storm* are at about the lower limit of duration for nouns. Hopi, you see, actually has a classification of events (or linguistic isolates) by duration type, something strange to our modes of thought. On the other hand, in Nootka, a language of Vancouver Island, all words seem to us to be verbs, but really there are no classes 1 and 2; we have, as it were, a monistic view of nature that gives us only one class of word for all kinds of events. "A house occurs" or "it houses" is the way of saying *house*, exactly like "a flame occurs" or "it burns." These terms seem to us like verbs because they are inflected for durational and temporal nuances, so that the suffixes of the word for *house event* make it mean "long-lasting house," "temporary house," "future house," "house that used to be," "what started out to be a house," and so on.

Figure 2

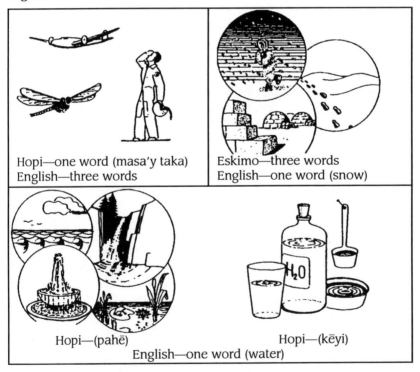

Hopi—one word (masa'y taka)
English—three words

Eskimo—three words
English—one word (snow)

Hopi—(pahē)
Hopi—(kēyi)
English—one word (water)

Languages classify items of experience differently. The class corresponding to one word and one thought in language A may be regarded by language B as two or more classes corresponding to two or more words and thoughts.

Hopi has one noun that covers every thing or being that flies, with the exception of birds, whose class is denoted by another noun. The former noun may be said to denote the class (FC-B)—flying class minus bird. The Hopi actually call *insect*, *airplane*, and *aviator* all by the same word and feel no difficulty about it. The situation, of course, decides any possible confusion among very disparate members of a broad linguistic class, such as this class (FC-B). This class seems to us too large and inclusive, but so would our class *snow* to an Eskimo. We have the same word for falling snow, snow on the ground, snow packed hard like ice, slushy snow, wind-driven flying snow—whatever the situation may be. To an Eskimo, this all-inclusive word would be almost unthinkable; he would say that falling snow, slushy snow, and so on are sensuously and operationally different, different things to contend with; he uses different words for them and for other kinds of snow. The Aztecs go even further than we in the opposite direction, with *cold*, *ice*, and *snow* all represented by the same basic word with different terminations; *ice* is the noun form; *cold*, the adjectival form; and for *snow*, "ice mist."

What surprises most is to find that various grand generalizations of the Western world such as time, velocity, and matter are not essential to the construction of a consistent picture of the universe. The psychic experiences that we class under these headings are, of course, not destroyed; rather, categories derived from other kinds of experiences take over the rulership of the cosmology and seem to function just as well. Hopi may be called a timeless language. It recognizes psychological time, which is much like Bergson's "duration," but this "time" is quite unlike the mathematical time, T, used by our physicists. Among the peculiar properties of Hopi time are that it varies with each observer, does not permit of simultaneity, and has zero dimensions (i.e., it cannot be given a number greater than one). The Hopi do not say "I stayed five days," but "I left on the fifth day." A word referring to this kind of time, like the word *day*, can have no plural. The puzzle picture (Figure 3, page 94) will give mental exercise to anyone who would like to figure out how the Hopi verb gets along without tenses. Actually, the only practical use of our tenses, in one-verb sentences, is to distinguish among five typical situations, which are symbolized in the picture. The timeless Hopi verb does not distinguish between the present, past, and future of the event itself but must always indicate what type of validity the speaker intends the statement to have: (a) report of an event (situations 1, 2, 3 in the picture); (b) expectation of an event (situation 4); (c) generalization or law about events (situation 5). Situation 1, where the speaker and listener are in contact with the same objective field, is divided by our language into the two conditions, 1a and 1b, which it calls present and past, respectively. This division is unnecessary for a language which assures one that the statement is a report.

Figure 3

Objective Field	Speaker (sender)	Hearer (receiver)	Handling of Topic Running of Third Person	
Situation 1a			English	"he is running"
			Hopi	"wari" (running, statement of fact)
Situation 1b Objective field blank devoid of running			English	"he ran"
			Hopi	"wari" (running, statement of fact)
Situation 2			English	"he is running"
			Hopi	"wari" (running, statement of fact)
Situation 3 Objective field blank			English	"he ran"
			Hopi	"era wari" (running, statement of fact from memory)
Situation 4 Objective field blank			English	"he will run"
			Hopi	"warikni" (running, statement of expectation)
Situation 5 Objective field blank			English	"he runs" (e.g., on the track team)
			Hopi	"warikngwe" (running, statement of law)

Contrast between a "temporal" language (English) and a "timeless" language (Hopi). What are to English differences of time are to Hopi differences in the kind of validity.

One significant contribution to science from the linguistic point of view may be the greater development of our sense of perspective. We shall no longer be able to see a few recent dialects of the Indo-European family, and the rationalizing techniques elaborated from their patterns, as the apex of the evolution of the human mind, nor their present wide spread as due to any survival from fitness or to anything but a few events of history— events that could be called fortunate only from the parochial point of view of the favored parties. They, and our own thought processes with them, can no longer be envisioned as spanning the gamut of reason and knowledge but only as one constellation in a galactic expanse. A fair realization of the incredible degree of diversity of linguistic system that ranges over the globe leaves one with an inescapable feeling that the human spirit is inconceivably old; that the few thousand years of history covered by our written records are no more than the thickness of a pencil mark on the scale that measures our past experience on this planet; that the events of these recent millenniums spell nothing in an evolutionary sense, that the race has taken no sudden spurt, achieved no commanding synthesis during recent millenniums, but has only played a little with a few of the linguistic formulations and views of nature bequeathed from an inexpressibly longer past. Yet neither this feeling nor the sense of precarious dependence of all we know upon linguistic tools which themselves are largely unknown need be discouraging to science but should, rather, foster that humility which accompanies the true scientific spirit, and thus forbid that arrogance of the mind which hinders real scientific curiosity and detachment.

Culture:
A Perceptual Approach

Marshall R. Singer

᪥᪥᪥᪥᪥᪥᪥᪥᪥᪥᪥᪥᪥᪥᪥᪥᪥᪥᪥᪥᪥᪥᪥᪥᪥᪥᪥᪥᪥᪥᪥᪥᪥᪥᪥᪥᪥

The Perceptual Model[1]

It is a basic premise of this article that people behave as they do because of the ways in which they perceive the external world. By *perception* I mean here the process by which an individual selects, evaluates, and organizes stimuli from the external environment.[2]

While individuals and the groups they constitute can only act or react on the basis of their perceptions, the important point is that the "same" stimuli are often perceived differently by different individuals and groups. Whether or not an objective "reality" exists apart from a person's perception of that reality need not concern us here. In terms of human behavior, however, there exists (for people) only subjective reality—that is, the universe as individuals perceive it. The question then becomes: how do people form their perceptions of the external world and how do those perceptions affect their behavior?

We would argue (rather simplistically here, because it is not the main purpose of the article) that humans are inescapably social animals. Particularly in their earliest years, but throughout their entire lives as well, people must exist in relationship with other human beings. Each of the humans with whom we come into contact brings to that relationship his or her own perceptual view of the universe. More important, perhaps, each of the groups in which we have been raised will have conditioned us to view the world from its perspective. Will I regurgitate or salivate at the thought of eating the flesh of a cow or of a kitten? It will depend on how thoroughly I have internalized the attitudes and values which I have been taught by my groups. Not only the languages I speak and the way in which I think, but even what I see, hear, taste, touch, and smell are conditioned by the cultures[3] in which I have been raised.

Benjamin Lee Whorf, the noted linguist, has written, "We are thus introduced to a new principle of relativity, which holds that all observers are not led by the same physical evidence to the same picture of the universe, unless their linguistic backgrounds are similar, or can in some way be calibrated."[4] I would go a step further and substitute the word *perceptual* for the word *linguistic*. I would argue that every culture has its own language[5] or code, to be sure, but that a language is the manifestation—verbal or otherwise—of the perceptions which the group holds. Language, once established, further constrains the individual to perceive in certain ways, but I would insist that language is merely one of the ways in which groups maintain and reinforce similarity of perception.

Specifically my model is based on the following set of premises, some of which are quite generally accepted; some of which are, at this stage, only hypotheses; and others of which are merely definitional. As the model is refined and further developed, some of these will undoubtedly be dropped, others will probably be rephrased, and still others may be added. While I believe that the approach is more important than the specific components, I present them here in order to make my model as explicit as is possible.[6]

1. Individual patterns of behavior are based on individual perceptions[7] of the external world, which are largely learned.

2. Because of biological and experiential differences, no two individuals can perceive the external world exactly identically.

3. The greater the biological and experiential differences between individuals, the greater is the disparity in perceptions likely to be. Conversely, the more similar the biological and experiential background, the more similarly are individuals likely to perceive.

4. A *perceptual group* may be defined as a number of individuals who perceive some aspects of the external world more or less similarly.[8]
5. A number of people who perceive some aspects of the external world more or less similarly and recognize (communicate) that they share this similarity of perception may be termed an *identity group*.
6. The higher the degree of similarity of perception that exists among a number of individuals, other things being equal, (a) the easier is communication among them likely to be, (b) the more communication among them is likely to occur, and (c) the more likely it is that this similarity of perception will be recognized—that an identity group will form.[9]
7. Ease of communication will allow for constant increase in degree of similarity of perception (through feedback mechanisms), which in turn allows for still further ease of communication. Thus, there tends to be a constant reinforcement of group identity.[10]
8. The greater the number and the degree of intensity of perceptual groups that individuals share—the more overlapping of important perceptual groups that exists among a number of individuals—the more likely they are to have a high degree of group identity.[11]
9. A pattern of perceptions, values, attitudes, and behaviors that is accepted and expected by an identity group is called a *culture*. Since by definition each identity group has its own pattern of behavioral norms, each group may be said to have its own culture.[12]
10. Since communication tends to be easiest among individuals who identify most closely with each other and most difficult among individuals who perceive more or less dissimilarly, this tends to reinforce and exacerbate awareness of group differences. Any "we" (identity group) comes into much sharper focus when juxtaposed against "they" (a different identity group).
11. An individual must inevitably be a member of a myriad of different perceptual and identity groups simultaneously, by definition. However, one shares a higher degree of similarity of perception, and a higher degree of group identity, with some groups than with others. Consciously or otherwise, one rank-orders one's various group identities.[13]

12. Because environmental and biological facts are ever changing, perceptions, attitudes, and values are ever changing.
Consequently, the rank-ordering of group identities is ever
changing, and new perceptual groups are constantly being
formed, while existing groups are constantly in a state of flux.[14]

We know from the study of genetics that no two individuals
are physiologically completely identical. Certainly if the skin on
the tips of the fingers is different for each individual, then each
person's sense of touch must be presumed to be individual and
unique. Yet, far more important for the way people view the universe are the still unanswered questions of physical variations in
other sensory receptors. What about the configuration of cones
and rods in the retina of the eye, or taste buds on the tongue, or
fibers in the ear, or any of the other physical receptors of external stimuli? If no two individuals have identical receptors of
stimuli, then it must follow, on the basis of physiological evidence alone, that no two individuals perceive the external world
completely identically. Yet biological differences probably account
for only the smallest fraction of the perceptual distinctions made
by people.

Far more important in determining an individual's perceptions of the external world are the factors involved in the incorporation, organization, and processing of sensory data. Geneti-
cally, we inherit from our parents those physical characteristics
that distinguish us as their offspring. Admittedly there is a good
deal of individual variation biologically and environmentally, but
there is also a good deal of similarity. Given two white parents,
the overwhelming probability is that the offspring will be white.
Given two English-speaking parents, the overwhelming probability is that the offspring will speak English. The difference is that
biological identity is—within a given range of probability—fixed,
while environmental identity is not. The daughter of two white
parents will always remain white no matter what happens to her
after birth, but the daughter of two English-speaking parents may
never speak English if immediately after birth she is raised by a
totally non-English-speaking group. Thus, while biological inheritance is relatively immutable, environmental inheritance is
ever changing. Nevertheless, while there is theoretically an almost infinite number of possibilities for environmental conditioning, the number of environmental factors to which most individuals are exposed is amazingly limited. While there may be a
whole world to explore, the overwhelming majority of individuals who inhabit this planet never stray more than a few miles

from their place of birth. Indeed each of us is a member of a finite, and comparatively small, number of different identity groups.

If, for biological and environmental reasons, it is not possible for any two individuals to perceive the universe 100 percent similarly, neither is it possible—for the same reasons—for them to share absolutely no similarity of perception. Hence I am postulating here a continuum of similarity of perception among individuals. At one end we can approach—but never reach—zero; at the other we can approach—but never reach—100 percent. Actually, degree of similarity of perception can probably best be measured not as a point of a continuum but rather as a range of points. Thus, for example,[15] two Catholics—one from a third-generation wealthy Boston family, and the other from an illiterate and impoverished small village in the Congo—may share, as Catholics, no more than perhaps a 10 to 15 percent similarity of perception. Yet I would argue that to the degree that they share an identity (recognize a similarity of perception) as Catholics, they are a part of the broad identity group called "Catholics." Teachers, considered as a group, may share an average range of 20 to 25 percent similarity of perception. If I narrow the group to include only college teachers, the range of similarity of perception may increase to from 40 to 50 percent. If I further specify that the group consists of only Catholic, male, heterosexual college teachers of quantum physics, with Ph.D.s from M.I.T. between the ages of thirty-five and forty, the range of similarity of perception might well increase to perhaps 75 to 80 percent. Notice that while I have decreased the number of people who can be included in the group, I have increased the number of group identities which the members of this group share. By doing so I have greatly increased the likelihood of their sharing still greater similarities of perception in the future. It is no wonder that the smaller the group, the greater the group cohesion is likely to be.

By communication I mean here that one individual, or a group of individuals, more or less understands another's message. Since no two individuals perceive 100 percent identically, it follows that no individual will perceive another's message 100 percent as the sender intended it to be understood. When one couples this with what Claude E. Shannon and Warren Weaver[16] have said about the ever-present distortion in the communication process, it is easy to recognize the potentially high degree of noncommunication inherent in the process. Fortunately, it is not imperative to the functioning of groups that communication be perceived 100 percent accurately. Fortunately, too, there are corrective devices inherent in almost any communication system. One such device is the "feedback mechanism," which may allow for continuous testing of accuracy of perception.[17] Another is redundancy. Most verbal languages are themselves more than one-half redundant. Thus, if part of the message is lost either due to differing perceptions or to distortions within the system, enough of the message usually gets through to convey the general meaning intended. At least in face-to-face communication and to some extent in television and movies, there is repetition of the same message over a number of channels. Thus, both audio and visual channels may simultaneously convey and reinforce the same message. Regardless of the type of media available in any society, however, face-to-face communication will remain the most effective form of communication.

But verbal communication comprises only a portion—and it may perhaps be the smallest portion—of the communication that goes on in any society. Far more important are the silent, nonverbal communications which we only half consciously or unconsciously transmit and receive. Perhaps a million persons intersect at the corner of Broadway and 42nd Street in New York City each day, and yet the nonverbal communication process is so accurate that without a word being spoken they filter past each other in orderly fashion, only rarely touching. A glance, a shrug, time and spatial communication,[18] indeed an endless number of nonverbal cues which are often too subtle even to be conscious, may communicate far more than words. There is mounting evidence that within any given group nonverbal communication may account for the overwhelming majority of the communication which occurs. It is precisely because we communicate and perceive so well within our own groups that we feel so comfortable there. We can communicate effectively with a minimum of effort and frustration because the patterns of behavior of the members of our own groups are so predictable to us that a minimum of effort is required for effective functioning.

It is exactly such shared, often unarticulated and sometimes unarticulable, patterns of perception, communication, and behavior which are referred to as "a culture." But group identities do not necessarily recognize the integrity of national boundaries. In the hypothetical case of the college teachers of quantum physics cited above, no mention was made of nationality. To be sure, if I were to stipulate that they all be Americans, the percentage of their shared similarity of perception would probably rise still higher. But the fact is that there is a considerably higher degree of similarity of perception among college teachers of quantum physics—regardless of nationality—than there could possibly be between them and, let's say, uneducated sharecroppers or perhaps barbers in the same society. It is for this reason that I consider each group as having its own culture, rather than attempting to consider only each society as having its own culture, and then being forced to consider deviations from the societal norms as "subcultural."[19] This is not to say that societal cultures do not exist. On the contrary, to the degree that an entire society shares and communicates certain similarities of perception and behavior it must be considered as an identity group—and thus, of course, to have a common culture of its own. There is no question that there are American, French, Japanese, and other cultures.

But, I would argue, there is greater analytical and operational utility in considering each society as the aggregate of the identity (cultural) groups which exist within it. From there one may proceed to compare and analyze whole societies to determine which identity groups are present in each and

1. how the presence or absence of certain groups in a given society affects that entire society;

2. what other clusters of groups may always, often, rarely, or never be found in societies containing certain groups;

3. what the differences and similarities are between the same groups in different societies[20]—why they are different, how they relate to the whole society, and how the whole society is related to them; and

4. which differences and similarities exist between different groups in the same society.

While I believe that the implications of this formulation of the problem to the study of the process of social change are indeed significant, they fall outside the scope of this article.[21]

Implications for Intercultural Communication

Implicit in the perceptual model outlined above is the proposition that an individual is in fact functioning somewhat "interculturally" whenever he or she communicates with another individual. The fewer group identities one shares (and the less intensely held the identities which exist) with the individuals with whom one must communicate, the more "intercultural" is the communication. We are dealing here with a continuum and not with dichotomies. The important point to note, however, is that some *intranational* communications can be far more intercultural than other *international* communications.

Workers in various antipoverty programs have sometimes been chagrined and shocked to find their well-intentioned plans utterly rejected by the very people whom they were intended to help. What they have often overlooked—and what any experienced social worker knows—is the fact that the urban, middle-class, well-educated professional probably has a totally different set of perceptions (and hence values, attitudes, and modes of behavior) from his or her inner-city or rural, lower-class, uneducated client.[22] Merely because the professional sees merit in a particular proposal in no way ensures that clients will view the proposal in the same way. Indeed, it would be nearly miraculous if they did. It is precisely because of this that the demand has grown for greater participation of clients in the planning of proposals intended for their benefit. To some degree this may alleviate the problem. But until the cause of the problem is recognized clearly, it is doubtful that significant progress will be made. Until one of the groups concerned (and it can only be the professional group) recognizes that its perceptions differ markedly from those of the other—and recognizes that different is not the same as bad—and makes a concerted attempt to understand the other's perceptions, the incidence of friction and frustration is likely to continue. What is more, now that African American, Hispanic, and other ethnic identity groups in the United States are actively defending the validity of their identities, the Anglo population has begun to sense an urgency for understanding these perceptions.

International intercultural operations are often more complicated and more difficult than domestic intercultural operations—not necessarily because the individuals involved share fewer perceptions, but rather because it is often extremely difficult to adjust levels of expectation of communication in unfamiliar environments. Within our own society there are a multitude of familiar, silent, and/or subtle cues that tell us at which levels of sophistication we may communicate. When a male physicist talks to his male barber in the United States, he knows that he is expected to discuss baseball and the weather. He also knows that it would be futile for him to attempt to discuss quantum physics. Thus, he adjusts his communication expectations accordingly and leaves the barbershop a little wiser about the league standing of the home team and perhaps a little apprehensive about the impending winter. But he certainly has no feeling of frustration at not having been able to discuss physics. He knows with whom he may discuss baseball and with whom he may discuss physics. In a foreign environment, on the other hand, it is difficult—particularly for the newcomer—to assess at which level one may communicate. The same American male physicist operating outside of his own country may be pleasantly surprised to find that his foreign counterpart not only speaks English, but *appears* to have the same problems, aspirations, and values as he himself has. He therefore expects to be readily understood, even when discussing the most complicated intellectual problems. If he later finds that he was not completely understood, he may feel hurt, cheated, and frustrated. Because of the outward *appearance* of similarity based on common perceptions which the two share as quantum physicists, the American may not have taken into account the fact that there are a myriad of other group identities— and consequently many other patterns of perception and behavior—which they do *not* have in common.

But there is another reason for the increased difficulty of international intercultural operations. While two individuals in the same society may be a cultural world away from each other educationally, physically they may reside in the same city, in the same mass culture. If I were to eat in my barber's house in the United States, I would know approximately what to expect and how to behave—the food and utensils would be familiar. When I left the barber's house I would drive down familiar streets, with familiar faces, places, and smells, to the security and comfort of my own home. On the other hand, in the home of another professor in, say, Bombay, I will not only have to remember the specifics of not eating strange foods with my left hand (and any other specific intercultural data that I may have acquired) but I must also be prepared for the totally unexpected. It is simply not possible to teach someone from one ethnic culture the perhaps hundreds of millions of discrete "bits" of information one would have to know to truly understand another ethnic culture. Yet it is precisely because we do not know what it is about another culture that we do not know that our anxiety level must perforce be high. Further, as soon as I leave the home of my counterpart in Bombay, I must wander through strange streets, with strange faces, places, and smells. All the silent little cues which would come to me subliminally in the United States would be missing. In Bombay it would be necessary for me to expend an enormous amount of energy merely making explicit all of those myriad little cues which, in my own culture, can remain implicit and subconscious. But, obviously, the lack of reception of silent cues is not all that complicates international intercultural operations. The matter of adjusting to unfamiliar food, climate, and other physical differences can be a very real problem. Further, there is the additional real burden of functioning in a society in which one may be totally or partially unfamiliar with the spoken or written language.

There is one additional factor which tends to make international intercultural operations more emotionally taxing than most domestic cross-cultural operations. While I have argued that, analytically, all communications are to some degree intercultural, within our own society contact with significantly different groups can be kept to a minimum. At home we tend to spend most of our leisure time, at least, surrounded by individuals who perceive more or less as we do. Even if our work is of a nature which forces us to deal with people significantly different from ourselves during the day, in the evening we can retreat to the comfort and ease of our groups. Internationally, this is not always possible.[23] Aside from possible contact with fellow compatriots (the connotation of the term *landsmann* is significant here) when working or living in a foreign environment, one can expect no relief from the strain of uncertainty—either until the task is accomplished and one returns home or until one has lived in that environment long enough to increase one's own range of similarity of perception with those around one, to the point where, if not everything, at least most things need no longer be made conscious and explicit.

In sum, while some communications within the same society can be more intercultural than some international communications, international intercultural communication tends to be significantly more difficult because we tend to share a higher degree of similarity of perception with more groups in our own society than we do in a foreign environment.

There is one additional concept I would like to introduce here. Every communication relationship has a power component attached to it. We might as well recognize that and deal with it openly and consciously. Until now very few communication specialists have been prepared to deal with the power aspect of the communication process. On the other hand, most political scientists have failed to recognize the importance of cultural differences in the situations they study. It is one of my most deeply held convictions that the study of intercultural communication informs the study of political behavior. It is also my contention that any study of communication relationships that ignores the power aspect of those relationships is one that misses a very important element of all communication.[24]

To conclude, I am arguing here that a pattern of learned, group-related perceptions—including both verbal and nonverbal language, attitudes, values, belief systems, and behaviors—that is accepted and expected by an identity group is called a culture. Since, by definition, each identity group has its own pattern of perceptions and behavioral norms and its own language or code (understood most clearly by members of that group), each identity group may be said to have its own culture.

Further, I am arguing that no two people can perceive 100 percent identically and that the groups with which we either have been, or are, associated for most of our lives determine what and how we perceive. Each of the groups with which we identify (either consciously or unconsciously) teaches us its own definitions of good and bad, beautiful and ugly, right and wrong. We may come to deviate from the norms of some of the groups with which we identify—that is, to identify less with them than with some other groups—but to the extent that we do identify with any particular group, to that degree we are likely to accept that group's attitudes, values, beliefs, and so forth. Further, the more group identities we share with others, the greater similarity of perception we are likely to share; the fewer group identities we share, the less similarly we are likely to perceive. The more group identities we share with someone, the less intercultural (and hence easier and probably more accurate) the communication is likely to be. The fewer group identities we share, the more intercultural (and hence the more difficult and probably more inaccurate) the communication is likely to be. But all is not bleak. It is possible to learn about other cultures and in so doing we begin to share more similar perceptions, and we begin to communicate more effectively. We just have to make a greater effort.

---

[1] The perceptual model presented here, as well as several applications of that model, was subsequently developed in considerably more detail by the author and was later published in a number of different places, most significantly in my book, *Intercultural Communication: A Perceptual Approach* (Englewood Cliffs, NJ: Prentice-Hall, 1987). The original version of this article appeared in *Vidya*, no. 3 (Spring 1969) and was later reproduced in *Readings in Intercultural Communication*, vol. 1, edited by David S. Hoopes (Pittsburgh: Intercultural Communications Network, 1975), 6-20.

[2] Thus, our use of the term *perception* includes "memory" (in the cybernetic sense) and "cognition" in the interpretative sense.

[3] In our list of propositions presented below, we define each group as having its own culture.

[4] From *Collected Papers on Metalinguistics,* quoted by Franklin Fearing in "An Examination of the Conceptions of Benjamin Whorf in the Light of Theories on Perception and Cognition," in *Language in Culture,* edited by Harry Hoijer (Chicago: University of Chicago Press, 1954), 48.

[5] Here we are using *language* in the broadest sense. This may include the jargon or symbols used by social scientists or mathematicians, for example, to express the concepts peculiar to their group.

[6] These premises draw rather heavily on the extensive literature produced by cultural anthropologists, sociologists, psychologists, communications theorists, and linguists. In particular the model is strongly influenced by the notion of perceptual constancies. See Franklin P. Kilpatrick, ed., *Explorations in Transactional Psychology* (New York: New York University Press, 1961).

[7] As used here *perception* includes attitudes and values.

[8] While the terms *more* and *less* are vaguely quantitative, they are clearly inadequate for a precise science of social action. Unfortunately, they are often the best that the social scientist can produce, given the current state of our knowledge. A good deal of serious research being done by psychologists today, however, indicates that they are finding ways of measuring perceptions more and more precisely. For some suggestive approaches to this problem, see Bernard Berelson and Gary Steiner, *Human Behavior: An Inventory of Scientific Findings* (New York: Harcourt Brace and World, 1964).

[9] The converse of this is also true.

[10] Where there is little or no communication among individuals, there tends to be a decrease in similarity of perception, which in turn tends to make further communication difficult (see premise 10).

[11] In most societies the family enjoys the highest degree of group identity. Among the reasons that this is so is the fact that the family tends to combine a great many different perceptual groups simultaneously. Thus, with rare exception, all adult members of the family speak the same language, are from the same place of residence, are of the same religious persuasion, have approximately the same educational level, are of the same socioeconomic class, are very likely to be employed in the same occupational grouping, and so on at incredible length. In other words, the family enjoys one of the highest possible degrees of group identity precisely because the members of that group are also concurrently members of so many other perceptual groups. Indeed, family identity as the superordinate identification for the individual tends to break down precisely in those more mobile societies (particularly in urban, industrial areas) where the family combines fewer similarities of perception.

[12] For a further discussion of this approach, see below.

[13] It often happens that individuals and/or groups exist, having internalized elements of several differing or even conflicting value systems simultaneously. Individuals and groups are able to survive and function under these conditions primarily because (a) they are able to identify in differing degrees—and at differing levels of consciousness—with each of the value systems which they identify, and (b) because most group identities which are simultaneously held only rarely come into direct *conscious* conflict. When two equally held value systems do come into conflict, a high degree of personal and/or group anxiety (conscious or otherwise) may result. The individual and/or group often seeks some third identity which can accommodate, neutralize, rationalize, and/or synthesize these conflicting value systems. For some individuals and/or groups it could produce an inability to act. For still others, it might mean rather erratic behavior, alternately overstressing one value sys-

tem at the expense of the other. In any one of these cases, however, it would probably be diagnosed as ambivalence.

[14] Small, isolated, and relatively undifferentiated societies may often seem to be almost totally unchanging and unchangeable just because there is a high degree of shared perceptions among most of the members of those societies. It is precisely because there is a high degree of reinforcement of similarity of perception that it is so difficult to introduce change into those societies.

[15] Any figures used in our examples are completely hypothetical and are included merely to illustrate a concept. They are not based on any known research.

[16] See Claude E. Shannon and Warren Weaver, *The Mathematical Theory of Communication* (Champagne-Urbana: University of Illinois Press, 1949).

[17] For a dramatic demonstration of the necessity of feedback for even partial similarity of perception between sender and receiver, see Harold Levitt, *Managerial Psychology,* 2d ed. (Chicago: University of Chicago Press, 1964), chapter 9.

[18] See Edward T. Hall, *The Silent Language* (1959; reprint, New York: Anchor/Doubleday, 1981).

[19] By the 1990s we have come to recognize this and now call it "cultural diversity."

[20] For example, the family, students, businessmen, industrial workers, bureaucrats, the military, the clergy, and so forth in different societies.

[21] To some degree this aspect of the problem has been discussed in the author's "Group Perception and Social Change in Ceylon," *International Journal of Comparative Sociology* 7, no. 1 (March 1967).

[22] The extreme contrast is used here merely for illustrative purposes. Although perhaps in differing degrees, the same holds true for clients from other groups as well.

[23] It does help to explain, however, the prevalence of the American, German, British, and other foreign ghettos and clubs one finds abroad.

[24] This paragraph did not appear in the original article published in 1967. It is taken from my later book *Intercultural Communication: A Perceptual Approach.*

Interactions between North Americans[1] and Japanese: Considerations of Communication Style[2]

Sheila J. Ramsey

🔲🔲🔲🔲🔲🔲🔲🔲🔲🔲🔲🔲🔲🔲🔲🔲🔲🔲🔲🔲🔲🔲🔲🔲🔲🔲🔲🔲🔲🔲🔲🔲🔲🔲

Introduction

This discussion of communication style is grounded in the primary assumption that those who are successfully prepared will be able to accomplish their tasks while developing and maintaining satisfying interpersonal relationships with Japanese friends and colleagues. The emphasis is upon face-to-face interaction within the business context. The theoretical groundwork for this emphasis can be found in Dell Hymes'[3] and J. M. Wiemann's[4] work in communicative competence, which is carried into intercultural contexts by Fredrick Erickson,[5] John J. Gumperz,[6] John J. Gumperz and C. Roberts,[7] and Brent D. Reuben.[8] An attempt is made to present monocultural values and behaviors as well as to comment upon the dynamics created within face-to-face intercultural interaction.

Throughout this inquiry, special attention is given to the following questions of direct concern for face-to-face interaction:

1. To what extent and in what areas should people consciously step outside their cultural styles and presuppositions to make allowances for, or assume, nonnative behavior patterns? Are there some interaction models that can be set up as goals for preparing North Americans to interact with Japanese?

2. What are particular friction points or areas needing special attention that commonly emerge for North Americans in everyday interaction with Japanese?

Communication style has tremendous impact upon the dynamics of face-to-face encounters. Erickson speaks specifically about interethnic counseling situations:

> Shared or divergent communication styles influence a gatekeeping encounter by affecting its behavioral organization, that is, whether a conversation proceeds smoothly or by fits and starts, whether a counselor and student continually interrupt each other or are both able to talk simultaneously without interrupting and whether their styles of listening match.[9]

Differences in ethnic background coupled with those of communication style, says Erickson, probably increase chances that implicit unverbalized matters will be overlooked or misinterpreted.[10]

On the surface, differences in communication styles between Japanese and North Americans are readily apparent:

> Somehow whenever I get into a group discussion with Japanese, the questions I ask and the timing of my statements seem to cause them to clam up. I am the only one left speaking, even when I sincerely try to encourage others to speak.... Apparently, many Japanese people place a high value on nonassertiveness when speaking or writing. I, too, consider it rather rude to blatantly assert disagreements or to boorishly assert my own ideas without regard for others. But to thoughtfully ask another person questions and to logically analyze their statements would seem to me not in the least selfish or assertive, but rather, it would be considered the heart and soul of intellectual discussion.[11]

Coming to grips with deeper and more sophisticated effects of style differences can take years. Many of the attitudes expressed in Table 1, as stereotypical as some may be, emerge in face-to-face interaction and can be analyzed from the perspective of communication style. In exploring such differences of "the other," one cannot help but come to understand the cultural factors that have shaped one's own style.

Table 1. Intercultural Communication Blocks between Japanese and Non-Japanese

Problem Areas	Foreigners' Reactions to Japanese	Japanese Reactions to Foreigners
Direct/Indirect	It is irritating and a waste of time that they don't say yes or no or what they really think, clearly and directly. They seem immature and cowardly....	They seem childish and unpolished when they pay little attention to others' feelings and say too directly what they think.
Individuals/Groups	They don't express their own opinions but keep silent in public, as if they were stupid.... There is terrifying conformity but no individuality or originality.	They often justify themselves without admitting their faults. It is hard to live in a meritocratic society when one has to advertise one's ability all the time. Because of extremes in individualism, there is a lack of cooperation resulting in inefficient work.
Decision Making	It takes time to get an answer to the simplest question. It is ambiguous who is the decision maker and who is responsible for what, and so who should be accused when a contract is not observed.	Responsibility is clearly assigned to each person, and it is not interchangeable. They seem to be very stubborn and inflexible.
Discussion	There isn't any discussion in the true sense of the word. Their opinions are sorted out ahead of time and pre-arrangements made; the "discussion" is just a formality.	They discuss thoroughly and act upon the decision in common, although it doesn't reach 100% accord. They also conceive of discussion as a game, which is very embarrassing.[12]

Components of Communication Style

What are the components of this rather loosely applied label, "communication style"? In his classic study of communication style in the United States and Japan, Dean Barnlund includes "topics people prefer to discuss, their favorite forms of interaction—ritual, repartee, argument, and self-disclosure—and the depth of involvement they demand, as well as the channel people rely upon."[13] In examining the counseling encounter, Erickson includes such behaviors as gesticulation, eye contact, speech and kinetic rhythm, and listening behavior within the topic of communication style.[14] Studying culturally patterned differences of discussion between Americans and Indians, E. S. Johnson chooses to examine interruptions, pauses, laughter, inductive and deductive statements, and types of questions.[15]

In this discussion, three variables are suggested as a core around which to explore communication style: (1) orientation to interaction, (2) code preference, and (3) interaction format.[16]

To emphasize the possibility of movement and flexibility, these three variables of communication style are presented as orientations and in the form of continua in Table 2. These are not to be understood as stereotyped descriptions of all members of any cultural group but rather as stylistic preferences of the cultural group as a whole.

Erickson makes the point that "encounters are partially bounded in the sense that some of the rules are shared with the large society, while others are generated *ad hoc* by the participants."[17] He stresses the existence of ethnic diversity and explains that theories of communication style must allow for situational exceptions.[18] Erving Goffman's work also emphasizes that interpersonal competence should not be understood as a static concept or list of characteristics but rather as a quality which arises in the process of interaction.[19] The competent communicator arrives at "self/situation definition through a process of interpersonal negotiation."[20] For W. F. Owens a person is competent, as defined by those present, in a particular situation.[21] Communication style orientations are anchored in cultural standards but allow for individual movement depending upon the situation and certain cultural constraints.

Table 2. Comparison of Communication Styles: North Americans and Japanese

	North Americans	Japanese
1. Orientation to Interaction	Self: Individualistic Reality: Objective	Interpersonal Subjective
2. Code Preference	Verbal (and nonverbal)	Nonverbal (and verbal)
3. Interaction Format	Persuasive Quantitative Pragmatic	Harmonizing Holistic Process-oriented

1. Orientation to Interaction

	North Americans	Japanese
Locus of Self	Individualistic	Interpersonal
View of Reality	Objective	Subjective

The North American frontier movement was built upon the values of self-sufficiency and independence. American human potential movements facilitate the search for self; it is important to acknowledge differences of experience, ability, and opinion which separate individuals and highlight who we are. Japanese are less anchored by an internally identified self-concept as moored by lines leading to friends, colleagues, and family. For the Japanese, a parallel to the American sense of loss of self is a sense of not belonging.[22] Other contrasts are apparent in corporate settings.

The orientation brought to North American organizations by European immigrants has been one of objectivity, emphasizing a belief in cause and effect and in linear determinism. From this perspective, it is theoretically possible and desirable to remove subjective elements from research design and decision making. Validity and reliability are prerequisites of "solid" research; conclusions or action plans should follow clearly from premises and needs analyses.

In contrast, Japanese have traditionally been more oriented toward a human relations (*ningen kankei*) reality: "In order to attain an end, whether social or nonsocial, the creation, maintenance, or manipulation of a relevant social relationship is a foremost and indispensable means."[23]

Takie Sugiyama Lebra provides helpful insight into these two cultural approaches. She speaks of a Japanese *social* preoccupation as compared with a North American *action* preoccupation that focuses on symbols or physical objects. In the latter case, the actor is more likely to see "influence flowing unilaterally from center to periphery and focus on a prime mover."[24] She describes this as *unilateral determinism*. Examples include a monotheistic religion, absolute principles of right and wrong, and theories of the sanctity of the individual. A person's behavior may be justified as follows: "So and so told him to do it"; "It is so written in the Bible"; or "Because I wanted to."[25] There is a compulsion to differentiate elements: yes or no, black or white, win or lose, true or false.

She labels the Japanese orientation toward social preoccupation as *interactional relativism*. An actor is indifferent to the existence of a prime mover, and influence flows both ways between self and object. Behavior is a result of interaction, and overall balance is crucial—"It all depends"—and thus an understanding of context is vital. Japanese deal with what the West considers almost sacred symbols from a relative point of view. For example, a statement's "truth" is tied to social bonds and loyalty; "justice" is tied to indications of sincere repentance, and "love of nature" is an interactive view that supports the attitude of improving upon nature. In accordance with Lebra, Kinhide Mushakoji calls Japan an *awase* (adjusting) culture and the United States an *erabi* (selecting) culture.[26]

These differing orientations appear throughout *The Chrysanthemum and the Bat*,[27] an examination of the world of Japanese baseball. Robert Whiting contrasts the Japanese and American attitudes toward training. In the United States a player is left to design his own, individually tailored training program. While there is a general team workout, personal training is paramount; coaches do help out, but the individual is responsible for self-development. In Japan, coaches make all decisions and all players train together. "Seldom is anything left to the player's imagination."[28] This contrast is highlighted in a dialogue between a Japanese baseball manager and his American player who is just off the injury list:

Manager:	Ask him if he can pinch-hit tonight.
Team Interpreter:	Can you pinch-hit tonight?
American:	Sure—no problem. I can play the whole game.
Team Interpreter:	He says he would be honored if you would allow him to play the whole game...
Manager:	(Serious thoughtful expression) Tell him that if he feels he is going to hit into a double play, he should strike out instead. That's better for the team.
Team Interpreter:	The manager says if you have the feeling you are going to hit into a double play, you should try to strike out.

American: (Astonished) What? Strike out? He must be crazy. I've never struck out intentionally in my life and I'm not about to start now. If he wants me to strike out, tell him not to put me in the game. I've never heard of anything so stupid.

Team Interpreter: (Ahem) He says he thinks it is very difficult to strike out intentionally...and that perhaps there might be other players on the team who could do it better than he.[29]

This illustrates an individualistic orientation in contrast with a group orientation. The American's approach also emphasizes the personal distress of striking out rather than the value of the more symbolic meaning striking out would have. A view that stresses the team relationship is not appreciated, since it seems irrational. It is also instructive in this example to note the cultural modifications that the team interpreter finds it necessary to make.

The contrast between individual and group interaction orientations is also seen within the context of business in the work of Lewis Austin. His *Saints and Samurai*[30] is a study of the political culture of the Japanese and North Americans as represented by Caucasian male executives. He asks, "Why is it sometimes good to hide our true feelings about others?" as well as questions about conflict resolution and personal fears. He concludes that the American males in the sample were most fearful of personal failure, and Japanese males of the failure or malice of others. Likewise, reasons for being less open with others were more individually oriented for Americans and more socially oriented for the Japanese. For the Japanese,

Dissension or difference of opinion must not appear in the open because the group's harmony might seem to be damaged. Together with the importance of the group goes the deepest fear of the individual member of it: exclusion. And so no one must seem to be left out of the process of charting the direction in which the group decides to move.[31]

The contrasts of individualistic/interpersonal and objective/ subjective styles are highlighted in a comparison of interpersonal criticism in Japan and the United States. The Japanese preferred passive-withdrawing forms that allowed interpersonal accommodation with the target person. The North Americans frequently chose more individualistic, active-aggressive forms of criticism and focused on the objective problem rather than the person.[32]

Within the two cultural ideals presented, certainly there is evidence of change. North Americans are being criticized for their extreme focus on self and urged to consider the rewards of more collective attitudes. The Japanese too are becoming aware that intergroup competition and intragroup divisiveness can be paralyzing; they are beginning to recognize the importance of being more objective in planning and problem solving.

2. Code Preference

North Americans	Japanese
Verbal (and nonverbal)	Nonverbal (and verbal)

For anyone whose identity emerges from being separate and unique, differences between self and others are emphasized. As a North American new on a job, I "make my mark" by making changes. Primers for effective communication warn against making assumptions about others' needs or wants and stress speaking for yourself. North American intercultural trainers remind trainees to consciously separate fact, inference, and judgment, and they suggest withholding judgment upon entering a new culture. Trainees are admonished not to fill in meaning before checking it out. Assuming difference, I expect you to speak for yourself and hold up your end of the conversation. Statements such as "Don't expect me to read your mind" and "I can't help if he doesn't tell me what he wants" are based upon such assumptions. It is, of course, also assumed that only through detailed verbalization can one most concretely and most accurately "check out" what the other means.

The United States continues to grow as a nation made up of ethnically diverse people who must work and live together. Reliance upon symbolic coding of experience has become a necessary survival skill. It remains true, however, that among certain groups talk is negatively valued, as is clearly shown in Gerry Phillipsen's ethnography of a blue-collar neighborhood in South Chicago[33] and Mirra Komarovsky's description of blue-collar marriages.[34] Noel Perrin's descriptions of New England rural communities are illustrative of many comments made here about Japanese communicative styles.[35] There is a vast difference between a primary emphasis upon verbalization or written forms and a primary emphasis upon what can be sensed, guessed at, and inferred from the total situation before verbalization. Masao Kunihiro describes this as a difference between language as *a* means of communication and language as *the* means of communication.[36] When asked why something is done thus and so, the Japanese answer will often begin with "We Japanese" or "The Japanese way is to...." Despite the fact that the Japanese in Okinawa are linguistically very different from those in Sapporo and that there are about six hundred thousand foreign residents in Japan, the Japanese find comfort in thinking of themselves as a homogeneous "we."

Japanese prefer a style of communicating that appreciates and employs assumptions about the opinions and feelings of their compatriots. While such a style is common in long-term familiar relationships in any culture, it is significant that an entire cultural group values and practices this style in everyday transactions. The following is representative of this view:

> Others have tried to qualify Japan's homogeneity.... In spite of all this, no one would deny that present-day Japan is more homogeneous than any other major country in the world...the members share a great many aspects of their daily life and consciousness. Thus, explanations through the medium of language often become unnecessary, and the intuitive, nonverbal communication of the sort that develops among family members living under the same roof spreads throughout the society.[37]

An impressive rather than expressive emphasis places high value on the person who can "hear one and understand ten."[38] The basic attitude toward verbal skills and the feeling that fewer words are better than more are prevalent traditionally. Although speaking is no longer considered a vice, the concept of *enryo* translates into a hesitancy to speak frankly and immediately and shows concern over being labeled thoughtless or brash.

A common perception is that Japanese are more comfortable with silence than are many North Americans. Certainly, Japanese who are not well acquainted with one another can be very uncomfortable with the silence which occurs when an American professor asks "Are there any questions?" However, silence also has a very acceptable place within Japanese communication style. Akiora Hoshino has documented silences of up to thirty minutes in a Japanese T-group;[39] in Japanese television dramas and radio programs, silences of up to one minute are acceptable to audiences.[40]

It is critical that silence not be interpreted as the absence of thought. It may have many situational meanings: time to formulate an opinion or consider the appropriate form or content of a remark; a gathering of courage to speak in English; a space while waiting for a *sempai* (senior) to speak first; or the formation of a generally less confrontative, softer way to convey disagreement.[41] For more effective interaction, non-Japanese must learn to become more comfortable in situations of silence and refrain from filling in the space with questions or small talk. It is also imperative to be able to wait longer than one is accustomed to after inquiring about understanding or asking for a suggestion before assuming that no response will be forthcoming. One must not automatically assume that a silent group member should be pulled into the discussion.

Related to the attitudes and assumptions about verbalization are those concerning the importance of form. Even during a brief stay in Japan, it will be clear that the form of an event or the manner in which a task is carried out is invariably as important as, if not sometimes more important than, the content of the task or the message. The "how" of form relates to timing, physical appearance, order, actors' roles or affiliations, and atmosphere. There are abundant examples: arrangement of food; combinations of food and serving dishes for the season; uniforms worn by shopkeepers, bus drivers, hikers, skiers, or golfers; and indicators of status and role in seating arrangements and the use of *meishi,* or name cards. (An ad in the Tokyo National Railways for a printing company read, "Your Name Card Is Your Face.") Regarding language, there are set phrases for apologies, excuses, requests, condolences, greetings, and farewells which continue to be used, in part, because of their time-tested appropriateness.

A reliance upon form or ritualized behavior has many functions. It is a buffer against surprise, a sign of membership, a sign of predictability, a mechanism for building and maintaining harmony, and a window into the character of the person, group, or organization. An advertising strategy for Japan Air Lines calls on such associations between form and character in saying, "The Way We Are Is the Way We Fly," implying that inferences about service and quality can be made from behavior and appearance. If one does not understand the significance of form in some situations, there may be negative social consequences, even for a foreigner.

North Americans may perceive the Japanese to be shallow, insincere game players who are only concerned with the surface aspects of reality, or they may perceive that Japanese pry into private affairs. For example, a landlady's inquiry, "Where are you going?" can seem nosy if it is not understood as an *aisatsu* or "lubricant" expression that can be answered with *chotto soko made*—"just over there" or "out for a while." To answer in more detail would be like a visitor to the United States answering in detail the question "How are you?" When crossing cultural boundaries a common problem is the inability to distinguish between the literal and more figurative or ritualistic meanings of a phrase or behavior. While this is a universal problem, a newcomer to Japan is especially confronted with this issue because of the cultural emphasis on form.

If one does not attend to dictates of form, one may feel foolish and embarrassed by sticking out in situations where differences draw undue attention. In such instances, it is possible to embarrass Japanese companions or to inadvertently communicate lack of respect. One might also make the mistake of deciding not to attend functions when actually one's presence alone would be helpful or emotionally supportive. Although attendance might seem a waste of time, one may go to a meeting conducted mostly in Japanese, not so much to be an active part of the task completion but for more symbolic reasons that relate to role and the organization one represents. The act of being present and sharing in the process, even by physical presence only, can be the more important message.

Kejime (demarcation) is an important concept in Japan. The boundaries that mark events determine context and thus the behavior that is appropriate to the situation. Many activities in Japan that might "just happen" in the United States are made into events, bounded in time and space and by rules of decorum. The way parties are held illustrates this difference. Whether an end of the year party (*bonenkai*), a farewell party for students graduating (*sobetsukai*), a party after a tennis tournament, or a New Year greeting party, beginnings and endings are clearly marked. One doesn't begin to eat or drink until after the group toast (*kampai*) or speech. When leaving, one does not just sneak out or drift away; good-byes or apologies for leaving early are important rituals that are directed toward the entire group. This can be contrasted with the North American expectation that people will circulate or comfortably talk in separate groups or couples and entertain themselves. It is very common for the entire Japanese group to listen to individuals who tell stories or to engage in group games. The entire event is arranged so that no one is left out; one is neither the hit of the party nor a wallflower. A common North American reaction to Japanese parties may be "too much structure" and "very childish." It can, however, be very reassuring to enjoy the security and relaxation that shared responsibility can bring. Those new to this perspective would be well advised to have a repertoire of favorite songs, skits, or games to use when called upon to take a turn as group leader.

Participation in ritualized events such as *Cha-no-yu* (tea ceremony), *Shichi-go-san* (seven-five-three ceremony), *Ohinamatsuri* (girls' day), and *Oboe* (the end of summer return of souls) can be understood as a process of socialization. The young newcomers to a company may be sent to a Zen temple to build self-understanding within the group context while the group spirit is fostered. A businessman returning from years of work overseas may readjust himself to Japan by studying *aikido*, a martial art, or Cha-no-yu; a graduate student studying abroad may keep his "cultural center" by writing haiku. Such events also serve as psychological supports for entry into new phases of life such as getting married, entering college, or taking a job. These events emphasize learning by doing and rely heavily on visual representations of reality.

The inability to learn quickly about the forms and rituals of Japan by asking the right question and getting the right answer is in part the basis for perceptions that Japan is an ambiguous and mysterious culture. Indeed, "context cracking" can be something like solving a mystery. Being able to comprehend the interplay among significant situational variables and being able to assess how one fits into the overall situation is critical in creating successful face-to-face interactions with Japanese friends and colleagues.

3. Interaction Format

North Americans	Japanese
Persuasive	Harmonizing
Quantitative	Holistic
Pragmatic	Process-oriented

The persuasive function is highly emphasized in North American corporate communication style. Selling a product or promoting an action relies heavily on the assumption that if one can be shown the facts, the numbers, the details, or the direct correlation between cause and effect logically and objectively, he or she will accept the point. Resistance to the point can imply that the receiver is unreasonable, illogical, irrational, too emotional, or stubborn. It is enlightening in this regard to examine the label "pointless." There seems to be an analogic relationship between the symbol and its meaning. A pointless remark is not directly aimed at the target or goal; there is no obvious cause-and-effect relationship. As such, the term implies that the comment is negatively valued.

In deliberate marketing as well as in satisfying conversation, Americans feel that "two-way contrast is a point of departure."[42] All parties to a conversation are responsible for their own opinions; active give-and-take is expected. Opinions and proposals bounce off one another in counterpoint. With the idea or task as the prime focus, only the lack of individual verbal skills or intellectual prowess should prevent one from affecting others' thoughts. However, with an emphasis on output and the importance of the sender's role, an effective communicator will tailor his or her content and presentation style to an audience. Needs analysis is an important step before giving a speech or workshop to ensure a good fit between sender and receiver and to increase the acceptability of the sender's message.

The Japanese concept of conversation includes an attitude of sharing, of "I start my sentence and you finish it" rather than "I finish my sentence and you say yours."[43] Not based so much in differentiation of dualistic concepts, Japanese are "masters of combination."[44] For Japanese,

> no matter how much one negotiates, there is no concrete result, no agreement on the basis of a thorough statement from both sides as to where differences lie.... The individual and the whole are organically integrated, and as long as one is following the prescribed route, not only communication of ideas but everything else follows without disruption.[45]

Kunihiro also suggests that the Japanese language is rather awkward in situations involving confrontation; a lack of familiarity in dealing with an "all or nothing" logic can produce an overly rigid, uncompromising posture when used in a "friend or foe" type of situation.

Japanese do, of course, interact in persuasive modes. Today's university students are becoming more interested in formal debate. Traditionally, however, one is not persuaded solely by verbal skills or logical construction of an argument. Rather, one can be "brought over" by another's status and age, or by an emotional, empathetic feeling that the situation or the relationship might call forth.

From assumptions about and value placed on difference, North Americans work toward similarity through persuasion. From assumptions about and value placed on homogeneity, Japanese allow individual difference as long as the group can run smoothly on parallel tracks toward a common goal. In their subjectivity, the Japanese employ a very objective and less binding approach to interpersonal relations. A traditional college professor or speech maker will deliver a presentation without great concern about adapting the material to the audience. It is the student's responsibility to react, study, and, finally, ask questions to ensure comprehension. Especially in conflict resolution or unpleasant situations, negative meaning will be implied rather than made explicit. The receiver is expected to be sensitive to the overall situation.

Rather than expressing a judgment or opinion, Japanese often prefer to give the other person space to react and draw his or her own conclusions. This preference is evident in the purely descriptive poetry form of haiku, in which the poet presents experience and observations rather than evaluation. In reacting and filling in the gaps, the reader is drawn in. The reader's involvement is much less when an author thinks for his or her audience or does all the emotional work and provides abundant detail. When this is done, one can be drawn to dichotomous reactions—accept or reject, agree or disagree. The Japanese may perceive the filling in of details as a lack of consideration for the listener and a refusal to let the listener really participate. This emphasis upon the receiver's role is at the heart of different approaches to media advertising in the two cultures.[46]

A common Japanese approach to both writing and speaking is to describe the context of an event or situation long before stating an opinion about the event or giving a reason for the comment. A common North American approach assumes just the opposite order of speaking. It is not unusual for a North American to become very frustrated while waiting for the "main point," which may never be explicitly stated. From the Japanese perspective, the direct and clear statement of opinion or intention feels invasive and pushy. This subjective, "it depends" approach to reality and interpersonal relationships (which can have a very objective consequence) is one of the many intriguing paradoxes of Japanese communication style.

For North American businesspeople the ultimate purpose of communication is often pragmatic. Behavior accumulates and contributes to accomplishing an end result. Experience must be quantified so that the most expedient logical action can be taken. The ideal is to know exactly how much for exactly how long to accomplish exactly what. A manager/teacher cannot be sure a job/lesson will be done correctly without having a checklist or clearly defined objectives. Evaluation, too, must be in the form of numbers, not feelings. For instance, complete appreciation of the Washington Monument includes knowing how high it is and how long it took to build. Businesspeople new to Japan want to know exactly how long it will take to get a handle on Japan. It can be hard for a Japanese potter to understand and to accept that Americans need to know answers to questions like "How long did it take to make a tea bowl?" or "How many platters can you make in a month?" as part of appreciating the craft.

What Americans may quantify, Japanese may deal with as common sense. The Japanese don't put a percentage on managerial readiness, for example. Americans may rely on a detailed checklist approach to safety training, while Japanese would prefer an end-of-day discussion and then resolve as individuals and as a group to "do better" tomorrow. Following a drop in productivity, an entire Japanese group might spend a weekend together away from work in an atmosphere that encourages individual meditation and group discussion about improvement.

The Japanese place emphasis on the process of doing something as well as on the product or end result. The hour-long hike to get to the shrine is as important as, if not more important than, getting to the shrine, which may have "nothing" inside. Emphasis upon the result is typified by an American tourist who was overheard to ask, "Well, is it worth it when we get there?" as he climbed toward a waterfall where a Japanese prince once took water to make tea. A Japanese manager who helps his or her subordinate correct a mistake emphasizes the correction process as more educational perhaps than the correction itself. Events are not separated from the process or from the people involved.

In regard to planning, execution, and evaluation of an event, Japanese and Americans seem to proportion their time and effort differently. The Japanese are more comfortable when an event is thoroughly planned in detail before it is executed; the *hanseikai* (evaluation) is an important time for members to discuss and give feedback to each other to decide what could have been better executed and to judge which members have the interest and capabilities to take certain responsibilities next time. Many North American managers are comfortable with a play-it-by-ear attitude about preplanning and execution. Sometimes planning overlaps the execution stage, since plans often change during execution. The evaluation, if done at all, may be the least-emphasized component.

In the world of business this is translated into a well-known difference—it seems to take the Japanese forever to make a decision, but once something is decided, it is implemented rapidly and completely. North American businesspeople seem to reach a decision very quickly, but implementation takes forever. Being bound, in a sense, by preplanned details may contribute to the perception that Japanese behavior is out of step with what is happening. For example, after I had delivered an hour's lecture on intercultural communication to a group of Japanese college students, the first question from the audience was "Why should we study intercultural communication?" This could be interpreted in a totally self-defeating way: "They didn't understand anything I have just been talking about." A more accurate interpretation is that the question was prepared in advance, not necessarily to be modified by my lecture. The process of asking a question should also be understood as a compliment, irrespective of the question's content.

The variable of "interaction format" greatly influences the establishment and maintenance of relationships between Japanese and North Americans. It is important to realize that in Japan one rarely accomplishes anything by oneself. Although one person may carry the majority of responsibility, it is vital to continually involve others so that an overall feeling of group effort and achievement is shared. Determining who these "appropriate others" are and learning how to include them can be a long and involved process. Inability to handle these "how" and "who" aspects can contribute to discomfort and bewilderment for those wishing to work within a Japanese context.

In Japan, another aspect of maintaining relationships is sharing information. "Touching base" must be done continually, not just at the beginning or end of a project. While it may be only a symbolic gesture, it should not seem to be so. Ideally, it should not be done via memo or telephone but is best accomplished in person. When a North American manager complains of not getting enough information from his Japanese section chiefs, he or she might well expect the reply, "If you didn't have a mailbox, you would see me a lot more and learn more." The Japanese office arrangement of many desks together in the same room encourages face-to-face communication. It is a very high-context situation, in which people can learn not only by asking why and how, but also by watching and listening to seasoned office mates doing their jobs. Japanese department managers do not sit in an office and wait for people to walk in to discuss a problem or give feedback. Most likely the manager's desk is in a back corner of the large room so that he or she can easily observe the work progress of all. If the manager does have a private office for special conferences, he or she will also have a desk in the common room. Managers must become familiar with nonverbal behaviors of their subordinates, which might indicate confusion, misunderstanding, or need for help. Such familiarity grows as they learn about each employee's personality and family.

Getting feedback from Japanese during the course of a conversation or meeting can be one of the more difficult aspects of communicating with them. "They don't give me any feedback"; "They don't ask any questions"; "I need to know if I'm getting through. I don't want a blank stare"; "I understand what I said, but I'm not sure they did." These kinds of comments are common from North Americans. It is interesting to compare these with typical Japanese comments: "I smile and catch as much as I can"; "We Japanese don't confirm. You Americans always clarify and so on"; "I don't want to say 'Let me check.' That is checking the person. Maybe I would say, 'Let me repeat'." Difficulties in following a discussion or formulating questions or taking turns in English often contribute to the lack of verbal feedback. Japanese tend to provide one another with much more back-channel reinforcement during conversations than do North Americans. Lack of nonverbal feedback from Americans can cause Japanese to feel rather separate and distant during an interaction. For a North American, being able to provide more frequent back-channel signals to a Japanese listener is a part of developing that necessary reciprocal orientation. Anyone who expects Japanese subordinates to walk into the office, sit down, and give verbal feedback about a project may never find out what is going on until it is too late to help. It is necessary to develop alternative ways to get feedback about work progress and one's own performance. Rarely will feedback be given in a direct verbal form.

In summary, assumptions about communication style can be deeply buried and can be the source of subtle ethnocentric attitudes and behaviors. North Americans who envision effective task accomplishment and the development of long-term relationships with the Japanese are encouraged to explore the norms of their home culture and those of the Japanese, and to value differing approaches as well as the consequences of disregarding the Japanese perspective. It can be informative and quite revealing to focus such a process around variables of communication style. With such a vision, a "common place"[47] can be created in which Japanese and North Americans can live and work together.

---

[1] Although many of the comments made may be applicable to various segments of the Canadian population, in using "North American" the reference is to long-term residents of the United States who are strongly influenced by the Anglo-Saxon tradition. Recently arrived Asian immigrants may be more closely described by the comments made about Japanese than those describing North Americans.

[2] This article is an adapted version of "Preparation of Americans for Interaction with Japanese: Considerations of Language and Communication Style" by Sheila J. Ramsey and Judy Birk. It appeared in *The Handbook of Intercultural Training*, vol. 3, edited by Dan Landis and Richard Brislin (Elmsford, NY: Pergamon Press, 1983).

[3] Dell Hymes, "On Communicative Competence," in *Sociolinguistics*, edited by John B. Pride and J. Holmes (London: Penguin Books, 1972).

[4] John M. Wiemann, "Explication and Test of a Model of Communicative Competence," *Human Communication Research* 3, no. 3 (1977): 195-213.

[5] Fredrick Erickson, "Gatekeeping and the Melting Pot: Interaction in Counseling Encounters," *Harvard Educational Review* 1975 45(1), 44-70.

[6] John J. Gumperz, "The Linguistic Basis of Communicative Competence," paper presented at Georgetown University Round Table, 1981.

[7] John J. Gumperz and Celia Roberts, "Developing Awareness Skills for Interethnic Communication," National Center for Industrial Language Training, Southall, Middlesex, England, 1978. Available as Occasional Paper #12 from Seamo Regional Language Center, RELC Building, 30 Orange Grove Road, Singapore 1025, Republic of Singapore.

[8] Brent D. Reuben, "Assessing Communication Competency for Intercultural Adaptation," *Group and Organizational Studies* 1, no. 3 (1976): 334-54.

[9] Erickson, "Gatekeeping and the Melting Pot," 52.

[10] Ibid., 55.

[11] This remark is abstracted from a student research paper completed for an intercultural communication course at International Christian University, Tokyo, Spring 1980.

[12] Reiko Naotsuka, *Mutual Understanding of Different Cultures* (Osaka, Japan: Educational Science Institute of Osaka Prefecture, 1978), 2.

[13] Dean Barnlund, *Public and Private Self in Japan and the United States* (Tokyo: Simul Press, 1975; Yarmouth, ME: Intercultural Press, 1989), 15.

[14] Erickson, "Gatekeeping and the Melting Pot."

15 E. S. Johnson, "A Technique of Studying Culturally Patterned Differences between Indian and American Discussion Style" (master's thesis, University of Hawaii, 1966).

16 These three variables encompass ideas presented in John C. Condon's "Contrasting Communication Styles of Japanese and Americans," in Clifford Clarke's "Communication Style Continuum of Japanese and Americans," and in the classic reference work by Dean Barnlund, *Public and Private Self.*

17 Erickson, "Gatekeeping and the Melting Pot," 50.

18 Ibid., 55.

19 Erving Goffman, *The Presentation of Self in Everyday Life* (Garden City, NY: Doubleday/Anchor, 1959).

20 Wiemann, "Explication," 196.

21 W. F. Owens, "Interpersonal Communication Competence: A Transcultural Model," *Speech Education* (1979): 1-12.

22 Richard T. Pascale and Anthony G. Athos, *The Art of Japanese Management Applications for American Executives* (New York: Simon and Schuster, 1981), 122.

23 Takie Sugiyama Lebra, *Japanese Patterns of Behavior* (Honolulu: University of Hawaii Press, 1976), 4.

24 Ibid., 7-8.

25 Ibid., 8.

26 Kinhide Mushakoji, "The Cultural Premise of Japanese Diplomacy," in *The Silent Power: Japan's Identity and World Role* (Tokyo: Simul Press, 1976), 39.

27 Robert Whiting, *The Chrysanthemum and the Bat* (Tokyo: The Permanent Press, 1977).

28 Ibid., 41.

29 Ibid., 181.

30 Lewis Austin, *Saints and Samurai: The Political Culture of the American and Japanese Elites* (New Haven: Yale University Press, 1975).

31 Ibid., 125-26.

32 Naoki Nomura, "Patterns of Interpersonal Criticism in Japan and the U.S." (master's thesis, San Francisco State University, 1980).

33 Gerry Phillipsen, "Speaking like a Man in Teamsterville: Culture Patterns of Role Enactment in an Urban Neighborhood," *Quarterly Journal of Speech* (1975): 15-25.

34 Mirra Komarovsky, *Blue-Collar Marriage* (New York: Vintage Press, 1967).

35 Noel Perrin, *Second Person Rural* (Boston: David R. Godine, 1980).

36 Masao Kunihiro, ed., "The Japanese Language and Intercultural Communication," in *The Silent Power: Japan's Identity and World Role* (Tokyo: Simul Press, 1976), 56.

37 Ibid., 53.

38 John C. Condon, "Contrasting Assumptions and Styles of Communication." Unpublished paper, 1976, Tokyo.

39 Akiora Hoshino, "The Characteristics of Japanese Self-Expression," *Eigo Kyoiku* 22, no. 3 (1973):16-18.

40 M. Wayne, "The Meaning of Silence in Conversations in Three Cultures," in *Patterns of Communication In and Out of Japan* (Tokyo: ICU Communication Department, 1974).

41 K. Ueda, "Sixteen Ways to Avoid Saying 'No' in Japan: A Survey of the Function and Frequency of Japanese Patterns of Declining Requests," in *Patterns of Communication In and Out of Japan* (Tokyo, ICU Communication Department, 1974); Wayne, "Meaning of Silence."

[42] Kunihiro, "Japanese Language," 69.
[43] N. Mizutani, *Communication in Japanese...Characteristic Features in Japanese Language Behavior Patterns,* paper presented at Japan Society, Tokyo, November 1979.
[44] Kunihiro, "Japanese Language," 65.
[45] Ibid., 60-62.
[46] Sheila J. Ramsey, "Cultural Differences and Similarities in Print Advertising: Japan and the United States," paper presented in 1981.
[47] Kunihiro, "Japanese Language," 71.

Black and White Cultural Styles in Pluralistic Perspective

Thomas Kochman

ᗶᗶ

Introduction

American society is presently in a period of social transition from a structurally pluralistic society to a culturally pluralistic one. The difference between the two kinds of pluralism is in the political arrangement of their culturally heterogeneous parts. Within structural pluralism the socially subordinate cultural person or group unilaterally accommodates the dominant (Anglo-American male) cultural group on the latter's terms. This pattern of accommodation can be said to have constituted an American policy orientation regarding the integration of immigrants and (with further important qualification) indigenous and other minorities into the larger American society. As Theodore Roosevelt said in 1919: "If the immigrant who comes here in good faith becomes an American and assimilates himself to us he shall be treated on an exact equality with everyone else."[1]

The "us" or "American" in Roosevelt's statement represents the socially dominant Anglo-American male, only recently (within the framework of cultural pluralism) identified as a "hyphenated" American too, alongside Afro-American, Irish-American, Polish-American, Italian-American, Jewish-American, et al., but having (within the framework of structural pluralism) effectively preempted the unhyphenated term *American* for themselves, with

others being less "American" to the extent that they were "hyphenated." As Roosevelt said in the same speech: "But this [equal-
ity] is predicated on the man's becoming in very fact an American and nothing but an American.... There can be no divided
allegiance here. Any man who says he is an American but something else also, isn't an American at all."

Equity within structural pluralism is seen as treating everyone the same. This serves both the social interest of cultural assimilation to Anglo-American male norms—to benefit equally
from the same treatment one has to become like the (Anglo-
American male) person for whom that treatment was designed—
and the social interest of economy and efficiency: officials need
only to choose the one "best" way, with individuals held responsible for adapting themselves as best they can to that same "best"
treatment. The fact that the same treatment might produce unequal effects, a point emphasized in the Bilingual Education Act
of 1968, was indifferently accepted as the unavoidable "fallout"
of this form of equity:

> There is no equality of treatment merely by pro-
> viding students with the same facilities, textbooks,
> teachers, and curriculum; for students who do not
> understand English are effectively foreclosed from
> any meaningful education.[2]

The structural arrangement within cultural pluralism reflects
greater political equality among the culturally heterogeneous
units. "Anglo-Americans" are one group among other "hyphenated" Americans, and the accommodation process among different culturally distinctive groups is reciprocal rather than unilateral. As with structural pluralism, the public arena again provides the stage within which culturally pluralist issues are developed and negotiated (as, for example, with regard to what intergroup "reciprocity" would constitute). The dominant metaphor
within cultural pluralism is the "salad bowl," not the "melting
pot," in which the identity and integrity of the culturally distinctive units remain intact while contributing to the overall quality,
effect, and purpose of the whole.

Equity within cultural pluralism moves from treating everyone
the same—an equality of input (comparable to giving every flower
in a garden the same amount of sunshine, fertilizer, and water,
which guarantees that only certain flowers will fully grow)—to an
equality of effect. Following the agricultural metaphor and model,
this would amount to allowing variable treatments so long as
they were or could be demonstrated to be equivalent.

The golden rule of "doing unto others what you would have done unto you," which the news columnist Sidney J. Harris[3] has pointed out may conceal a cultural bias—it assumes that others want what you want for yourself—also needs to be refashioned within cultural pluralism to become "do unto others as they would want done unto them."

Cultural Pluralism and Black and White Cultural Differences

Insofar as present mainstream American attitudes toward cultural diversity by and large have been those generated by structural pluralism, differences in Black and White mainstream linguistic and cultural patterns, perspectives, and values are likely to be seen through a mindset that attaches greater social respectability, if not conceptual validity, to the White mainstream cultural style. The ubiquity of such a mindset becomes obvious when we realize that Black and White cultural and linguistic differences are manifested in approaches to assessing others and being assessed oneself in terms of ability and performance in school, college, and the workplace (for example, consider judgments and inferences which follow an emotionally heated confrontation as an instance of Black functional "truth-seeking" style, described below). Indeed, through its school system and other social agencies, the dominant social group still insists upon "linguistic and cultural assimilation as a prerequisite to social incorporation," thereby instituting a policy and program whereby pressures are brought to bear upon Blacks and members of other minority groups to accommodate the dominant social group exclusively on the latter's terms. And in fact, when interest has been shown in American minority languages and cultures in the past it has generally been geared to understanding them *for the purpose of easing their social and cultural transition into the American mainstream,*[4] an attitudinal stance consistent with the "melting pot" concept within structural pluralism.

What disturbs me about this accommodation process is its unidirectional and nonreciprocal character. Those members of minority cultures who wish to become socially incorporated into the American mainstream do need to learn about mainstream American linguistic and cultural patterns. In some instances, it might even benefit them to use and embrace such patterns as necessity or desire might dictate.

But what about the needs of the American mainstream? The nonreciprocal nature of the process of cultural assimilation of minorities does not permit the mainstream American culture to learn about minority cultural traditions or benefit from their official social incorporation. It also suggests an unwarranted social arrogance: that mainstream American society has already reached a state of perfection and cannot benefit from being exposed to and learning from other (minority) cultural traditions. I reject that assumption, and I demonstrate that in the stance I take here by promoting a view of the culturally different patterns and perspectives of Blacks and mainstream Whites from a social standpoint that regards them as equally respectable and valid (of course, therefore, also equally accountable to criticism, as on functional grounds, when such may be warranted).[5]

Styles of Work and Play

The following sections will detail the contents of some of the culturally different patterns as they appear in the domains of work and play. An overview is presented in Figure 1 below.

Figure 1. Styles of Work and Play

BLACK	WHITE
PATTERNS	
Mental "Reflex"	Mental "Set"
Spontaneous	Methodical
Improvisational	Systematic
Exaggerated	Understated
Expressive	Restrained
Personalized	Role-Oriented

ISSUES
Being/Doing: Individuality
Teamwork/Play: Individuality; Functionality

Being and Doing

In American mainstream culture Whites (especially males) are taught to see themselves as individuals rather than as members of a group. Yet when they become members of an organization or team, they are frequently called upon to subordinate their individuality to fit the hierarchy and role requirements established by the group. The nature of the subordination process takes the form of seeing the group as more important than oneself ("There is no letter *I* in the word *team*"). This process often leads to a fused self or identity (organized around what mainstream individuals do professionally) such as when White males talk about themselves in terms of a corporate "we" rather than as an individual "I."

Organizational culture also qualifies individuality in other respects. White mainstream American cultural style in the areas of organized work and play is serious, methodical, and systematic, characterized by what Paul C. Harrison[6] has called "mental set": a stance or attitude in which action or activity (doing) is seen to evolve out of a tightly structured plan, schedule, or procedure. The conception and implementation of the plan is comprehensive (attempts are made beforehand to take all relevant variables into account and control for them), prescribed (from top management on down), and systematized (through standard operating procedures). The purpose of mental set is to render processes and outcomes orderly and predictable.

Within this role-oriented structure, individuals operating within and through mental set are taught to see themselves in essentially instrumental terms ("You are what you do!"). Those parts of the self that are drawn upon are those mental and physical skills that functionally contribute (in some direct way) to organizational objectives. Aspects of the self that cannot be justified as directly contributing to the established task are disallowed as not only nonfunctional but as subversive. They are seen to promote and sustain individual allegiance to nonwork-related values, which, among other things, White mainstreamers believe, threaten the undivided attention to task necessary to do work well. Individuals with similar skills, roles, and tasks are seen within the team or organizational framework as "interchangeable" parts. As a result of these social pressures within the organization, the more distinctive aspects of White male individuality (self and identity) within mainstream American culture are more often realized in isolation: outside the context of a work group, rather than within it.

The relationship between the individual and the plan within the framework of "mental set" is analogous to that between the performer and the text within the "compositional" tradition in the performing arts. The principal interaction there is between the performer and the text or composition.[7] The role and responsibility of the performer are with regard to the text: the revelation of its "embodied meaning," and consequently, with a sense of fidelity to the author's or composer's original conception. Thus, performers are constrained in their interpretation and rendition of the text so as not to take "undue liberties." Chicago Symphony oboist Ray Still makes this point in the context of objecting to the tradition (apparently as a result of his having been influenced by jazz music values):

> It's almost an unwritten law that we're not sup-
> posed to glissando—sliding from one note to an-
> other, as jazz musicians do so often—on a wind
> instrument. Only string instruments and the voice
> are supposed to do it. When I do it—I like my
> glisses—some eyebrows are raised. They say, "Oh,
> Ray is bending his instrument, now, trying to show
> his jazz technique." But that tradition burns me
> up. Why shouldn't we do it?[8]

Black cultural style in work and play evolves out of a conception that sees "change" rather than "set" as the constant aspect
of cosmic and social order. Consequently, the Black cultural
psyche operates out of "mental reflex,"[9] one oriented to "move
through changes" as changing modes or circumstances determine. In conjunction with the Black penchant for generating powerful imagery, change becomes that aspect of order that "revital-
izes an event."[10] The cultural style that Blacks have developed
that serves "going through changes" is improvisation. And the
force within the individual that motivates and complements improvisation is spontaneity ("I'm not a prizefighter, I'm a *surprise*
fighter").

Consistent with this view of cosmic and social order, Black
cultural style evolves out of a performance (as opposed to compositional) tradition;[11] consequently, the principal interaction is
between the performer and the audience (the goal there being
"engendered feeling"[12]). Within this tradition, performers are
granted great license to improvise with regard to the text—in
effect to generate new "text" as they go along—and, through the
simultaneous and direct demonstration of the individual
performer's virtuoso ability and powers of evocation, to produce
"engendered feeling" in the audience.[13]

There is, of course, a performance dimension within the Western compositional tradition, too, that aims at "engendered feeling," but, as Charles Keil argues, with "music composed for repetition, 'engendered feeling' has less chance [than when] music
is left in the hands of the performer" (improvised).[14]

Critical differences between the compositional and performance traditions, then, are those of substance, principal focus,
and direction. As Keil says, "a good composer gives some spontaneity to his form and, conversely, a good improviser tries to
give some form to his spontaneity."[15] Likewise, as Harrison notes,
actors in the White American theater aim at generating *affective
memory,* which allows them to repeat the same emotion night

after night. In the Black theater, on the other hand, actors try to generate *effective memory*, which allows them to produce real, spontaneously conceived emotions, so as to produce (as the *context* rather than the *text* demands) the truest emotional response capable of galvanizing the (audience's) collective unconscious.[16] Thus, where White mainstream cultural style is oriented to shape the context to fit the text, Black cultural style is oriented, rather, to shape the text to fit the context.

Black individuality is realized within the framework of strong interpersonal connectedness, but, as Virginia H. Young states, "not with absorption or acceptance of group identity as higher than individual identity."[17] Moreover, while there is emphasis on instrumental forms of doing, focus is also on individual character and style ("doing one's *own* thing"), leading to more personalized and idiosyncratic expressions of doing (as opposed to the more routine, uniform, and impersonal [role-oriented] forms of doing characteristic of self-presentation within White mainstream organizational culture).

Stylistic Self-Expression

Stylistic self-expression within White mainstream culture is minimalist in character: "a style of no style";[18] thus, characterized by economy and efficiency ("the shortest distance between two points," "no wasted moves") and modest (self-effacing) understatement and restraint ("If you've got it, you don't need to flaunt it").

Stylistic self-expression within Black culture is characterized by dramatic self-conscious flair. A nice descriptive example comes from Janet Milhomme's portrait of Felix Toya, Ghana's dancing traffic policeman:

> Dubbed "Toyota" or "Life Boy" by the city's taxi drivers, Constable Toya attracts as much pedestrian traffic as he directs vehicles. Lookers applaud and cheer, drivers toot their horns and sometimes take an extra turn on the roundabout as Felix oscillates and gyrates, lifts, bends and pirouettes, making an art form out of his assigned task, never missing a step or a signal change. Few Ghanians own Walkmans, but in the privacy of his own mind, Constable Toya creates a symphony of sounds and rhythms to which he moves with grace and precision. He is the ultimate street performer, taking cues from his environment and entertaining a diverse audience of fleeting yet appreciative fans.[19]

Black stylistic self-expression is also characterized by inventive (humorously ironic) exaggeration as in the self-promotion of demonstrably capable aspects of self ("If you've got it, flaunt it") or even by less demonstrably positive capabilities ("If you don't have it, flaunt it anyway"), which is all part of Afro-American boasting: the "making of one's noise."[20] As "Hollywood" Henderson said, "I put a lot of pressure on myself to see if I can play up to my mouth."[21] But exaggeration also serves to characterize (and neutralize the impact of) negative situations, such as poverty ("The soles on my shoes are so thin, I can step on a dime and tell you whether it's heads or tails").

Conflict and Confluence

Individuality/Functionality

The functional rule for getting things done follows the norms for appropriate stylistic self-presentation and expression within the two cultures. The White mainstream cultural rule is governed by the principles of economy and efficiency, which serve to promote the uniform, impersonal, minimalist, and instrumental (role-oriented) style considered standard within mainstream White organized work and play. Thus the rule here is "make only moves that are necessary to getting the job done."

The Black cultural rule serves to promote the standards within the Black performance tradition, which is, as Roger D. Abrahams[22] has said, for individual performers to bring about an experience in which their creative energies and the vitality of others may find expression. Blacks accomplish this by executing tasks with bold originality and dramatic flair. Insofar as it is in "how" things get done that the energetic involvement of others and stylistic self-expression occur, rather than in "what" gets done, Blacks say (to protect the individual right of original self-expression), "Tell me what to do but not how to do it." Consonant with this purpose, the functional rule for Blacks is "so long as the moves that are made do not interfere with getting the job done, they should be allowed."

These two different cultural rules clash in the workplace and on the playground with great regularity.[23] One example of this clash is in the restrictions set forth in the professional football rules governing "spiking" the football (throwing it forcefully to the ground): a self-celebrating expression of personal accomplishment (resembling an exclamation point [!]) by which Black players punctuate their achievement. Were a player to "spike" the football after scoring an important first down, he would be penalized. The official reason given for assessing the penalty is "delay of game." In actuality there is no real "delay of game" because after a team scores a first down the line markers have to be moved, and a new football is thrown in from the sidelines; there may even be a TV commercial. At issue is the different aesthetic standard governing stylistic self-expression within Black and White mainstream culture. "Spiking" the football is permitted in the end zone after a touchdown, but only by the player who actually scores the touchdown. So when the White quarterback of the Chicago Bears, Jim McMahon, scored a touchdown and gave the football to one of the linemen to spike (in recognition of his cooperative and instrumental role in the touchdown), the officials assessed a penalty on the ensuing kickoff. As a measure of the acceptance of the Black cultural view on such matters in professional sports, it is significant that the reaction of both White announcers at the time of its occurrence and of Bear quarterback Jim McMahon, when interviewed afterward, was to regard the penalty assessment as "stupid."

Other aspects of cultural conflict center around the issue of individual entitlement for stylistic self-expression and authorization for making changes in how a task is to be done. In White mainstream organizational culture, stylistic self-expression, when it occurs at all, tends to be a function of rank. Consequently, it is often the chief executive male officer in the organization who, in manner or dress, "shows off" or otherwise demonstrates a more individually expressive (noninstrumental?!) style (for example, Lee Iacocca, Ray Kroc, Douglas MacArthur, and so forth).

In Black culture, however, stylistic self-expression is an individual entitlement. Consequently, one does not have to be the president of the company to drive an expensive top-of-the-line car or wear fashionable clothes. However, this cultural pattern often gets Blacks into trouble in White mainstream organizations, since the latter interpret such individual stylistic self-expression as a presumption: a laying claim to a greater rank or title in the organization than the Black person actually holds.

As to authorization for how a task is to be accomplished, the Black dictum "Tell me what to do, but not how to do it," while establishing a protection for the individual right to self-expression, also asserts that the final authority for the implementation of a task rests with the doer/performer. However, White mainstream organizational culture, through the framework of "mental set," sees the authorization of a standard protocol or procedure to rest with the designer of the plan: the manager/composer. This difference also gets Blacks into trouble in the organization because they get accused here once again either of arrogating to themselves authority to which their rank or role in the organization does not entitle them, or of being insubordinate or uncooperative, even when they do the task differently in the interests of getting the job done, when doing it in the way it was officially prescribed would have failed.

The Role and Function of Competition

In organized work and play within White mainstream culture, the role and function of competition is to provide a climate and context to determine which pair of adversaries (individual or group) can dominate the other. The role and function of competition in organized work and play within Black culture is twofold. It is not only to set the stage for determining which opponent can dominate the other (though it is also that, and intensely so), but also for each individual or group to use its opponent (as a foil is used in theater) to show off their skill in the process of doing so. The cultural difference is one of focus and emphasis. For Blacks, as Abrahams has said, competition provides the atmosphere in which performers can best perform.[24] The Black goal therefore is divided between winning (dominating one's opponent) and showboating (displaying one's ability vis-à-vis one's opposition so as to show it off at its highest level of accomplishment). This display function sets competition within Black culture apart from its counterpart in White mainstream culture. As basketball player Lloyd Free said,

> The fans have the right idea about pro basketball's regular season.... They know there are too many games and it's silly to play all that time to eliminate so few teams from the playoffs.
>
> So why do they even come to our games?... They come to see a show and that's why guys like myself and Dr. J and David Thompson are so popular. We make the fun and the excitement. Man, you just don't get serious in this business until the playoffs.[25]

This divided function of competition (winning and showboating) together with another cultural pattern, that of individual identity not being subordinate to group identity (the individual can succeed even if the team does not), leads to a more diffuse focus in competitive play. This diminishes somewhat the singular importance attached to team winning that exists within White main-stream culture, represented by the assertion attributed to Vince Lombardi: "Winning may not be everything. But losing isn't any-thing." It especially takes the hard edge off losing. (As Blacks say, "The best you can do is the best you can do.") In the following passage, Red Holzman responds to a question about frequent reports that today's players don't take defeat as hard as yesterday's heroes. Without attributing this different attitude directly to Black cultural influence, he nonetheless supports the culturally dichoto-mous view presented here (albeit within the framework of differ-ences in "older" and "newer" player attitudes toward losing):

> When I first started to coach in the pros, guys would come into the locker room after a tough loss and break up the furniture or brood or act like there was no tomorrow. It was like they had committed a crime by losing.
>
> Now as a coach, I certainly don't want my play-ers to take any defeat lightly. But when you're part of an 82 game schedule, you're playing five times in the next six nights, and you're rushing to catch an airplane. I don't think it's too smart to carry those kinds of feelings with you. In that respect, I think today's players handle things a lot better emotionally.[26]

Also, Blacks attach some importance to "having fun" in orga-nized play, which also translates into winning and losing not being taken as seriously as in White mainstream culture, as Lloyd Free's comments above also suggest. The different Black cultural view on the nature and function of competition, combined with atti-tudes toward individual display and showmanship and losing and "having fun" in organized play, has no doubt helped shape the more general public attitude often expressed today that tends to regard baseball and basketball as being as much "entertainment" as "sport."

The element of "fun" and "showboating" that Blacks bring into organized competitive play is negatively valued by Whites, except perhaps where it has commercial value (cf. the Harlem Globetrotters), especially insofar as Whites tend to see organized or competitive play as more like work: serious (even somber) and important, and therefore, prescriptive, patient, methodical, systematic, role-oriented, and so on. It is as though Whites are bringing work-related values into organized competitive play, thereby making play resemble work, while Blacks are bringing play-related values (such as spontaneity, improvisation, and fun) into organized competitive play, thereby making work resemble play. Also, insofar as Blacks introduce these values alongside stylistic self-expression—also regarded as "extracurricular" within the strictly functional White cultural mindset—Blacks would be regarded by Whites as not sufficiently "serious" or "interested" in getting the job or task accomplished.

Concentration

This interpretation is reinforced by the different meaning that Blacks and Whites give to "concentration to task." For White mainstreamers *concentration* means undivided attention: focusing upon one thing and one thing only. For Blacks, *concentration* means divided attention: attending to task accomplishment while simultaneously concentrating on doing it with flair or expressive style. Because Black attention is divided here, Whites believe that the focus on style is *at the expense of* focus on task to the ultimate detriment of task accomplishment. But this view misrepresents the Black cultural pattern which inherently protects against that happenstance by giving no credit for stylistic self-expression *if the person does not succeed in accomplishing the task.* Thus, in the above description of the "dancing policeman" Felix Toya, it was very important that he never missed a signal change even as he never missed a step. As Grace Sims Holt said with regard to Black (functionally) expressive performance, "everything must come together."[27]

Of course, the White view that sees Black divided attention to task as dysfunctional with regard to task accomplishment may in some instances simply be a pretext for discrediting Black preoccupation with stylistic self-expression. This view is based upon the value orientation within White mainstream culture that sees allegiance to nonwork-related values (as it defines *work*) as corrosive of the American commitment to the work ethic. There is no question that Black preoccupation with stylistic self-expression does express an allegiance to values other than those promoted by and within White mainstream American culture. But so far, that allegiance has not sacrificed task accomplishment, nor is there any indication to lead one to suppose that it will. Moreover, the Black introduction of these other "play" values (such as "fun") into the workplace may ultimately have a revitalizing effect and in the end constitute a real contribution to mainstream American organized work and play culture.

Examples

The following two descriptive accounts are especially illustrative of conflict and confluence in Black and White mainstream cultural styles, especially so in showing the interaction of several of the cultural themes listed and discussed above. They are taken from Carol C. Koogler's description of two events involving the same kindergarten class consisting of twenty-one White children (twelve females and nine males) and eight Black children (three females and five males).[28] The first event, a "Valentine Dance," was led by the class's regular White female teacher. The second event, a music room activity, was led by a Black female teacher, whose contact with children occurred in the music room where she provided special music activities for all of the elementary classes. The accounts of the two events as observed and reported by Koogler are as follows:

Event 1—"The Valentine Dance"

The teacher gathered all of the children on the rug as she started a record of valentine dance music. She directed the children to form two parallel lines, boys in one, girls in the other. Boys were then asked to face the girls. The person one was facing was considered one's partner.

The teacher demonstrated the patterned group dance using the following order of action: boys would walk to the midpoint between the parallel lines, facing their respective partners, each bowing. They would return to their starting position and repeat. This time the girls would meet their respective partners at the midpoint. Partners would then join hands, dance around in a circle, singing "I want you to be my valentine."

Following the demonstration, class members tried to imitate the dance. The Black children (with the exception of one female) left their positions, ran to one end of the parallel lines and clustered together, giggling. Soon after, they began "hand slapping" and "finger snapping" in time with the music.

While the White children attempted to dance, one Black boy left the cluster and ran between the lines of children singing, "Be mine, be mine, you sweetie valentine." With this, he threw kisses, clapped his hands, and stopped periodically to engage in rhythmic body movements of the hips and shoulders. Then he ran around several of the White boys, stopping periodically to rearrange their positions, thus pairing them with different girls. When he approached his closest friend, he said: "Man, you don't want her. Let's move you around." With this, his friend (a White boy) left the dance and joined the cluster of Black children.

The teacher, angered by the behavior of the Black boy, escorted him to the principal's office. He tried to physically resist, then pleaded with her to allow him to stay. The teacher continued to remove him. Meanwhile, the student teacher tried to coax the remainder of the nonparticipating children to join in the dance. Finally, two Black girls reluctantly decided to join as partners, only to be ridiculed by the Black males.

The student teacher reprimanded the males, who were trying desperately to stop giggling. She sent one of the boys behind a partition as punishment. He became angered and threw objects into the dance area. The dance began to break up as children began hitting each other and running around the room.

The teacher reentered the classroom and began separating fighting children.

Event 2—Music Room Activity

The music teacher started the musical activity by playing a song on the piano. The children clustered on the floor as the teacher sang and played the familiar song. Soon the children joined in the singing.

Shortly, the same Black male who had been escorted to the principal's office during the Valentine Dance ran to the front of the group and began rhythmic body movements, snapping his fingers as he slowly changed the tempo of the tune. A Black girl responded, "Cool man, you're cool," as she joined him, snapping her fingers. The teacher, still playing the piano, changed her timing to coincide with the finger snapping.

As the music continued, some of the White children stopped singing to listen and watch the performance. A few Whites joined in, stamping their feet in a marching movement. (Some matched the tempo; others were unable to do so; nevertheless, they kept stamping their feet.) Black children then began clapping their hands and engaging in body movements as they followed the leader around the classroom. White children who had been watching gradually began singing and clapping. Several attempted rhythmic hip movements.

During the second part of the music period, the teacher asked the children to group themselves into four groups in order to sing parts of the song separately. The children divided into five groups (according to their friendship groupings, largely by sex and race), so she divided the song into five parts. As the teacher played the piano, she signaled each of the groups at the appropriate time. When she signaled a group of three Black boys, they were standing in front of the class with a set of drums. They acted out their portion of the song using percussion and shoulder movement.

Analysis

One of the clear issues leading to a conflict of cultural styles in Event 1 was the mainstream cultural orientation of "mental set," which sees activity evolving out of set patterns. This is exemplified by the Valentine Dance's predetermined, random pairing using sex as the pairing criterion and a highly patterned group dance which individual participants were not allowed to modify.[29] Attempts by the Black students to establish their own culturally expressive style pattern in gesture and dance were rejected insofar as they did not fit the "White" dance pattern. What is relevant here is not only the stylistic differences in the expressive patterns themselves but the inflexibility of the authority person (what Koogler calls interference stemming from too strong leadership). This inflexibility did not allow for either (1) variation with regard to the prescribed pattern, or (2) (a matter of authorization and entitlement) the right of students to initiate changes in a set plan (Koogler notes that the Black boy who ran between the lines was, consistent with Black cultural norms, "asserting leadership and soliciting audience participation"[30]).

In the first instance, the "variation" amounted to the introduction of a wholly different "Black" stylistic pattern, in part, as Koogler argues, because the Black students were unfamiliar with the kind of pattern they were required to perform. My own view, however, would be to see it as culturally consistent for the teacher to have been inflexible also in allowing individual students (while staying basically within the "White" cultural pattern) to try to shape it to their personal taste, were that to have happened. I say that based upon the impersonal and role-oriented nature of the predetermined pairing, which suggests support of the mainstream cultural view of individuals as (except for sex) "interchangeable parts," and, going along with that orientation, a tendency to regard uniform processing through standard operating procedures to be the appropriate way to execute the set arrangement laid out in the original composition of the dance structure. The teacher (as part of the White mainstream compositional tradition herself) might even see her own authority and role to be subordinate and restricted here: one bound to represent literally the set plan as conceived by the composer, rather than (more flexibly) as a basis for improvisation.

Event 2 was free of cultural conflict because the Black music teacher was responsive both to the right of students to initiate changes in a set plan (for example, changing the number of parts from four to five, organizing themselves according to race as well as sex, allowing spontaneous student leadership to emerge) and more generally to allow for individual variation by letting students define for themselves the stylistic character of their respective individual contributions.[31]

Styles of Discourse

Truth-Creating Processes

Argument versus Discussion. Black and White "truth-creating processes" are those protocols and procedures that each cultural group has established as appropriate for the working through of disagreements and disputes or for otherwise "getting at the truth." For Blacks, the appropriate truth-creating process is "sincere" argument (as opposed to the form of argument that is quarreling, which Blacks also have). For White mainstream people, discussion rather than argument is the idealized (if not always realized) truth-creating process. Thus, a White middle-class couple will say that they had a "discussion that 'deteriorated' into an argument," therein showing that argument is more like quarreling than a sincere attempt at truth seeking. Notwithstanding the occasional failures by those in the American mainstream to realize discussion norms, the cultural standards are there nonetheless to structure attitudes and otherwise serve as a social barometer for evaluating verbal behavior or discourse style, either that of oneself or others. The same holds true for Blacks in those social contexts where sincere argument rather than discussion is the cultural standard for expressing disagreement and resolving disputes.

Black argument as a cultural style is (as for other ethnic groups) confronting, personal, advocating, and issue-oriented. White discussion style is nonconfronting, impersonal, representing, and peace- or process-oriented, the latter expressed by such concepts as "compromise" and "agreeing to disagree." An overview of these differences is shown in Figure 2.

The issues that divide Blacks and Whites culturally and account for how they assess each other's behavior—Blacks regard Whites here as "insincere" and "devious"; Whites see Blacks as "argumentative" and "threatening"— revolve around the value of contentiousness or struggle, the separation (or fusion) of reason and emotion, the separation (or fusion) of truth and belief, and finally, self-control. I will briefly consider each of these in turn.[32]

Struggle. In the context of truth seeking, struggle or contentiousness is unifying for Blacks, polarizing for Whites. Blacks view struggle or contentiousness as positive, while Whites view it as negative. A metaphor to describe the difference would be individuals holding opposite ends of a rope while pulling against each other. Whites essentially see only the opposition: individuals pulling in opposite directions. Blacks see individuals pulling in opposite directions, to be sure, but more tellingly, also being held together by the same rope (that is, the individuals are cooperating in their opposition, and cooperating more than they are opposing).

Figure 2. Truth-Creating Processes

Black	White
Argument	Discussion

PATTERNS

Confronting	Nonconfronting
Personal	Impersonal
Advocating	Representing
Truth- or issue-oriented	Peace- or process-oriented

ISSUES
Struggle
Reason/Emotion
Truth/Belief
Self-control

BEHAVIORAL MEANINGS

Black	White
"Whites are insincere and devious"	"Blacks are argumentative and threatening"

Black and White attitudes toward the value of struggle stem from these different positions. Thus, if disagreement at a meeting were likely to generate heat and strong emotions, Whites would say it was better not to contend than to contend ("I can't talk to you now. You're too emotional!"); on the other hand, Blacks would say it was better to contend than not to contend. This is because Whites see the prevention of potential damage to the harmony of social relationships as taking precedence over the expression of their individual views. If they were to threaten such harmony (however contrived or artificial), Whites would see this as "selfish," "self-indulgent," or "impolite." For Blacks, on the other hand, the powerful expression of one's personal views takes precedence over sustaining a surface harmony that may have no real (sincere) foundation, which Blacks would see as "hypocritical" or a "charade."

The attitudes of Whites and Blacks are also based in part on their respectively different (culturally determined) capacities to manage emotionally charged disagreements. Both attitudes and capacities are directly linked in turn to systems of etiquette within the two cultures.[33]

For example, the etiquette system governing social interaction in the public arena within White mainstream culture declares that (except under certain socially "marked" occasions, like a "talk" or "lecture") the social rights of the receiver deserve greater consideration than the rights of the "assertor." As a consequence, mainstream Americans are socialized to regard the protection of their own and other people's sensibilities (when they are in the receiver role) as deserving principal consideration, even when that may be at the expense of their own or others' feelings (emotions) when they or others are in the assertor role. This pattern within the mainstream American etiquette system generates (relative to Black culture) a low offense/low defense pattern of public social interaction. This is because protecting the sensibilities of themselves and others requires mainstreamers to moderate the intensity level of their self-assertion to the level that "others" (that is, receivers) can comfortably manage. And insofar as the intensity level that mainstream receivers can comfortably manage is culturally programmed to be low ("sensitive"), the level of self-assertion must also be commensurately low. Thus, low defense generates low offense. In turn, low offense (under the rubric of *protecting* sensibilities) maintains low defense because it withholds from mainstreamers regular exposure to the more potent stimuli that would enable them to learn how to manage intense interactions more effectively (at least so as not to be overwhelmed by them).

By way of contrast, Black culture generates a (relatively) high offense/high defense pattern of public social interaction. This comes about as a result of the culture granting the assertor rights that are at least equal to, and often greater than (especially when aroused), the rights of the receiver. As Harrison said,

> Blacks are not known...to ever be totally desensitized, defused, or repressed in their emotions when dealing with definable antagonisms. A Black per-

son would not pussyfoot with an insult from a
White—or a Black—if rendered with the slightest
edge of an acerbity that might threaten one's security: the response would be fully acted out, regardless of the name of the game which deems it
necessary to be sensitive to the other feller.[34]

Thus, where the process of accommodation in White mainstream culture is for assertors to consider the sensibilities of receivers first, even at the expense of their own feelings (emotions),
the process of accommodation in Black culture is the reverse: for
receivers to accommodate assertors' feelings (emotions), especially when they are charged (as when following the "impulse
toward truth" in sincere argument).

And it is the greater priority given to feelings (emotions) over
sensibilities within Black culture that produces the high offense/
high defense pattern. The receivers' orientation to accommodate
self-presentations of high emotional intensity exposes them to
such presentations on a regular basis, which, in turn, improves
their capacity to manage them effectively. In such a way does
high offense generate high defense. Reciprocally, the greater capacity of receivers to manage emotionally charged self-presentations allows individuals to assert their feelings (emotions) more
freely with the confidence that others can receive them without
becoming overwhelmed by them. In such a way does high defense sustain and promote high offense.

Comparatively, then, the psychological consequences of these
different sociocultural orientations are that for Whites it hurts
them more to hear something unfavorable than it hurts them not
to express their feelings (as in abandoning themselves to the "impulse toward truth"). For Blacks, it hurts them more not to express their feelings than to hear something unfavorable.

These different attitudes and capacities generate different
levels of comfort and tolerance among Blacks and Whites when
meetings become emotionally charged and lead to directly opposite evaluations of such proceedings. Thus, at one such meeting among Black and White staff at a local psychological clinic in
Chicago, Blacks left saying that was the "best" staff meeting that
they had ever had. Whites left saying that it was the "worst" staff
meeting that they had ever had.

Another way of characterizing Black and White attitudes toward struggle is that Blacks put truth before peace whereas Whites
put peace before truth. In the mainstream American political
arena, to be "peace"-oriented ultimately means to accommodate

established political arrangements, before which truth is sacrificed in the form of compromise. The Black orientation in the political arena is, as with interpersonal disagreements and disputes, again to put truth before peace, which is to say, to keep the truth intact and politicize on its behalf.

It is also possible to look at the White mainstream and Black cultural styles as situationally (as well as ethnoculturally) determined. In this view, the priorities within the White mainstream cultural pattern (that sacrifices truth to accommodate political realities) are consistent with an establishment (in-power) social orientation. Similarly, the priorities within the Black cultural pattern (that keeps the truth intact and seeks to politicize on its behalf) are consistent with a nonestablishment (out-of-power) social orientation. Thus, when the Equal Rights Amendment became an issue for White middle-class women, they reversed their usual socially mainstream priorities of placing peace before truth by putting truth before peace and also by replacing their customary discussion mode with sincere argument.

Reason and Emotion/Truth and Belief. Mainstream American culture believes that truth is objective, which is to say, external to the self; consequently, it is something to be discovered rather than possessed. This assumption has led mainstream Americans to view themselves instrumentally as objective truth seekers following the model and method of cognitive science in getting at (scientific) truth. In that instrumental view the means must be consistent with the end: one needs a rational means to produce a rational (reliable) result, one that also would be replicable from person to person insofar as individuals applied the same (rational/scientific) method to the truth-seeking process. Replicability of method would also ensure a standard or uniform mental process leading to a predictable outcome (see the discussion under "mental set" above).

The emphasis on replication and standardization of method produces a generalized focus and concern with process, also leading individuals to come to see themselves in processual terms and to regard as intrusive those aspects of self that would interfere with the instrumentalization of themselves as neutrally objective (rational) truth seekers. Emotion and belief are especially suspect: those elements of self that were part of an earlier traditional view that saw truth as subjective, as something internal, to be possessed, as in belief (and defended through argument),[35] as opposed to something objective, external, and discoverable. This has led mainstream Americans to see emotion and belief as contaminants that undermine their neutrally objective self/stance that defines and regulates rational (scientific) engagement and inquiry. The effort to free reason and truth from the contaminating influence of emotion and belief has led people to define reason and objective truth seeking *in terms of* the other category: not by virtue of what rationality is (a mental process characterized by a clear, accurate, and logical progression of thought), but by what it is not. So practically speaking, people now consider themselves and others "rational" to the extent that they are *not* emotional. And insofar as "rationality" is promoted at the expense of emotionality, people socialized to realize "rational" self-presentations are often, in reality, becoming socialized to realize unemotional self-presentations instead.

The above mainstream American cultural attitude and practice ultimately lead to the separation of reason and emotion. Likewise, the following line of reasoning on the relationship of objective truth seeking and belief leads to the cultural separation of truth and belief. Mainstream Americans say "no one person has a monopoly on the truth," and "the more strongly individuals believe that they do own the truth, the less likely it is to be the truth." The first of these statements asserts that individuals vary in their points of view, that the best that individuals can have is a point of view, and that any individual point of view can only be part of the truth (the more complete or "whole" truth theoretically constituting a sum of all of the different points of view that are or can be brought to bear upon the overall topic or situation). Expressed in mathematical terms, a truth that contains the perspectives of individuals A and B is more complete (and therefore "better") than a truth that contains only the point of view of individual A or individual B. This view ultimately leads mainstreamers, such as news journalists, to define appropriate truth seeking as a balance of opposing viewpoints.[36]

The second statement ("the more strongly individuals believe that they do own the truth, the less likely it is to be the truth") incorporates the views expressed in the first and also says something about the nature of the self as objective truth seeker. In addition to being rational, individuals are obliged to be sufficiently open-minded to receive and reflect upon points of view other than their own. Implicit in this view is the implication that to the extent that individuals believe that their point of view is *the* truth, they will be less likely to be so receptive or considerate. So strongly held beliefs in themselves have also come to be seen as polarizing and defeating of the kind of interactional cooperation individuals need to realize for the objective truth-seeking process to work. This is in spite of the fact that it may be other attributes—those that accompany the assertion of owned truths (beliefs/convictions)—that more directly account for such "closed-minded" resistance, not the fact of having strong convictions, per se, or expressing them in a certain (as opposed to tentative) manner. Nonetheless, the public presumption that strongly held views disable the objective truth-seeking process has led individuals to view positively those who do not hold or express strong views whether those individuals are actually engaged in objective truth seeking or not—their stance evokes the "open-minded" attitude of the objective (scientific) truth seeker. So personnel forms test for mental "rigidity" or its converse, "flexibility," by asking recommenders to rate individuals on whether they are "respectful and accepting of others," insofar as they adapt their thinking "to allow for other persons' points of view." Individuals who are less able to adapt their thinking to allow for other points of view are presumably rated as *less* respectful of others.[37]

Evaluations of Behavioral Meanings

The separation of reason and emotion and truth and belief by Whites when they engage in disagreements and disputes produces the more detached and impersonal style of self-presentation characteristic of discussion, which, in conjunction with the avoidance of direct confrontation, Blacks personally characterize as "insincere" and generally consider to be dysfunctional of the truth-creating process. The Black characterization of Whites as "insincere" refers both to their impersonal self-presentation style when engaging in disagreement (it seems as though Whites do not believe what they are saying themselves) as well as to White unwillingness to engage in direct confrontation, or any kind of dialogue at all, as when things begin to get emotionally charged.

Blacks also have characterized the White discussion style as "devious," perhaps a more severe indictment even than "insincere." This characterization stems from Whites frequently not owning the position they are representing, nor seeing such ownership as a requirement when engaging in disagreement or debate. The basis for the White style and attitude has its roots in the mainstream culture that (as discussed above) gives credit for "authoritative" views, not the individual's own view (often discredited as simply "opinion"). Such "authoritative views" have become established within White mainstream culture as making one's self-presentations more persuasive. From the Black stand-point, however, only those views that an individual takes own-ership of are admissible when engaging in disagreement or de-bate. This is because Blacks believe that all points have to be processed through the crucible of argument, even those of es-tablished "authority." Whites often see such authoritative views as above challenge (at least by nonexperts). Moreover, in not accepting them as their own, Whites also do not accept respon-sibility for the validity of the view that they are representing and whose contents they are being challenged on. (White student: "It wasn't me that said it." Black student: "But you introduced it.") Blacks see the White behavior here as "cheating," as attempting to get credit for a particular view without allowing such a view to be processed through the crucible of argument. Thus, when White students would say, "Well, Marshall McLuhan said...," Black stu-dents would interrupt, "Wait a minute! Marshall McLuhan's not here. If he were here, I'd be arguing with him. Are you willing to accept the view that you are representing as your own [to allow it to be processed through argument]?" The White student is then caught up short, saying, "I haven't thought enough about it to have a personal position on it." Blacks tend to view such com-ments with great suspicion.

In some instances, Blacks do not believe that Whites do not have a position on what they are (re)presenting, but rather, be-lieve that Whites are trying to avoid the anticipated challenge to the position by claiming not to own the position that they, in fact, do have. And *that,* Blacks would allege, is "cowardly" and "devi-ous."

Finally, the Black characterization of the nonconfronting, impersonal, representational, "peace" (process)-oriented White presentation style here as "devious" derives from its similarity to the pattern of self-presentation that Blacks adopt when they are "lying," as one Black woman put it. The White style for Blacks is the opposite of the "for real" style (which for Blacks is confront-ing, personal, advocating, and truth (issue)-oriented). Thus, the White "discussion" style here is the one that Blacks adopt when "they do not care enough about the person or issue to want to waste the energy on it" or when "it is too dangerous to say what they truly feel and believe." This often occurs for Blacks in those situations where they cannot be "for real" and have to "front" (that is, hide their true feelings and opinions).

Whites characterize the Black style as "argumentative." This characterization stems from the personal approach that Blacks use when engaging in argument. Blacks do not just debate the idea, as Whites do. They debate the person debating the idea. Thus, in such a context, your idea is only as good as your personal ability to argue it.[38]

The White view of Black style as "argumentative" also stems from the Black view that insists that Whites own and defend the position that they may only be representing, which Whites may be unwilling or unable to do, for reasons given above.

More seriously, Whites also characterize the Black argumentative style as "threatening," as when meetings get emotionally charged. This view has its origin in differences in White and Black cultural views of "self-control" as well as what constitutes "threatening" behavior.

Briefly, emotional *self-control* in White mainstream culture is characterized and practiced as self-restraint: containing or reining in emotional impulses.

Consequently, when emotions are "out," they are perceived by Whites (as they function for Whites) as "out of control." For Blacks, self-control is characterized and practiced as control over emotions, not only at the level of containment but also at the level of emotionally intense self-expression. The Black cultural concept for controlling one's emotions is "being 'cool'." And the caveat "to be cool" is often invoked in situations that are "hot."[39] But "being cool" in such situations does not mean realizing a state of emotional self-denial or restrained emotional expression, but rather being in control of one's emotional heat and intensity (whether laughter, joy, or anger). So in Black culture it is possible for individuals to be "hot" and "cool" at the same time (instigating performers who try to heat up the scene while "proclaiming [their] own cool").[40] So what constitutes a state of "out of control" for Whites constitutes an "in-control" state for Blacks.

The White view of Black emotional behavior as "threatening" also stems from Blacks and Whites having different conceptions of what constitutes a "threat," which is linked in turn to different cultural conceptions about when a "fight" begins. For Whites a "fight" begins when emotional confrontation gets intense (as when opponents raise angry voices, get insulting, and utter threats). For Blacks a "fight" begins when, in the context of such an angry confrontation, *someone makes a provocative move.* Were neither of the opponents to "make [such] a move," notwithstanding the loud, angry, confrontive, insulting, intimidating talk, from the Black standpoint, they are still only "talking."[41] A "threat" for Whites, then, begins when a person *says* they are going to do something. A "threat" for Blacks begins when a person actually *makes a move* to do something. Verbal threats, from the Black standpoint, are still "only talk."

[1] Theodore Roosevelt, "Editorial: Keep Up the Fight for Americanism," *El Grito: A Journal of Mexican American Thought* 1, no. 2 (1919; reprint 1968), 5.

[2] *United States Statutes at Large,* vol. 81, 817, quoted in Kenji Hakuta, *The Mirror of Language: The Debate on Bilingualism* (New York: Basic Books, 1986), 198.

[3] Sidney J. Harris, "We Tarnish Golden Rule by Inflicting Cultural Bias," *Chicago Sun-Times,* 20 June 1983.

[4] Miles V. Zintz, *Education across Cultures* (Des Moines, IA: Wm. C. Brown, 1963); Alfred A. Aarons, Barbara Y. Gordon, and William A. Stewart, eds., "Linguistic-Cultural Differences and American Education," *Florida FL Reporter* 7, no. 1 (1969); Courtney B. Cazden, Vera P. John, and Dell Hymes, eds., *Functions of Language in the Classroom* (New York: Teachers College Press, 1972).

[5] Thomas Kochman, *Black and White Styles in Conflict* (Chicago: University of Chicago Press, 1981), 34-35; 151.

[6] Paul C. Harrison, *The Drama of Nommo* (New York: Grove, 1972), 35-37.

[7] Charles Keil, "Motion and Feeling in Music," in *Rappin' and Stylin' Out,* edited by Thomas Kochman (Urbana: University of Illinois Press, 1972): 83ff.

[8] Florence H. Levinsohn, "Still the Oboist," *Reader [Chicago's Free Weekly]* 16, no. 3 (1986): 20.

[9] Harrison, *Drama of Nommo,* 35.

[10] Ibid., 7.

[11] Keil, "Motion and Feeling," 84-85.

[12] Ibid., 86.

[13] Ibid., 86.

[14] Ibid., 86, n. 6.

[15] Ibid., 85-86.

[16] Harrison, *Drama of Nommo,* 157.

[17] Virginia H. Young, "Family and Childhood in a Southern Negro Community," *American Anthropologist* 72 (1970): 255; See also Diane K. Lewis, "The Black Family: Socialization and Sex Roles," *Phylon* 36, no. 3 (1975): 225.

[18] Roger D. Abrahams, interview with author; see also Roger D. Abrahams, *Talking Back* (Rowley, MA: Newbury, 1976): 8-9; 90-91.

[19] Janet Milhomme, "Break dancing in Accra," *LA Extra,* May 1986, 16-22.

[20] Karl Reisman, "Noise and Order," in *Language in Its Social Setting,* edited by William W. Gage (Washington, DC: Anthropological Society of Washington, 1974), 60; Kochman, *Black and White Styles,* 65.

[21] Ross Atkin, "'Hollywood Henderson' at Super Bowl," *Christian Science Monitor,* 18 January 1979, 16.

[22] Abrahams, *Talking Back,* 9.

[23] Kochman, *Black and White Styles,* 145-52.

[24] Roger D. Abrahams, *Positively Black* (Englewood Cliffs, NJ: Prentice-Hall, 1970), 42.

[25] Phil Elderkin, "The Serious Side of a Supershowman," *Christian Science Monitor,* 4 April 1979, 17.

[26] Phil Elderkin, "Red Holzman—the Marco Polo of Pro Basketball," *Christian Science Monitor,* 5 March 1981, 16.

[27] Grace Sims Holt, "Communication in Black Culture: The Other Side of Silence," *Language Research Reports* 6 (1972): 60; see also Kochman, *Black and White Styles,* 138ff.

28 Carol C. Koogler, "Behavioral Style Differences and Crisis in an Integrated Kindergarten Classroom," *Contemporary Education* 51, no. 3 (1980): 127ff.
29 Ibid., 129.
30 Ibid.
31 For other examples of conflict and confluence between Black and White cultural styles, including patterns of self-presentation, performance, and value orientation, see Susan Houston, "Black English," *Psychology Today*, March 1973, 45-48; Kochman, *Black and White Styles*, 153ff.
32 For a more complete discussion see Kochman, *Black and White Styles*, 16-42.
33 See Kochman, *Black and White Styles*, 106-129; see also Thomas Kochman, "The Politics of Politeness," in *Meaning, Form and Use in Context: Linguistic Applications*, edited by Deborah Schiffrin, Georgetown University Roundtable on Languages and Linguistics (Washington, DC: Georgetown University Press, 1984).
34 Harrison, *Drama of Nommo*, 150.
35 Walter J. Ong, S. J., *Orality and Literacy: The Technologizing of the Word* (New York: Methuen, 1982).
36 The positions are assumed a priori to have an equal claim on the truth regardless of the respective merits of the position. The moral goal is to realize a fair and equitable process rather than to proselytize on behalf of one or another particular position.
37 Note that being "objective" is equated here with being open to other people's viewpoints *regardless of how those other viewpoints were arrived at*. The effect of only one individual being "open-minded" and/or "neutrally objective" does not necessarily promote *objective* truth. It may simply weaken the self by allowing for a unilateral *adaptation to another person's* "closed-minded," non-negotiable assertions.
38 This also means that it would be inappropriate for others to jump in to support the person who, because of personal inadequacy, cannot marshal enough support for his or her own position. Such attempts are rebuffed, usually by the person who is winning the argument, by "Wait a minute. I am arguing with *him* [that person being the one who has been temporarily caught short-handed in coming back with a reply]. When I'm through arguing with *him*, I'll argue with *you*."
39 Abrahams, *Talking Back*, 84-85.
40 Ibid., 84.
41 See Kochman, *Black and White Styles*, 43ff for a complete discussion.

Cultural Assumptions and Values

Edward C. Stewart, Jack Danielian, and Robert J. Foster

For purposes of analysis, culture may be examined at four levels: concrete *behavior*, *values*, *assumptions*, and generalized *cultural forms*. The last three are necessarily derived from observations of behavior but can be usefully treated as a motivational explanation underlying most human behavior. Viewed at the individual level they are, in effect, internalized components of personality that are generally shared with other members of the cultural group.

Values are relatively concrete, discrete, and specific; for instance, typical American values are the sanctity of private property, the desirability of physical comfort, and the need for tangible measures of success. Values also have a quality of "oughtness" and are relatively available to individual awareness.[1] A person will often discuss values when explaining his or her own or others' feelings or behavior.

Assumptions, on the other hand, are more abstract and more outside of conscious awareness. They represent the predispositions the individual employs to pattern the world and are usually felt by the individual to be an aspect of the world itself and not simply his or her perception of it. Examples of American assumptions are a predisposition to see the self as separate from the world and the usual endorsement of "doing" as the preferred means of self-expression.[2]

Assumptions provide a person with a sense of reality—which is only one of several possible realities—and values provide a basis for choice and evaluation. However, assumptions and values merge into one another. What is an assumption for one individual, or for one culture, may be a value for another individual or for another culture. Any one concept held by a person is likely to combine aspects of both assumptions and values; hence it is difficult, and often unimportant, to determine whether it is one or the other.

In some cases the cognitive processes underlying cultural thinking are so abstract and lacking in substantive reference that they are probably best distinguished from assumptions and called *cultural forms*. Examples include assumptions about time, space, essence, energy, and logical process. Cultural forms tend to overlap with assumptions and, to a lesser degree, values. For training purposes it is probably not critical to be able to make firm distinctions; consequently, after the nature of forms, assumptions, and values is illustrated, these concepts will generally be treated under the label "value and assumption" or, where it seems more appropriate, "predisposition." Occasionally, "perspective" or "frame of reference" will be used with more or less the same meaning.

A frequent objection made to efforts to analyze any culture is that people differ from one another in many ways, even within a culture, and any attempt to describe a people according to broad generalizations, such as cultural characteristics, results in stereotypes. It is clear that people differ widely with respect to any particular behavior or value. Nevertheless, certain values and assumptions are dominant in, for example, American culture and are shared to one degree or another by most members. Thus, when we speak of an American value (or assumption), we refer to a peak or modal tendency for a range (distribution) of that value in the culture. All points on the distribution can be found in any society; thus, when two cultures are compared on a given dimension, there is overlap (i.e., some members of Culture A will be more typical of Culture B than many members of Culture B who may be far from the modal point of their culture).

In addition, an individual's reactions will vary from situation to situation and from time to time in the same situation. However, there is a relative internal integration and stability in behavior over time and situation. Variations, thus, should not obscure systematic differences which do exist or the validity of stereotypes (modal tendencies) in understanding intercultural phenomena.

Cultural patterns, including their variations, may be seen as guides to "a limited number of common human problems for which all peoples at all times must find some solution."[3] These problem areas can be used as a framework for identifying inclusive cultural dimensions on which all cultures can be plotted.[4] The common human problems covered by such a system of assumptions and values can be classified under five categories: activity, social relations, motivation, perception of the world, and perception of the self and of the individual. Each category is briefly identified by describing *some* American values and assumptions, together with non-Western alternatives, which fall within each category. Their identification follows the work of Florence R. Kluckhohn, with a few divergencies.

Activity

Self-expression is a problem common to all humans; Kluckhohn refers to this as the activity modality.[5] In American society, the dominant mode of activity is *doing*. Doing refers to the assumption that activity should result in externalized, visible accomplishment as exemplified by the stock American phrase, "getting things done." The contrasting mode is *being*, which, however, does not connote passivity, since a person with a being orientation can be very active. The being orientation refers to the spontaneous expression of what is regarded as the given nature of human personality. It values the phenomenological experience of humanity rather than tangible accomplishments and is associated with the notion of having a natural and given position in society. A third possible orientation to activity, which stresses development of all aspects of the integrated person—*being-in-becoming*—is similar to being in its stress on experience rather than accomplishment, but it is dynamic.

Another area of activity that can be analyzed according to several dimensions is problem-solving decision making. In some cultures, decisions are more likely to be made by an individual because of the role he or she occupies; under this condition, decisions are much more likely to be influenced by the characteristics of the role than by the preferences or commitments of the individual. Another possibility is for decision making to be a function of a group, and for no one individual or role occupant to assume responsibility for it. This last alternative, for example, is more typical of Japanese culture than of American culture.[6]

The concept of what constitutes decision making varies from culture to culture and thus requires some alteration when examined within different cultural frameworks. In American society the process of decision making unfolds primarily through the anticipation of the consequences of alternative courses of action. In some other cultures, however, the function of the decision maker or makers is to evaluate a situation by classifying it according to preestablished categories. Whatever action ensues, or whatever decisions are made, will follow automatically from this traditional classifying activity.[7] Perhaps it is such a process of classification that leads some Western observers to conclude that in the underdeveloped world few decisions are required. This example illustrates the difficulty of getting outside of one's own cultural framework when one is required to examine parallel processes from culture to culture.

The distinctions between different ways of organizing activity also have important implications for learning or teaching.[8] For example, Americans implicitly assume that learning is an *active* process requiring performance by the learner, whose incentive to learn is either a future reward or the avoidance of punishment; thus, learning is regarded as a process of shaping the responses of the learner and building upon them. In some cultures the learner is assumed to be passive and the chief technique used is serial rote learning;[9] learning is assumed to be an automatic process occurring in a highly structured situation. From this perspective, events in the natural and social world of the learner occur automatically in response to his or her actions. Since the world is considered as overwhelming, highly structured, and impervious to the initiative of the individual, no stress is put on spontaneity or upon the characteristics of the learner. This kind of learning corresponds to a Pavlovian situation, and is more prevalent in Bali, for example, than in the United States.[10]

These brief descriptions of some possible alternative values and assumptions underlying different expressions of activity call attention to the necessity for using several dimensions to explain any specific behavior. In speaking of decision making and learning, for instance, allusions to perception of the self, perception of the world, and motivation are required.

Social Relationships

A chief characteristic of social relationships among Americans of the middle class is equality.[11] Its ramifications are so profound that it should be considered an assumption of American culture, even though as an expressed value there is no uniform application to all segments of the society. In nearly every other culture there is a much greater emphasis on inequality of persons.[12] To assume that everyone is equal and should be treated alike is considered, in some cultures, to be demeaning to the individuality of the person. Inequality underlies social conventions and etiquette and clearly defined reciprocity among persons engaged in social interactions.

In American culture social conventions tend to be more informal and social reciprocities much less clearly defined. For example, equality removes the need for elaborate forms of social address, since one of the functions of formality is to call attention to the participants' respective status and ascriptions. Americans usually tend to ignore these qualities of social intercourse, quickly achieve a first-name basis with others, and conduct both business and social intercourse with directness and informality. Unlike members of other cultures such as the Thai, Americans prefer direct contact with others in either business or social affairs and hence seldom have need of a third person, an intermediary, as do the Thai.

Despite the emphasis on equality and informality, there is an element of depersonalization in relationships between Americans. Americans have many friends, but these are often associated with a given situation or time.[13] Furthermore, the word *friend* may serve to describe anyone from a passing acquaintance to a lifetime associate. American friendship differs from that found in many parts of the world, where an individual may have few friends but is likely to have a total, rather than a selective, commitment to them. Individuals may be disinclined to share a friend with other friends, since both the quality of friendship and the number of friends are considered limited and hence not to be squandered.[14]

Americans tend to be relatively impartial and objective in the conduct of social relations, compared to the personalized interactions found in many parts of the world. Examples of the former are large charitable fund-raising efforts, objective standards of promotion, and the uneasiness about gift giving in business. Examples of personalized interaction are found in the paternal benevolence of the Japanese and Latin Americans, personal leadership of the Latin *caudillos*, and the nepotism endemic to Asia, Africa, and Latin America.[15]

The depersonalized predisposition of Americans combines with other values to nurture competition in which each individual strives for his or her own personal goals. For example, "joshing," "one-upmanship," "repartee," and a "friendly suggestion" are subtle forms of competition. Although this sort of behavior in interpersonal relations usually seems innocuous to Americans, such actions are perceived as subtle coercion in many other cultures.[16]

Motivation

A third category of assumptions and values is motivation. Achievement is generally agreed to be a chief motivating force in American culture. It is the force which gives the culture its quality of "driveness."[17] An American's identity and, to a large degree, worth are established by accomplishments; an American *is* what an American achieves. Furthermore, accomplishments should be objective, visible, and measurable, since the culture does not readily provide a means of evaluating and knowing the self except through external performance.

Relative to members of many other societies, Americans do not attribute particular meaning to place of birth, family, heritage, traditional status, or other prescriptive considerations which can be used to define the self. American culture, then, emphasizes personal achievement through externally documented accomplishments while many other societies emphasize ascription with its attendant concern for the traditionally fixed status of the individual.[18]

An American's investment in material and visible signs of success leads one to inquire about American notions about failure. For Americans the concept is difficult to accept and hence is usually avoided or rationalized. A typical response is to rationalize the failure as an inevitable part of the learning process leading to future accomplishment or to regard the situation as the fault of others.

Perception of the World

A dominant perception in American culture assumes that the world is material rather than spirit (or idea, essence, will, or process), and should be exploited for the material benefit of humanity. This perception implies a clear separation between humans and all other forms of life and nature. Men's and women's quality of humanness endows them with a value absent in other forms of life; they are unique because of their souls. Nature and the physical world, although often referred to as living, are conceived of as material and mechanistic.

This perspective is distinct from assumptions held in some other parts of the world (and variant assumptions in American culture) that humanity is inseparable from the environment and should strive for harmony with it.[19] Nature is perceived as alive and animistic; animals and even inanimate objects have their own essence. Hence, no clear dividing line separates plants, rocks, rivers, and mountains from humans. Consequently, they should strive for unity and integration with nature and the physical world rather than attempt to control these forces.

Control and exploitation of the environment are closely associated with the concept of progress, a notion relatively absent in many parts of the world. There is a prevalent notion among Americans that a person and especially an organization must progress or cease to exist; one cannot stand still and continue to function.

Bound up with the idea of progress and achievement motivation in American culture is a feeling of general optimism toward the future. Most Americans feel that through their efforts a better future can be brought about which will not compromise the welfare and progress of others.[20] There is enough for everyone. Such a system of values and assumptions, of course, receives repeated reinforcement, since Americans live in a country with an expanding economy and resources. These assumptions contrast with the concept of "limited good" and fatalism found in many parts of the world.[21]

The American's high valuation of material aspects of the world, in combination with values associated with the self as an *individual,* forms cultural underpinnings for a strong and salient cultural concept of private property.

Perception of Self and the Individual

The concept of an individualistic self is an integral assumption of American culture so deeply ingrained that Americans ordinarily do not question it. They naturally assume that each person has his or her own separate identity. However, since this cultural assumption is implicit and generally outside the awareness of the American, the nature of self-identity is somewhat elusive. An individual's relatively diffuse identity is, in part, a consequence of the absence of clear ascriptive classifications such as *caste* and *class* found in other cultures.[22]

Stress on the individual begins at a very early age when the American child is encouraged to be autonomous. It is an accepted value that children (and adults) should be encouraged to make decisions for themselves, develop their own opinions, solve their own problems, have their own possessions. The concepts of freedom of choice and self-autonomy are, however, moderated by social control mechanisms in the form of expectations that the individual will choose according to the wishes of others.

An important consequence of this emphasis on the individual is that the American tends to resist formal authoritative control.[23] The concept of ideal authority for the American is one that is minimal and exercised informally by means of persuasion and appeals to the individual, rather than by coercion or by expectation of compliance to tradition, as is the case in many other cultures.

Another consequence of the American's individuality is that his or her self-concept is not easily merged with a group; any group, ranging from a small one to the nation, is conceived as a collection of individuals. The American resists becoming lost in a group or expresses concern about the nonperson emphasis of a cause or abstract ideology.

This avoidance of nonperson is tied to the fact that in the American culture ideas and concepts are typically made meaningful by using the individual as a point of reference. For example, concepts of dignity and human nature are most likely to take the form of self-respect, personal needs, and individual goals. With emphasis on concrete and self-referring terms, Americans are uncomfortable when referring to concepts that do not have a clear reference to the individual.

Another dimension of the perception of self and others revolves around the wholeness-divisibility of the person and is closely related to the American's emphasis on objectives rather than personal relationships. Americans tend to fragment personalities. They do not have to accept other people in totality to be able to work with them; an American may disapprove of the politics, hobbies, or personal life of an associate and still work effectively with him or her. An individual with ascriptive motivation, however, tends to react to others as total or whole persons and, consequently, often cannot work or cooperate with a person of different religion, belief system, or ethical code.

Action, thoughts, and intent are separately evaluated in American culture. For example, the individual cannot be held legally liable for harboring undesirable thoughts. In parts of the non-West (perhaps China is the best example), there is no such clear differentiation. Instead, action, thoughts, feelings, and intents are synthesized in a total assessment of the person. Thus, an indication of "wrong thoughts" would be grounds for censure even though undesirable action did not actually occur.

Generalized Cultural Forms

When the assumptions underlying cultural thinking are pervasive and lack substantive reference, they are probably best called cultural forms or form cognitions. While forms tend to merge with values and assumptions, they are discussed separately for conceptual clarity even though the distinction is not emphasized in training.

For Americans, the cultural form of *time* may usually be regarded as lineal. American concepts of planning, progress, preventive measures in health and technology, and orientation to the future may be seen to be associated with a lineal concept of time. Progress, for example, is closely associated with the view that time flows in one direction, toward the future. "You've got to keep up with the times" is an American expression which illustrates this association. This concept of time is eminently suited to a rational view of the world. One can distinguish various events in time and note their relationship by calling the preceding moment "the cause" and the next one "an effect." Although this description is oversimplified, it identifies the American predilection for seeing the world in concrete and delimited cause-and-effect sequences and provides a firm foundation on which to base the dominant American beliefs in accomplishment, in one's ability to master one's environment.

Concepts concerning contiguity and location may be regarded as aspects of *space,* a second kind of cultural form. Concepts of using space show important cultural differences. It is clear that different cultures deploy living and working areas in different patterns. Some cultures, such as Chinese, have a strong sense of territorialism; in other cultures, American for instance, territorialism is less highly developed, and one might expect it to be nearly absent in some nomadic cultures. Spatial displacements of persons in face-to-face interactions are also noticeably and measurably different from culture to culture.[24] At the most abstract level, formal causes and correlational thinking may be considered expressions of spatial relations. Although they occur in American culture, they are not nearly so frequent as, for example, in Chinese culture.[25] Temporal concepts, and efficient and material causes, are usually preferred by Americans.

A third kind of cultural form refers to the definitions of *essence* and *energy*. Primarily, for Americans, the universe is conceived as matter, or as things; in contrast, some people from sub-Saharan Africa view the universe as consisting of a network of living forces. In their perspective, force is synonymous with being.[26]

The *relational* form, a fourth possible kind of form cognition, is the one which perhaps most clearly refers to process rather than to structure. A basic issue underlying human behavior is the relationship between the empirical world and the cognitive world. If the relationship is isometric, the empirical world can be apprehended directly. Americans tend to comprehend what they observe through intermediate explanatory concepts, whereas many non-Western people are more likely to apprehend experience directly through intuition and spontaneous reaction, without a need for "explanation" in the Western sense of the word.

The American is more likely to take a relativistic and pragmatic position than to assume the existence of a directly knowable reality. Another aspect of this contrast in relational forms is manifest in the American emphasis on analysis and logic as modes of expression rather than esthetic appreciation or sensitivity.[27]

Other cultural forms are related to those described above: for example, the American tendency toward inductive thinking and quantification in contrast to deduction and inherent qualities. Another important contrast is that between comparative judgment, which is typically American, and absolute judgment (i.e., comparison against an abstract standard).

A final additional example, the concept of limits, should be mentioned. George M. Foster has described a chief distinction between peasant and Western societies in terms of the concept of "limited good."[28] The concept, in the most general sense of a cultural form, refers to the tendency to conceive of the world in limited rather than expansive terms. The assumption of "unlimited good," in American culture, underlies achievement motivation, in which individuals see their opportunities and achievements as relatively unlimited and at least partly determined by their efforts. The value configuration is frequently referred to as "effort-optimism," a key concept in understanding American behavior. In peasant societies the basic motivation is ascription, maintenance and entrenchment of status, privileges, and prerogatives.[29] Underlying this value is the concept that the good in the world is limited and that gains for one individual are necessarily obtained at the expense of others. Foster describes the "image of the limited good" as

> one in which all of the desired things in life such as land, wealth, health, friendship and love, manliness and honor, respect and status, power and influence, security and safety, *exist in finite quan-*

tity, and *are always in short supply....* Not only do these and other "good things" exist in finite and limited quantities, but in addition *there is no way directly within peasant power to increase the available quantities.* It is as if the obvious fact of land shortage in a densely populated area applied to all other desired things: not enough to go around. "Good," like land, is seen as inherent in nature, there to be divided and redivided, if necessary, but not to be augmented.[30]

This concept of limits has far-reaching consequences in all aspects of the cultural pattern.

Table 1

Summary of Cultural Assumptions and Values[31]

American	Contrast-American

1. Definition of Activity

a. **How do people approach activity?**
  (1) concern with "doing," .... "being"
     progress, change

     external achievement .... spontaneous expression

  (2) optimistic, striving .... fatalistic

b. **What is the desirable pace of life?**
  (1) fast, busy .... steady, rhythmic
  (2) driving .... noncompulsive

c. **How important are goals in planning?**
  (1) stress means, ... stress final goals
     procedures, techniques

d. **What are important goals in life?**
  (1) material .... spiritual
  (2) comfort and absence .... fullness of pleasure
     of pain   and pain
  (3) activity .... experience

e. **Where does responsibility for decisions lie?**
  (1) responsibility lies with   function of a group or
     each individual .... resides in a role (*dual contrast*)

f. **At what level do people live?**
  (1) operational, goals .... experiential truth
     evaluated in terms of
     consequence

American	Contrast-American

g. **How do people assign value?**
    (1) utility (does it work?) .... essence (ideal)

h. **Who should make decisions?**
    (1) the people affected .... those with proper authority

i. **How do people solve problems?**
    (1) planning outcomes .... coping with outcomes
    (2) anticipating consequences .... classifying the situation

j. **How do people learn?**
    (1) actively .... passively
    (student-centered   (serial rote learning)
    learning)

2. Definition of Social Relations

a. **How are roles defined?**
    (1) attained .... ascribed
    (2) loosely .... tightly
    (3) generally .... specifically

b. **How do people relate to others whose status is different?**
    (1) stress equality, ... stress hierarchical ranks,
    minimize differences   stress differences
    (2) stress informality .... stress formality,
    and spontaneity   behavior more easily anticipated

c. **How are sex roles defined?**
    (1) similar, overlapping .... distinct
    (2) sex equality .... male superiority
    (3) friends of both sexes .... friends of same sex only
    (4) less legitimized .... legitimized

d. **What are members' rights and duties in a group?**
    (1) assume limited .... assume unlimited
    responsibility   responsibility
    (2) join group to .... accept constraint
    seek own goals   by group
    (3) active members can .... leader runs group,
    influence group   members do not

e. **How do people judge and relate to others?**
    (1) specific abilities or interests .... overall individuality of
                               person and his/her status
    (2) task-centered .... person-centered
    (3) limited involvement .... total involvement

American	Contrast-American

f. What is the meaning of friendship?

(1) social friendship .... intense friendship
(short-term commitment,   (long-term commitment,
friends shared)   friends are exclusive)

g. How do people regard friendly aggression in social interaction?

(1) acceptable, ... not acceptable,
interesting, fun   embarrassing

3. Motivation

a. What is the motivating force?

(1) achievement .... ascription

b. How is competition among humans evaluated?

(1) as constructive, healthy .... as destructive, antisocial

4. Perception of the World (Worldview)

a. What is the (natural) world like?

(1) physical .... spiritual

(2) mechanical .... organic

(3) subject to control .... not subject to control
by machines   by machines

b. How does the world operate?

(1) in a rational, learnable, ... in a mystically ordered,
controllable manner   spiritually conceived
     manner (fate, divination)

(2) through chance .... through fate
and probability

c. Where do humans stand in nature?

(1) apart from nature .... part of nature
or any hierarchy   or of some hierarchy
     (*dual contrast*)

(2) things are impermanent, ... things are permanent,
not fixed, changeable   fixed, not changeable

d. What are the relationships between people and nature?

(1) good is unlimited .... good is limited

(2) humanity should modify .... humanity should
nature for its ends   accept the natural order

(3) good health and .... some disease
material comforts   and material deprivation
expected and desired   are natural, expected

American	Contrast-American

e. What is truth? goodness?
  (1) tentative .... definite
  (2) relative to circumstances .... absolute
  (3) experience analyzed in separate .... experience
      components, dichotomies   apprehended as a whole

f. How is time defined? valued?
  (1) future (anticipation) .... past (remembrance) or
                                        present experience (*dual contrast*)
  (2) precise units .... undifferentiated
  (3) limited resource .... limitless resource
  (4) lineal .... circular, undifferentiated

g. What is the nature of property?
  (1) private ownership important........ use for "natural" purpose
      as extension of self   regardless of ownership

5. Perception of the Self and the Individual
  a. How is the self defined?
  (1) diffuse, changing................................ fixed, clearly defined
  (2) flexible behavior .... person located
                                                            in a social system

  b. Where does a person's identity seem to be?
  (1) within the self .... outside the self in roles,
      (achievement)   groups, family, clan, caste, society

  c. Nature of the individual
  (1) characteristics .... perceived as totality
      separable

  d. On whom should one rely?
  (1) self .... superiors, patron, others
  (2) impersonal organizations .... people
      abstract principles

  e. What are the qualities of a person who is valued and respected?
  (1) youthful (vigorous) .... aged (wise, experienced)

  f. What is the basis of social control?
  (1) persuasion, ... formal, authoritative
      appeal to the individual
  (2) guilt.. shame

Generalized Forms

a. lineal (time) .... nonlineal

b. efficient and material .... formal causes,
    cause-and-effect thinking (space)   correlative thinking

c. material substantive .... spirit, energy
    (essence and energy)

d. operationalism (implied observer) .... direct apprehension
    or formalism (*dual contrast*)

e. induction .... deduction or transduction
    (*dual contrast*)

f. judgment by comparison ....judgment against
    an absolute standard

---

[1]   Clyde Kluckhohn et al., "Values and Value-Orientations in the Theory of Action," in *Toward a General Theory of Action*, edited by Talcott Parsons and Edward A. Shils (Cambridge: Harvard University Press, 1951), 388-433.

[2]   Florence R. Kluckhohn and Fred L. Strodtbeck, *Variations in Value Orientations* (1961; reprint, Westport, CT: Greenwood Press, 1973).

[3]   Florence R. Kluckhohn, "Some Reflections on the Nature of Cultural Integration and Change," in *Sociological Theory, Values and Sociocultural Change: Essays in Honor of P. A. Sorokin*, edited by Edward A. Tiryakian (New York: Free Press, 1963), 221.

[4]   Ibid.

[5]   Kluckhohn and Strodtbeck, *Variations*.

[6]   Fred N. Kerlinger, "Decision-Making in Japan," *Social Forces* 30 (October 1951): 36-41.

[7]   Kalman H. Silvert, "National Values, Development, and Leaders and Followers," *UNESCO International Social Science Journal* 15, no. 4 (1963): 560-70.

[8]   Gregory Bateson, "Social Planning and the Concept of Deutero-Learning," in *Readings in Social Psychology*, edited by Theodore M. Newcomb and Eugene L. Hartley (New York: Henry Holt, 1947), 121-28.

[9]   Gerardo and Alicia Reichel-Dolmatoff, *The People of Aritama: The Cultural Personality of a Colombian Mestizo Village* (Chicago: University of Chicago Press, 1961).

[10] Bateson, *Social Planning*.

[11] Robin M. Williams Jr., *American Society: A Sociological Interpretation* (New York: Alfred A. Knopf, 1961), 415-26.

[12] Conrad M. Arensberg and Arthur H. Niehoff, *Introducing Social Change* (Chicago: Aldine Publishing, 1964).

[13] Clyde Kluckhohn, "American Culture—A General Description," in *Human Factors in Military Operations*, edited by Richard H. Williams, Technical Memorandum ORO-T-259, Operations Research Office, Johns Hopkins University, Chevy Chase, Maryland, 1957, 94-111.

[14] George M. Foster, "Peasant Society and the Image of Limited Good," *American Anthropologist* 67, no. 2 (April 1965): 293-315.

[15] In describing American social relations as "depersonalized" and those of others as "personalized," no invidious comparison is intended. Trust, goodwill, and acceptance of other people for what they are, for example, are American characteristics but they need not be personalized in their expression. Distrust and suspicion are quite personal and more common in many other parts of the world than in the United States.

[16] Rosalie H. Wax and Robert K. Thomas, "American Indians and White People," *Phylon* 22, no. 4 (Winter 1961): 305-17.

[17] Jules Henry, *Culture against Man* (New York: Random House, 1963).

[18] David M. Potter, *People of Plenty: Economic Abundance and the American Character* (Chicago: University of Chicago Press, 1954).

[19] Arensberg and Niehoff, *Introducing Social Change.*

[20] Clyde Kluckhohn and Florence R. Kluckhohn, "American Culture: Generalized Orientations and Class Patterns," in *Conflicts of Power in Modern Culture: Seventh Symposium*, edited by Lyman Bryson (New York: Harper and Row, 1947).

[21] Foster, "Peasant Society."

[22] Margaret Mead, "The Factor of Culture," in *The Selection of Personnel for International Services*, edited by Mottram Torre (Geneva: Federation for Mental Health, 1963), 3-22.

[23] Geoffrey Gorer, *The American People: A Study in National Character* (New York: W. W. Norton, 1948).

[24] Edward T. Hall, *The Hidden Dimension* (1966; reprint, New York: Anchor/Doubleday, 1982).

[25] Hajime Nakamura, *Ways of Thinking of Eastern Peoples: India-China-Tibet-Japan* (Honolulu: East-West Center Press, 1964).

[26] Janheinz Jahn, "Value Conceptions in Sub-Saharan Africa," in *Cross-Cultural Understanding: Epistemology in Anthropology*, edited by Filmer Stuart C. Northrop and Helen H. Livingston (New York: Harper and Row, 1964), 56.

[27] Filmer Stuart C. Northrop, *The Meeting of East and West, An Inquiry Concerning World Understanding* (New York: Macmillan, 1945).

[28] Foster, "Peasant Society."

[29] Foster, "Peasant Society"; Potter, *People of Plenty.*

[30] Foster, "Peasant Society," 296.

[31] The authors wish to acknowledge the contributions of Dr. Jasper Ingersoll, Department of Anthropology, Catholic University, to the development of this table.

Stumbling Blocks in Intercultural Communication

LaRay M. Barna

Why is it that contact with persons from other cultures is so often frustrating and fraught with misunderstanding? Good intentions, the use of what one considers to be a friendly approach, and even the possibility of mutual benefits don't seem to be sufficient to ensure success—to many people's surprise. A worse scenario is when rejection occurs just because the group to which a person belongs is "different." It's appropriate at this time of major changes in the international scene to take a hard look at some of the reasons for the disappointing results of attempts at communication. New proximity and new types of relationships are presenting communication challenges that few people are ready to meet.

The Six Stumbling Blocks

Assumption of Similarities

One answer to the question of why misunderstanding and/or rejection occurs is that many people naively assume there are sufficient similarities among peoples of the world to make communication easy. They expect that simply being human and having common requirements of food, shelter, security, and so on makes everyone alike. Unfortunately, they overlook the fact that the forms of adaptation to these common biological and social needs and the values, beliefs, and attitudes surrounding them are vastly different from culture to culture. The biological commonalities are not much help when it comes to communication, where we need to exchange ideas and information, find ways to live and work together, or just make the kind of impression we want to make.

Another reason many people are lured into thinking that "people are people" is that it reduces the discomfort of dealing with difference, of not knowing. The thought that everyone is the same, deep down, is comforting. If someone acts or looks "strange" (different from them), it is then possible to evaluate this as wrong and treat everyone ethnocentrically.

The assumption of similarity does not often extend to the expectation of a common verbal language but it does interfere with caution in decoding nonverbal symbols, signs, and signals. No cross-cultural studies have proven the existence of a common nonverbal language except those in support of Darwin's theory that facial expressions are universal.[1] Paul Ekman found that "the particular visible pattern on the face, the combination of muscles contracted for anger, fear, surprise, sadness, disgust, happiness (and probably also for interest) is the same for all members of our species."[2]

This seems helpful until we realize that a person's cultural upbringing determines whether or not the emotion will be displayed or suppressed as well as on which occasions and to what degree.[3] The situations that bring about the emotional feeling also differ from culture to culture; for example, the death of a loved one may be a cause for joy, sorrow, or some other emotion, depending upon the accepted cultural belief.

Since there seem to be no universals of "human nature" that can be used as a basis for automatic understanding, we must treat each encounter as an individual case, searching for whatever perceptions and communication means are held in common and proceed from there. This is summarized by Vinh The Do:

> If we realize that we are all culture bound and culturally modified, we will accept the fact that, being unlike, we do not really know what someone else "is." This is another way to view the "people are people" idea. We now have to find a way to sort out the cultural modifiers in each separate encounter to find similarity.[4]

Persons from the United States seem to hold this assumption of similarity more strongly than some other cultures do. The Japanese, for example, have the reverse belief that they are distinctively different from the rest of the world. This notion brings intercultural communication problems of its own. Expecting no similarities, they work hard to figure out the foreign stranger but do not expect foreigners to be able to understand them. This results in exclusionary attitudes and only passive efforts toward mutual understanding.[5]

As Western trappings permeate more and more of the world, the illusion of similarity increases. A look-alike facade deceives representatives from contrasting cultures when each wears Western dress, speaks English, and uses similar greeting rituals. It is like assuming that New York City, Tokyo, and Tehran are all alike because each has the appearance of a modern city. But without being alert to possible underlying differences and the need to learn new rules for functioning, persons going from one city to the other will be in immediate trouble, even when taking on such simple roles as pedestrian or driver. Also, unless a foreigner expects subtle differences, it will take a long time of noninsulated living in a new culture (not in an enclave of his or her own kind) before he or she can adjust to new perceptual and nonevaluative thinking.

The confidence that comes with the myth of similarity is much stronger than with the assumption of differences, the latter requiring tentative assumptions and behaviors and a willingness to accept the anxiety of not knowing. Only with the assumption of differences, however, can reactions and interpretations be adjusted to fit what is happening. Without it one is likely to misread signs and symbols and judge the scene ethnocentrically.

The stumbling block of assumed similarity is a "troublem," as one English learner expressed it, not only for the foreigner but for the people in the host country (United States or any other) with whom the international visitor comes into contact. The native inhabitants are likely to be lulled into the expectation that since the foreign person is dressed appropriately and speaks some of the native language, he or she will also have similar nonverbal codes, thoughts, and feelings. In the United States nodding, smiling, and affirmative comments will probably be confidently interpreted by straightforward, friendly Americans as meaning that they have informed, helped, and pleased the newcomer. It is likely, however, that the foreigner actually understood very little of the verbal and nonverbal content and was merely indicating polite interest or trying not to embarrass himself or herself or the host by trying to verbalize questions. The conversation may even have confirmed a stereotype that Americans are insensitive and ethnocentric.

In instances like this, parties seldom compare impressions and correct misinterpretations. One place where opportunities for achieving insights do occur is in an intercultural classroom. Here, for example, U.S. students often complain that international student members of a discussion or project group seem uncooperative or uninterested. One person who had been thus judged offered the following explanation:

> I was surrounded by Americans with whom I couldn't follow their tempo of discussion half of the time. I have difficulty to listen and speak, but also with the way they handle the group. I felt uncomfortable because sometimes they believe their opinion strongly. I had been very serious about the whole subject but I was afraid I would say something wrong. I had the idea but not the words.[6]

The classroom is also a good place to test whether one common nonverbal behavior, the smile, is actually the universal people assume it to be. The following enlightening comments came from international students newly arrived in the United States:[7]

> Japanese student: *On my way to and from school I have received a smile by non-acquaintance American girls several times. I have finally learned they have no interest for me; it means only a kind of greeting to a foreigner. If someone smiles at a stranger in Japan, especially [at] a girl, she can assume he is either a sexual maniac or an impolite person.*

> Korean student: *An American visited me in my country for one week. His inference was that people in Korea are not very friendly because they didn't smile or want to talk with foreign people. Most Korean people take time to get to be friendly with people. We never talk or smile at strangers.*

> Arab student: *When I walked around the campus my first day, many people smiled at me. I was very embarrassed and rushed to the men's room to see if I had made a mistake with my clothes. But I could find nothing for them to smile at. Now I am used to all the smiles.*

Vietnamese student: *The reason why certain foreigners may think that Americas are superficial—and
they are, some Americans even recognize this—is
that they talk and smile too much. For people who
come from placid cultures where nonverbal language
is more used, and where a silence, a smile, a glance
have their own meaning, it is true that Americans
speak a lot. The superficiality of Americans can also
be detected in their relations with others. Their friendships are, most of the time, so ephemeral compared
to the friendships we have at home. Americans make
friends very easily and leave their friends almost as
quickly, while in my country it takes a long time to
find out a possible friend and then she becomes your
friend—with a very strong sense of the term.*

Statements from two U.S. students follow.[8] The first comes
from someone who has learned to look for differing perceptions
and the second, unfortunately, reflects the stumbling block of
assumed similarity.

U.S. student: *I was waiting for my husband on a
downtown corner when a man with a baby and two
young children approached. Judging by small quirks
of fashion [I guessed] he had not been in the U.S.
long. I have a baby about the same age and in appreciation of his family and obvious involvement as
a father I smiled at him. Immediately I realized I did
the wrong thing as he stopped, looked me over from
head to toe and said, "Are you waiting for me? You
meet me later?" Apparently I had acted as a prosti-
tute would in his country.*

U.S. student: *In general it seems to me that foreign
people are not necessarily snobs but are very unfriendly. Some class members have told me that you
shouldn't smile at others while passing them by on
the street. To me I can't stop smiling. It's just natural
to be smiling and friendly. I can see now why so
many foreign people stick together. They are impossible to get to know. It's like the Americans are big
bad wolves. How do Americans break this barrier? I
want friends from all over the world but how do you
start to be friends without offending them or scaring
them off—like sheep?*

The discussion thus far threatens the popular expectation that increased contact with representatives of diverse cultures through travel, student exchange programs, joint business ventures, immigration, and so on will result in better understanding and friendship. Indeed, tests of that assumption have been disappointing.[9] For example, research has found that Vietnamese immigrants who speak English well and have the best jobs suffer more from psychosomatic complaints and psychological disorders and are less optimistic about the future than their counterparts who remain in ethnic enclaves without attempts to adjust to their new homeland. One explanation given by the researcher is that these persons, unlike the less acculturated immigrants, "spend considerable time in the mainstream of society, regularly facing the challenges and stresses of dealing with American attitudes."[10]

After twenty-four years of listening to conversations between international and U.S. students and professors and seeing the frustrations of both groups as they try to understand each other, I am inclined to agree with Charles Frankel, who says, "Tensions exist within nations and between nations that never would have existed were these nations not in such intensive cultural communication with one another."[11] Recent world events have proven this to be true.

From a communicative perspective, it doesn't have to be that way. Just as more opportunities now exist for cross-cultural contact, so does more information about how to meet this challenge. We now have access to more orientation and training programs around the world, more courses in intercultural communication in educational institutions, and more published material.[12] Until people can squarely face the likelihood of meeting up with difference and misunderstanding, however, they will not be motivated to take advantage of these resources.

Many potential travelers who do try to prepare for out-of-country travel (for business conferences, government negotiations, study tours, or whatever) might gather information about the customs of the other country and a smattering of the language. Behaviors and attitudes of its people are sometimes researched, but necessarily from a secondhand source, such as a friend who has "been there." Experts realize that information gained in this fashion is general, seldom sufficient, and may or may not be applicable to the specific situation a traveler encounters or an area that he or she visits. Also, knowing exactly "what to expect" often blinds the observer to all but that which confirms his or her image. Any contradictory evidence that does filter through the screens of preconception is likely to be treated as an exception and thus discounted.

A better approach is to begin by studying the history, political structure, art, literature, and language of the country as time permits. This provides a framework for on-site observations. It is even more important to develop an investigative, nonjudgmental attitude and a high tolerance for ambiguity—all of which require lowered defenses. Margaret Mead suggests sensitizing people to cross-cultural variables instead of developing behavior and attitude stereotypes. She reasons that there are individual differences in each encounter and that changes occur regularly in cultural patterns, making research information obsolete.[13]

Edward C. Stewart and Milton J. Bennett also warn against providing lists of "dos and don'ts" for travelers, mainly because behavior is ambiguous—the same action can have different meanings in different situations—and no one can be armed with prescriptions for every contingency. Instead they encourage people to learn to understand the assumptions and values on which their own behavior rests. This knowledge can then be compared with what is found in the other culture, and a "third culture" can be adopted based on expanded cross-cultural understanding.[14]

The remainder of this article will examine some of the variables of the intercultural communication process itself and point out danger zones therein.

Language Differences

The first stumbling block has already been discussed at length— the hazard of *assuming similarity instead of difference.* A second danger will surprise no one—*language difference.* Vocabulary, syntax, idioms, slang, dialects, and so on all cause difficulty, but the person struggling with a different language is at least aware of being in trouble.

A greater language problem is the tenacity with which some people will cling to just one meaning of a word or phrase in the new language, regardless of connotation or context. The variations in possible meaning, especially when inflection and tone are varied, are so difficult to cope with that they are often waved aside. This complacency will stop a search for understanding. The nationwide misinterpretation of Khrushchev's sentence "We will bury you" is a classic example. Even "yes" and "no" cause trouble. When a nonnative speaker first hears the English phrase, "Won't you have some tea?" he or she listens to the literal meaning of the sentence and answers, "No," meaning that he or she wants some. The U.S. hostess, on the other hand, ignores the double negative because of common usage, and the guest gets no tea. Also, in some cultures it is polite to refuse the first or second offer of refreshment. Many foreign guests have gone hungry because they never got a third offer. This is another case of where "no" means "yes."

There are other language problems, including the different styles of using language such as direct, indirect; expansive, succinct; argumentative, conciliatory; instrumental, harmonizing; and so on. These different styles can lead to wrong interpretations of intent and evaluations of insincerity, aggressiveness, deviousness, or arrogance, among others.

Nonverbal Misinterpretations

Learning the language, which most visitors to foreign countries consider their only barrier to understanding, is actually only the beginning. As Frankel says, "To enter into a culture is to be able to hear, in Lionel Trilling's phrase, its special 'hum and buzz of implication'."[15] This suggests the third stumbling block, *nonverbal misinterpretations*. People from different cultures inhabit different sensory realities. They see, hear, feel, and smell only that which has some meaning or importance for them. They abstract whatever fits into their personal world of recognition and then interpret it through the frame of reference of their own culture. An example follows:

> An Oregon girl in an intercultural communication class asked a young man from Saudi Arabia how he would nonverbally signal that he liked her. His response was to smooth back his hair, which to her was just a common nervous gesture signifying nothing. She repeated her question three times. He smoothed his hair three times. Then, realizing that she was not recognizing this movement as his reply to her question, he automatically ducked his head and stuck out his tongue slightly in embarrassment. This behavior *was* noticed by the girl and she expressed astonishment that he would show liking for someone by sticking out his tongue.

The misinterpretation of observable nonverbal signs and symbols—such as gestures, postures, and other body movements—is a definite communication barrier. But it is possible to learn the meanings of these observable messages, usually in informal rather than formal ways. It is more difficult to understand the less obvious unspoken codes of the other cultures, such as the handling of time and spatial relationships and the subtle signs of respect of formality.

Preconceptions and Stereotypes

The fourth stumbling block is the presence of *preconceptions and stereotypes.* If the label "inscrutable" has preceded the Japanese guests, their behaviors (including the constant and seemingly inappropriate smile) will probably be seen as such. The stereotype that Arabs are "inflammable" may cause U.S. students to keep their distance or even alert authorities when an animated and noisy group from the Middle East gathers. A professor who expects everyone from Indonesia, Mexico, and many other countries to "bargain" may unfairly interpret a hesitation or request from an international student as a move to manipulate preferential treatment.

Stereotypes help do what Ernest Becker says the anxiety-prone human race must do—reduce the threat of the unknown by making the world predictable.[16] Indeed, this is one of the basic functions of culture: to lay out a predictable world in which the individual is firmly oriented. Stereotypes are overgeneralized, secondhand beliefs that provide conceptual bases from which we make sense out of what goes on around us, whether or not they are accurate or fit the circumstances. In a foreign land their use increases our feeling of security. Stereotypes are psychologically necessary to the degree that we cannot tolerate ambiguity or the sense of helplessness resulting from our inability to understand and interact with people and situations beyond our comprehension.

Stereotypes are stumbling blocks for communicators because they interfere with objective viewing of stimuli—the sensitive search for cues to guide the imagination toward the other person's reality. They are not easy to overcome in ourselves or to correct in others, even with the presentation of evidence. Stereotypes persist because they are firmly established as myths or truisms by one's own national culture and because they sometimes rationalize prejudices. They are also sustained and fed by the tendency to perceive selectively only those pieces of new information that correspond to the image held. For example, a visitor who is accustomed to privation and the values of self-denial and self-help cannot fail to experience American culture as materialistic and wasteful. The stereotype for the visitor becomes a reality.

Tendency to Evaluate

The fifth stumbling block and deterrent to understanding between persons of differing cultures or ethnic groups is the *tendency to evaluate,* to approve or disapprove, the statements and actions of the other person or group. Rather than try to comprehend thoughts and feelings from the worldview of the other, we assume our own culture or way of life is the most natural. This bias prevents the open-mindedness needed to examine attitudes and behaviors from the other's point of view. A midday siesta changes from a "lazy habit" to a "pretty good idea" when someone listens long enough to realize the midday temperature in that country is 115 degrees Fahrenheit.

Fresh from a conference in Tokyo where Japanese professors had emphasized the preference of the people of Japan for simple natural settings of rocks, moss, and water and of muted greens and misty ethereal landscapes, I visited the Katsura Imperial Gardens in Kyoto. At the appointed time of the tour a young Japanese guide approached the group of twenty waiting Americans and remarked how fortunate it was that the day was cloudy. This brought hesitant smiles to the group, who were less than pleased at the prospect of a shower. The guide's next statement was that the timing of the summer visit was particularly appropriate in that the azalea and rhododendron blossoms were gone and the trees had not yet turned to their brilliant fall colors. The group laughed loudly, now convinced that the young man had a fine sense of humor. I winced at his bewildered expression, realizing that had I come before attending the conference, I would have shared the group's belief that he could not be serious.

The miscommunication caused by immediate evaluation is heightened when feelings and emotions are deeply involved; yet this is just the time when listening with understanding is most needed. As stated by Carolyn W. Sherif, Musafer Sherif, and Roger Nebergall, "A person's commitment to his religion, politics, values of his family, and his stand on the virtue of his way of life are ingredients in his self-picture—intimately felt and cherished."[17] It takes both an awareness of this tendency to close our minds and the courage to risk changing our own perceptions and values to dare to comprehend why someone thinks and acts differently from us. Religious wars and negotiation deadlocks everywhere are examples of this.

On an interpersonal level there are innumerable illustrations of the tendency to evaluate which result in a breach in intercultural relationships. Two follow:[18]

> U.S. student: *A Persian friend got offended because when we got in an argument with a third party, I didn't take his side. He says back home you are supposed to take a friend's or family's side even when they are wrong. When you get home then you can attack the "wrongdoer" but you are never supposed to go against a relative or friend to a stranger. This I found strange because even if it is my mother and I think she is wrong, I say so.*

> Korean student: *When I call on my American friend he said through window, "I am sorry. I have no time because of my study." Then he shut the window. I couldn't understand through my cultural background. House owner should have welcome visitor whether he likes or not and whether he is busy or not. Also the owner never speaks without opening his door.*

The admonition to resist the tendency to immediately evaluate does not mean that one should not develop one's own sense of right and wrong. The goal is to look and listen empathically rather than through the thick screen of value judgments that impede a fair and total understanding. Once comprehension is complete, it can be determined whether or not there is a clash in values or ideology. If so, some form of adjustment or conflict resolution can be put into place.

High Anxiety

High anxiety or *tension*, also known as *stress*, is common in cross-cultural experiences due to the number of uncertainties present. The two words, *anxiety* and *tension*, are linked because one cannot be mentally anxious without also being physically tense. Moderate tension and positive attitudes prepare one to meet challenges with energy. Too much anxiety or tension requires some form of relief, which too often comes in the form of defenses, such as the skewing of perceptions, withdrawal, or hostility. That's why it is considered a serious stumbling block. As stated by Young Y. Kim,

> Stress, indeed, is considered to be inherent in intercultural encounters, disturbing the internal equilibrium of the individual system. Accordingly, to be interculturally competent means to be able to manage such stress, regain internal balance, and carry out the communication process in such

a way that contributes to successful interaction outcomes.[19]

High anxiety or tension, unlike the other five stumbling blocks (assumption of similarity, language, nonverbal misinterpretations, preconceptions and stereotypes, and the practice of immediate evaluation), is not only distinct but often underlies and compounds the other stumbling blocks. The use of stereotypes and evaluations are defense mechanisms in themselves, used to alleviate the stress of the unknown. If the person were tense or anxious to begin with, these mechanisms would be used even more. Falling prey to the aura of similarity is also a protection from the stress of recognizing and accommodating to differences. Different language and nonverbal patterns are difficult to use or interpret under the best of conditions. The distraction of trying to reduce the feeling of anxiety (sometimes called "internal noise") makes mistakes even more likely. Jack R. Gibb remarks,

> Defense arousal prevents the listener from concentrating upon the message. Not only do defensive communicators send off multiple value, motive, and affect cues, but also defensive recipients distort what they receive. As a person becomes more and more defensive, he becomes less and less able to perceive accurately the motives, the values, and the emotions of the sender.[20]

Anxious feelings usually permeate both parties in an intercultural dialogue. The host national is uncomfortable when talking with a foreigner because he or she cannot maintain the normal flow of verbal and nonverbal interaction. There are language and perception barriers; silences are too long or too short; proxemic and other norms may be violated. He or she is also threatened by the other's unknown knowledge, experience, and evaluation—the visitor's potential for scrutiny and rejection of the person and/or the country. The inevitable question, "How do you like it here?" which the foreigner abhors, is a quest for reassurance or at least a "feeler" that reduces the unknown. The reply is usually more polite than honest, but this is seldom realized.

The foreign members of dyads are even more threatened. They feel strange and vulnerable, helpless to cope with messages that swamp them. Their own normal reactions are inappropriate. Their self-esteem is often intolerably undermined unless they employ such defenses as withdrawal into their own reference group or into themselves, screen out or misperceive stimuli, use rationalization or overcompensation, or become aggressive or hostile. None of these defenses leads to effective communication.

Culture Shock. If a person remains in a foreign culture over time, the stress of constantly being on guard to protect oneself against making "stupid mistakes" takes its toll and he or she will probably be affected by "culture fatigue," usually called *culture shock.* According to LaRay M. Barna,

> the innate physiological makeup of the human animal is such that discomfort of varying degrees occurs in the presence of alien stimuli. Without the normal props of one's own culture, there is unpredictability, helplessness, a threat to self-esteem, and a general feeling of "walking on ice"— all of which are stress producing.[21]

The result of several months of this sustained anxiety or tension (or excitation if the high activation is perceived positively) is that reserve energy supplies become depleted, the person's physical capacity is weakened, and a feeling of exhaustion, desperation, or depression may take over.[22] He or she consciously or unconsciously is then more likely to use psychological defenses, such as those described previously. If this temptation is resisted, the sojourner suffering from the strain of constant adjustment may find his or her body absorbing the stress in the form of stomach- or backaches, insomnia, inability to concentrate, or other stress-related illnesses.[23]

The following account by a sojourner to the United States illustrates the trauma of culture shock:

> Soon after arriving in the United States from Peru, I cried almost every day. I was so tense I heard without hearing, and this made me feel foolish. I also escaped into sleeping more than twelve hours at a time and dreamed of my life, family, and friends in Lima. After three months of isolating myself in the house and speaking to no one, I ventured out. I then began to have severe headaches. Finally I consulted a doctor, but she only gave me a lot of drugs to relieve the pain. Neither my doctor nor my teachers ever mentioned the two magic words that could have changed my life: culture shock! When I learned about this, I began to see things from a new point of view and was better able to accept myself and my feelings.

> I now realize most of the Americans I met in
> Lima before I came to the U.S. were also in one of
> the stages of culture shock. They demonstrated a
> somewhat hostile attitude toward Peru, which the
> Peruvians sensed and usually moved from an ini-
> tially friendly attitude to a defensive, aggressive
> attitude or to avoidance. The Americans mostly
> stayed within the safe cultural familiarity of the
> embassy compound. Many seemed to feel that the
> difficulties they were experiencing in Peru were
> specially created by Peruvians to create discom-
> fort for "gringos." In other words, they displaced
> their problem of adjustment and blamed every-
> thing on Peru.[24]

Culture shock is a state of dis-ease, and, like a disease, it has different effects, different degrees of severity, and different time spans for different people. It is the least troublesome to those who learn to accept cultural diversity with interest instead of anxiety and manage normal stress reactions by practicing posi-tive coping mechanisms, such as conscious physical relaxation.[25]

Physiological Reactions. Understanding the physiological com-ponent of the stumbling block of anxiety/tension helps in the search for ways to lessen its debilitating effects.[26] It is hard to circumvent because, as human animals, our biological system is set so that anything that is perceived as being "not normal" au-tomatically signals an alert.[27] Depending on how serious the po-tential threat seems to be, extra adrenaline and noradrenaline pour into the system; muscles tighten; the heart rate, blood pres-sure, and breathing rate increase; the digestive process turns off; and other changes occur.[28]

This "fight or flight" response was useful—actually a biologi-cal gift for survival or effective functioning—when the need was for vigorous action. However, if the danger is to one's social self, which is more often the case in today's world, too much anxiety or tension just gets in the way. This is particularly true in an in-tercultural setting, where the need is for understanding, calm deliberation, and empathy in order to untangle misperceptions and enter into smooth relationships.

All is not doom and gloom, however. As stated by Holger Ursin, "The bodily response to changes in the environment and to threatening stimuli is simply activation."[29] Researchers believe that individuals control their emotional response to that activa-tion by their own cognitions.[30] If a person expects something to be exciting rather than frightening, he or she is more likely to interpret the somatic changes of the body as excitement. Hans Selye would label that "the good stress," which does much less harm unless it continues for some time without relief.[31] Feeling "challenged" facilitates functioning as opposed to feeling "threatened."[32]

People also differ in their stress tolerance. Everyone knows people who, for whatever the reasons, "fall apart at the least thing" and others who seem unflappable in any crisis. If you are one of the former, there are positive ways to handle the stress of intercultural situations, whether these be one-time encounters or frequent dialogues in multicultural settings. For starters, you can find opportunities to become familiar with many types of people so that differences become normal and interesting instead of threatening. And you can practice body awareness so that changes that signify a stress reaction can be identified and counteracted.

Conclusion

Being aware of the six stumbling blocks is certainly the first step in avoiding them, but it isn't easy. For most people it takes insight, training, and sometimes an alteration of long-standing habits or thinking patterns before progress can be made. The increasing need for global understanding, however, gives all of us the responsibility for giving it our best effort.

We can study other languages and learn to expect differences in nonverbal forms and other cultural aspects. We can train ourselves to meet intercultural encounters with more attention to situational details. We can use an investigative approach rather than stereotypes and preconceptions. We can gradually expose ourselves to differences so that they become less threatening. We can even learn to lower our tension level when needed to avoid triggering defensive reactions.

The overall goal should be to achieve *intercultural communication competence*, which is defined by Kim as "the overall internal capability of an individual to manage key challenging features of intercultural communication: namely, cultural differences and unfamiliarity, intergroup posture, and the accompanying experience of stress."[33]

Roger Harrison adds a final thought:

> The communicator cannot stop at knowing that the people he is working with have different customs, goals, and thought patterns from his own.

He must be able to feel his way into intimate contact with these alien values, attitudes, and feelings. He must be able to work with them and within
them, neither losing his own values in the confrontation nor protecting himself behind a wall of
intellectual detachment.[34]

[1] See Charles Darwin, *The Expression of Emotions in Man and Animals* (New York: Appleton, 1872); Irenaus Eibl-Eibesfeldt, *Ethology: The Biology of Behavior* (New York: Holt, Rinehart & Winston, 1970); Paul Ekman and Wallace V. Friesen, "Constants across Cultures in the Face and Emotion," *Journal of Personality and Social Psychology* 17 (1971): 124-29.

[2] Paul Ekman, "Movements with Precise Meanings," *Journal of Communication* 26 (Summer 1976): 19-20.

[3] Paul Ekman and Wallace V. Friesen, "The Repertoire of Nonverbal Behavior—Categories, Origins, Usage, and Coding," *Semiotica* 1 (1969): 1.

[4] Personal correspondence. Mr. Do is a multicultural specialist, Portland Public Schools, Portland, Oregon.

[5] E. Tai, "Modification of the Western Approach to Intercultural Communication for the Japanese Context," master's thesis, Portland State University, Portland, Oregon, 1986: 45-47.

[6] Taken from student papers in a course in intercultural communication taught by the author.

[7] Ibid.

[8] Ibid.

[9] See, for example, Bryant Wedge, *Visitors to the United States and How They See Us* (Princeton, NJ: D. Van Nostrand, 1965); and Milton Miller et al., "The Cross-Cultural Student: Lessons in Human Nature," *Bulletin of Menninger Clinic* (March 1971).

[10] Jack D. Horn, "Vietnamese Immigrants: Doing Poorly by Doing Well," *Psychology Today* (June 1980): 103-04.

[11] Charles Frankel, *The Neglected Aspect of Foreign Affairs* (Washington, DC: Brookings Institution, 1965): 1.

[12] For information see newsletters and other material prepared by the Society for Intercultural Education, Training and Research (SIETAR), 1444 I Street NW, Suite 700, Washington, DC, 20005. Sources are also listed in the *International and Intercultural Communication Annual,* published by the National Communication Association, 5105 Backlick Rd., Suite E, Annandale, VA, 22003; the *International Journal of Intercultural Relations,* Department of Psychology, University of Mississippi, University, MS, 38677.

[13] Margaret Mead, "The Cultural Perspective," in *Communication or Conflict,* edited by Mary Capes (New York: Association Press, 1960).

[14] Edward C. Stewart and Milton J. Bennett, *American Cultural Patterns: A Cross-Cultural Perspective,* rev. ed. (Yarmouth, ME: Intercultural Press, 1991).

[15] Frankel, *Neglected Aspect of Foreign Affairs,* 103.

[16] Ernest Becker, *The Birth and Death of Meaning* (New York: Free Press, 1962), 84-89.

[17] Carolyn W. Sherif, Musafer Sherif, and Roger Nebergall, *Attitude and Attitude Change* (Philadelphia: W. B. Saunders, 1965), vi.

[18] Taken from student papers in a course in intercultural communication taught by the author.

[19] Young Y. Kim, "Intercultural Communication Competence: A Systems-Theoretic View," in *Cross-Cultural Interpersonal Communication*, vol. 15, edited by Stella Ting-Toomey and Felipe Korzenny, *International and Intercultural Communication Annual* (Newbury Park, CA: Sage, 1991).

[20] Jack R. Gibb "Defensive Communication," *Journal of Communication* 2 (September 1961): 141-48.

[21] LaRay M. Barna, "The Stress Factor in Intercultural Relations," in *Handbook of Intercultural Training*, vol. 2, edited by Dan Landis and Richard W. Brislin (New York: Pergamon Press, 1983), 42-43.

[22] Hans Selye, "Stress: It's a G.A.S.," *Psychology Today* (September 1969).

[23] Barna, "Stress Factor," 29-30.

[24] Personal correspondence.

[25] Barna, "Stress Factor," 33-39.

[26] Hans Selye, *Stress without Distress* (New York, J. B. Lippincott, 1974); Hans Selye, *The Stress of Life* (New York: McGraw-Hill, 1976).

[27] Alvin Toffler, *Future Shock* (New York: Bantam, 1970), 334-42; Holger Ursin, "Activation, Coping and Psychosomatics," in *Psychobiology of Stress: A Study of Coping Men*, edited by Eirind Baade, Seymour Levine, and Holger Ursin (New York: Academic Press, 1978).

[28] Donald Oken, "Stress—Our Friend, Our Foe," in *Blue Print for Health* (Chicago: Blue Cross, 1974).

[29] Ursin, "Activation, Coping and Psychosomatics," 219.

[30] B. B. Brown, "Perspectives on Social Stress," in *Selye's Guide to Stress Research*, vol. 1, edited by Hans Selye (New York: Van Nostrand Reinhold, 1980); J. P. Keating, "Environmental Stressors: Misplaced Emphasis Crowding as Stressor," in *Stress and Anxiety*, vol. 6, edited by Irwin G. Sarason and Charles D. Spielberger (Washington, DC: Hemisphere, 1979); Stanley Schachter and J. E. Singer, "Cognitive, Social and Physiological Determinants of Emotional State," *Psychological Review* 69 (1962).

[31] Hans Selye, "On the Real Benefits of Eustress," *Psychology Today* (March 1978).

[32] Richard S. Lazarus, "Positive Denial: The Case for Not Facing Reality," *Psychology Today* (November 1979).

[33] Kim, "Intercultural Communication Competence," 259.

[34] Roger Harrison, "The Design of Cross-Cultural Training: An Alternative to the University Model," in *Explorations in Human Relations Training and Research*, NEA, no. 2 (Bethesda, MD: National Training Laboratories, 1966), 4.

Overcoming the Golden Rule: Sympathy and Empathy

Milton J. Bennett

᠎᠎᠎

> *Therefore all things whatsoever ye would that men should do to you, do ye even so to them....*
>
> —Matthew 7:12

Many of the world's great religions include a dictum similar to the Golden Rule. So it is not surprising that the Rule embodies a basic truth: all of us are equally human, not just our family or compatriots. Yet we humans still flaunt the Rule in both the paroxysms of genocide and the everyday destructiveness of prejudice and bigotry. Why is the wisdom of the Golden Rule so elusive? One reason may be that we commonly apply the Rule in a way that actually obstructs our path toward intercultural understanding.

The Golden Rule is typically used as a kind of template for behavior. If I am unsure of how to treat you, I simply imagine how I myself would like to be treated, and then act in accordance. The positive value of this form of the Rule is virtually axiomatic in U.S. American culture, and so its underlying assumption frequently goes unstated: other people *want* to be treated as I do. And under this assumption lies another, more pernicious belief: all people are basically the same, and thus they really *should* want the same treatment (whether they admit it or not) as I would.

Simply stated, the Golden Rule in this form does not work

because people are actually different from one another. Not only are they individually different, but they are systematically different in terms of national culture, ethnic group, socioeconomic status, age, gender, sexual orientation, political allegiance, educational background, and profession, to name but a few possibilities. Associated with these differences in people are differences in values—values which cannot easily be generalized to all people from those of any given group.

That people are different may appear obvious to readers of this article, but it is simply not a widely held notion among people in general—including those who are well-educated. Many teachers and trainers of intercultural communication find that while most people acknowledge superficial behavioral differences in dress, custom, language, and so on, it takes but a scratch of this surface to encounter a basic belief in the essential similarity of all people. The statement indicative of this belief is, "Once you get used to their different (dress, manners, style), they're just like us!" Attempts to point out more fundamental value differences may even be met by hostility—an indication of how central the assumption of similarity is to our worldview.

In addition to denying difference, the Golden Rule is also a poor guide for effective communication. Assuming that others are like ourselves when we talk to them is tantamount to talking to ourselves. We fail to recognize the crucial differences to which our communication must be accommodated, and our efforts to understand and be understood are subverted by a facade of uniformity.

This effort to expose the bias of the Golden Rule will take us into some philosophical assumptions, some concepts of social organization, and some communication techniques, or strategies. On the philosophical level, we will consider first the *assumption of similarity* and its relationship to theories of *single-reality*. This philosophical orientation will be seen to manifest in the social concepts of the *melting pot* and *ethnocentrism*. The communication strategy associated with these ideas is *sympathy*. Contrasting on the philosophical level will be the *assumption of difference* and its relationship to theories of *multiple-reality*. Communication based on the assumption of difference is *empathy*. Finally, we will consider some ways in which empathy might be developed and implemented toward the goal of intercultural communication.

Similarity and Single-Reality

The strongest statement of the assumption of similarity holds that all human beings are basically the same. In this view, physiological, personality, and even cultural differences which might be observed are mainly superficial. Underlying these permutations is a basic "human nature" that transcends time, cultural boundaries, and individual predilection. The assumption of similarity is not just a passive perspective—it also defines what will be actively sought. Thus, the observer notes and imputes importance to human similarities while ignoring or downgrading the importance of human differences.

The assumption of similarity is represented in philosophy by both *idealists* and *empiricists*.[1] Idealists hold that the universe (including human beings) has a permanent, ideal form. Human beings may discover their true nature by perceiving this form and adapting themselves to it. The current resurgence of mysticism and fundamentalist religion is, in many ways, a reawakening of this Platonic idealism. Most mystics and charismatics teach that there is a true, transcendent reality which, when it is perceived, illuminates the seeker with the knowledge that this single-reality exists within each individual. In this view, differences among people are ephemeral phenomena of the lower planes of existence, superficial in relation to the essential unity of higher planes.

Empiricists take a different route to the assumption of similarity. There is no transcendent reality; there is only the observable world of matter and energy. While this observable reality would seem to be inherently diverse, there is a catch. The catch is that only that which is observed is diverse. The observers (people) are necessarily similar in their ability to observe the same thing, given similar circumstances. This is the essence of scientific replicability. If a phenomenon cannot be observed by many people, it is simply assumed not to exist. Of course, this necessitates the belief that all people, properly trained, can and do see the same real phenomena.

Most other forms of the assumption of similarity can be seen to derive from these two philosophical positions. For instance, evangelical religions such as many forms of Christianity and Islam take the idealist stance that there is one truth, and that all people should have a similar knowledge of it. The growing field of ethnobiology argues from an empirical base that people are similar one to another in their adherence to some basic primate behavior. Transformational linguistics suggests that people are essentially similar in basic language "competence"—an example of the Platonic ideal form. And, of course, social sciences such as psychology and sociology base their empirical observations on the statistical similarity of a normative population.

The theories mentioned above are only a few examples of a general category which can be called "single-reality" theory. The basic assumption inherent in this category is that there is *one* way that things really are. In this view, reality is not invented by our observational categories; it is *discovered* through either philosophical/religious (idealist) insight or through objective (empiricist) observation. An indicator of the idealist approach to single-reality is some form of the statement, "If only we develop sufficient (wisdom, faith, knowledge, discipline, insight), we will know the true nature of the universe." An indicator of the empiricist approach is the statement, "We don't know it all yet, but with sufficient (experiments, categorization, instrumentation, explanation) we will figure out how things really work."

The Golden Rule depends on single-reality theory to fuel its underlying assumption of similarity. If there were not a single, discoverable reality, we could never be sure whether the similarity we observed was "really" the case, or whether it was merely a function of our point of view. If similarity were only a matter of perspective, then we might have to consider that other people had *different* points of view, which might lead them to observe entirely different kinds of similarity (or difference) between themselves and us. In this case, the Golden Rule wouldn't work at all, and we would be thrust into a much more complex, relativistic world. So we preserve the comfortable assumptions of the Golden Rule and the single reality it represents.

The Melting Pot and Ethnocentrism

The ramifications of preserving the Golden Rule are not restricted to the abstractions of philosophy. There are several social consequences of single-reality theory and the assumption of similarity. Two of these consequences of interest to intercultural communication are "the melting pot" and "ethnocentrism." The melting-pot concept is a source of major concern to minorities in this country who might wish to maintain an ethnic identity different to some extent from the mainstream culture. The term *melting pot* was coined by Israel Zangwill in a play by that title written in 1921.

> America is God's Crucible, the great Melting Pot
> where all the races of Europe are melting and re-
> forming—Here you stand good folk...with your fifty

> languages and histories.... But you won't be long
> like that brothers, for these are the fires of God
> you come to—these are the fires of God.[2]

Unenlightened as it might sound today, the idea of the melting pot is actually a relatively liberal holdover from the colonial period of American history. In those days and up until World War I, many thought that the fusion of ethnic differences in America would lead to a great civilization of supermen.[3] But as a stronger mainstream culture developed, the original melting-pot idea transformed into the ideal of assimilation and Americanization.

Americanization is a specific case of cultural assimilation in general. The Americanizing melting pot did not merely amalgamate difference; it *molded* it into the prevailing American cultural pattern. So, although the end result of both kinds of melting was similarity, the original melting pot at least suggested a unique product. The more recent use of the concept seems clearly based on single-reality theory, where mainstream American culture is the one true frame of reference.

We hear today widespread disavowal of the melting pot in favor of some form of "cultural pluralism." A good part of this disavowal, when it comes from mainstreamers, may be insubstantially rhetorical. In most cases, it is simply not evident that there has occurred the philosophical shift away from a single-reality assumption that would necessarily underlie a strong commitment to pluralism. Such a commitment demands the kind of multiple-reality assumption discussed in a later section of this article. The best that can be hoped for under the single-reality theory is a kind of tolerance for "second-best" cultural patterns. This stance obviously does not address the severe negative value judgments that characterize so much interethnic and intercultural communication.

Related to the idea of an Americanizing melting pot is the concept of ethnocentrism. This tendency to see our own culture as the center of the universe—that is, as the true reality—affects all intercultural communication, including interethnic relations. In fact, ethnocentrism is the most appropriate label for the single-reality assumption of similarity in a cultural context. This can be seen clearly in Richard E. Porter and Larry A. Samovar's definition of the concept:

> A major source of cultural variance in attitudes is
> *ethnocentrism,* which is a tendency to view people
> unconsciously by using our own group and our
> own customs as the standard for all judgments....

> The greater their similarity to us, the nearer to us
> we place them; the greater the dissimilarity, [the]
> farther away they are.... We tend to see our own
> groups, our own country, our own culture as the
> best, as the most moral. This view also demands
> our first loyalty and produces a frame of reference
> that denies the existence of any other frame of
> reference. It is an absolute position that prohibits
> any other position from being appropriate for an-
> other culture.[4]

From the above description, it is understandable why Jon A.
Blubaugh and Dorothy L. Pennington state that "ethnocentrism
seems to be at the root of racism."[5]

In a parallel development to the rhetorical call for cultural
pluralism, we hear today a cry for "intercultural understanding."
Again, this cry is meaningless if it is not accompanied by a shift
away from that essential ingredient of ethnocentrism, the assumption of similarity. Unless we can accept that other groups of people
are truly different—that is, they are operating *successfully* according to different values and principles of reality—then we cannot
exhibit the sensitivity nor accord the respect to those differences
that will make intercultural communication and understanding
possible.

The continued existence of melting-pot ideas and ethnocentrism is facilitated by their inherent connection to the Golden
Rule. We really want to use our own values as the basis for our
behavior toward others. It is easier (we don't need to imagine
different values), and it somehow seems so moral. When we find,
no matter how much we try to ignore it, that many other people
don't respond to this treatment, we face a choice. Either we must
alter our behavior (and underlying assumptions), or we must alter the unresponsive people. Supported by the ethnocentric conviction that those other people are somehow wrong or ignorant,
we choose the latter course. Perhaps, we hope, after they are
educationally melted into the proper configuration, they will respond as they should to our Golden Rule behavior.

Of course, some people seem impervious to the fires of God.
For them, we have a different rule, which can be labeled the "Lead
Rule." The Lead Rule dictates "Do unto others as they deserve
having done unto them." If people are unresponsive to our well-
motivated Golden Rule behavior, and if they will not be helped to
become similar, then we may assume that they are "mad or bad."[6]
If we assume they are mad, we may extend our educational ef-

forts into therapy. A prime indicator of the Lead Rule being employed therapeutically is the statement, "We're only doing this for your own good." If we assume they are bad, we may try to punish them. If they do not respond to punishment, then we may be compelled to employ the full force of the Lead Rule, which is to kill them.

Sympathy

So far, we have been considering general behavior and its underlying philosophical assumptions. In situations of actual face-to-face interaction, these general behavioral tendencies take the form of specific communication techniques, or strategies. The strategy which is most closely allied with the Golden Rule and its attendant assumptions is *sympathy.*

Although the term *sympathy* is used variably, it will be used here to mean "the imaginative placing of ourselves in another person's position."[7] It should be understood by this definition that we are not taking the role of another person or imagining how the other person thinks or feels, but rather we are referencing how we ourselves might think or feel in similar circumstances. For instance, if I tell you that my aunt has recently died, you might sympathize by imagining how you would feel (or have felt) about your aunt dying. This definition is not restricted to cases of socially defined sorrow, however. It would also be sympathy if I tell you that I just inherited a million dollars, and you respond by imagining how you would feel as a millionaire.

In a following section, this definition of *sympathy* will be contrasted to the notion of *empathy.* For the time being, suffice it to say that empathy concerns how we might imagine the thoughts and feelings of other people from their own perspectives. This distinction is fairly consistent with Lauren G. Wispé in the *International Encyclopedia of the Social Sciences*: "In *empathy,* one attends to the feelings of another; in *sympathy* one attends to the suffering of another, but the feelings are one's own."[8] Note, however, that here sympathy is not restricted to cases of suffering. The difference between sympathy and empathy is not defined by either the degree or the subject of concern; it is defined by whose perspective is being assumed.

Probably the easiest way to think of sympathy is as projection. Following the assumption of similarity, we merely assume that the other person is like ourselves and therefore impute to him or her our own thoughts and feelings. In its least sophisticated form, sympathy projects both the self and the circumstances of the sympathizer onto the perceived situation. Imagine, for example, that a middle-class suburbanite is interacting with a poor person living in the inner city. Pure projection might lead the suburbanite to suggest that the poor person get a job and shop carefully for inexpensive groceries—an assumption that the suburban circumstances of job opportunity, competitive prices, and transportation are all available to the inner-city dweller, as well as the motivation assumed by the suburbanite herself. Projecting only self, the suburbanite might imagine how she herself would feel in the poor person's circumstances—perhaps frustrated, and certainly anxious to take the first opportunity to escape into a "better" environment. (Note that this might not be at all how the poor person feels.)

It is apparently possible to increase the sophistication of sympathy quickly. I once asked a group of (assumedly) upper-middle-class white high school students what they would do for recreation if they had grown up in a ghetto. Quickly, several students replied with such projective responses as "go bowling," or "go swimming," or "drive around." I suggested that they might have neither the facilities nor the money to do those things. There was a silence, and then one boy spoke up with a clearly more sophisticated sympathetic suggestion: "jog!"

The general category of projective sympathy can be divided into two major ways of responding sympathetically to another person: referencing our own memory, here referred to as *reminiscent sympathy;* and referencing our own imagination of self in different circumstances, here termed *imaginative sympathy.* Of these two, reminiscent sympathy is probably the most common.

With the technique of reminiscent sympathy, we search our past experience for circumstances that seem similar to those observed as connected to the other person's experience. For instance, if you report to me that you have a drinking problem, I might try to remember some time when I felt compelled to drink. Assuming that I find such a circumstance in my own life, I would then try to reconstruct my feelings at that time and attempt to use them as a guide for further conversation or counsel. An indicator of the reminiscent sympathy technique is the statement, "I know just how you feel—I was there myself." Note that my feelings about drinking may be totally dissimilar to yours, but the desire to assume similarity is strong.

The apparent unassailability of the reminiscent sympathy technique is part of the reason why reformed alcoholics, former prisoners, cured schizophrenics, and other "experienced" people are so frequently considered credible counselors in their respective areas of experience. A parallel to this belief in minority relations is the assumption that only a Latino American, Native American, or African American can speak credibly to the problems encountered by his or her respective ethnic group. This credibility is frequently not undeserved and many such "survivors" are apparently extremely effective in their work.[9] However, caution should be exercised in assuming that exposure to certain circumstances is a sufficient qualification for political, educational, or counseling expertise in the area. Having experienced a toothache does not make one a dentist.

There is also a danger that a strong experience, although potentially a valuable tool, can limit our consideration of different reactions to the same circumstances. For instance, some feminists seem to assume that all women do (or should) have the same reaction to being female in this culture. The failure to recognize different reactions is most likely when reminiscent sympathy is the only technique of understanding employed. When it is, the Golden Rule takes a kind of retroactive form, reading, "Do unto others as you would have liked to have had done unto you in similar circumstances."

Imaginative sympathy involves the referencing of our imagination of ourselves in different circumstances. This is probably a more sophisticated process than is the use of memory, but it involves a similar referencing of self rather than the other person. An example of imaginative sympathy might involve your informing me of your recent miraculous escape from an automobile accident. Having never had a serious automobile accident to remember, I might search for an appropriate response by imagining how I would feel in that circumstance. But no matter how I imagine I might feel, my response bears no necessary relationship to how you actually do feel. Nevertheless, as usual, it is likely that the Golden Rule will permit me the assumption of similarity necessary to think I understand your feelings. In these cases, the Rule reads "Do unto others as you imagine you would like to have done unto you in similar circumstances."

Fund appeals for humanitarian causes commonly attempt to elicit an imaginative sympathy reaction from readers. For instance, a recent issue of the *New Yorker* magazine displayed a fund appeal topped by a picture of a young Asian girl dressed in a dirty but frilly dress, her hair disheveled but beribboned, and her face set in a plaintive but cute expression. The large-type caption under the picture reads "Tina has never had a Teddy Bear."

I suspect that the creators of this appeal are assuming that most readers of the *New Yorker* had teddy bears in their childhood. Further assuming that these teddy bears are remembered fondly by the readers, the fund appealers ask the readers to imagine what it would be like not to have had a teddy bear. The discomfort occasioned by this imagining of a deprived self will then, it is hoped, motivate some check-writing behavior.

I don't really think there is anything wrong with this kind of sympathetic altruism. It is certainly well-motivated, and it probably doesn't do much harm. However, sympathetic altruism may not be addressing the real needs of those whom we want to help. We should at least ask, "But does Tina want a teddy bear?"

While a Peace Corps volunteer in Truk (Chuuk), Micronesia, I happened to be near the receiving end of several gestures of sympathetic altruism. One particularly amusing example was the annual Navy airdrop of Christmas presents. It was a great show: a giant airplane swooping low over the island and disgorging a bombardment of cosmetics, candy, and plastic toys. While the Navy's image was undoubtedly a factor in this action, it still was a pleasant enough thing to do. How much better it would have been, however, if the plane had dropped cloth, ballpoint pens, and perfume—the really valuable gifts from the Trukese point of view.

I'm afraid I was a part of another sympathetic gesture toward the Trukese. My training group decided that creating a water system for the island would be a great help to our hosts. Our hosts themselves seemed more inclined toward a school building, but since the island already had one school building and since we incidentally already had the plastic pipe, we pushed the water project. The island leaders finally gave a reluctant go-ahead and we began work, secure in the knowledge that the project's great sanitation and convenience benefits would soon become apparent. The Trukese men helped us with what I only later could recognize as a bemused and tolerant attitude.

The following events occurred in the next year: even after warnings, several plastic pipes were melted shut during field burning; the island children took to swimming and urinating in the water tanks; inter-village quarrels were punctuated by late-night machete raids on the pipes; the island women continued to lug their wash up the mountain to a stream, where they could socialize as before; and arguments occurred over who had the right to turn the water on and off. Finally, the water system died a merciful death and a school building project was begun. It was a wonderful lesson in the unplanned consequences of sympathetic altruism.

Advantages and Disadvantages of Sympathy

So far, we have seen a rather bleak picture of the sympathetic strategy. In this final consideration of sympathy, I will suggest some possible advantages of sympathy as well as summarize its disadvantages.

Advantages of using a sympathetic communication strategy include the following:

1. *Sympathy is easy.* Most of us are distressed to some extent by unfamiliarity, and we prefer to identify phenomena with pre-existing categories. With people, the most familiar frame of reference is ourselves, and so we prefer to generalize from ourselves to others—the basic process of assuming similarity. Depending on the situation, we may use reminiscent or imaginative sympathy techniques to enable this kind of generalization.

2. *Sympathy is credible.* Credibility is a major factor in the success of reminiscent sympathy. Because the assumption of similarity is widespread, many people really believe that similar circumstances yield similar experience. We are then likely to give credence to those who have "been through it." While experience may indeed give a person many valuable insights, much of the effectiveness of an experienced person may derive from the attribution of credibility itself. Given this credibility, we may even modify our own feelings to correspond with those of the experienced person.

3. *Sympathy is often accurate.* The accuracy of sympathetic understanding is not a function of its process. Rather, it derives from our tendency to surround ourselves with truly similar people. Attraction to similarity is a pervasive phenomenon.[10] Insofar as we interact mainly with truly similar people, our sympathetic generalizations yield relatively accurate assumptions about those carefully selected others. In these situations of similarity, accuracy should be greatest for imaginative sympathy because it can take into account minor differences in circumstance. Reminiscent sympathy should give second-best results because of its greater rigidity, but its greater credibility may equalize its effectiveness. As sympathy becomes increasingly less sophisticated, it yields accurate assumptions only in nearly identical situations with extremely similar people.

4. *Sympathy may be comforting.* Sometimes people are comforted by knowing that another person has encountered similar cir-

cumstances, even if his or her experience of the circumstances was different. This advantage of reminiscent sympathy seems most apparent in the case of illness, where the unique experience of a particular illness may be perceived as secondary in importance to the mere fact of the sympathizer having had the same disease. In addition, a sympathetic approach may be comfortable for people who would prefer not to disclose their actual, possibly different, feelings or thoughts about certain circumstances.

The disadvantages of a sympathetic communication strategy can be summarized as follows:

1. *Sympathy is insensitive to difference.* Despite our best efforts to interact only with truly similar people, we are frequently thrown into communication situations where others probably think and feel differently. These situations include at least communication with people from different national cultures, ethnic groups, socioeconomic status, age groups, genders, sexual orientation, political persuasion, educational background, and profession. In these and other situations, sympathetic understanding is likely to be inaccurate at best, and probably will impede effective communication.

2. *In the face of difference, sympathy is patronizing.* Generalizing exclusively from our own frame of reference carries with it all the connotations of ethnocentrism. One of these connotations is that our own experience is the best standard with which to measure the world. People with different views of the world may feel that their thoughts and feelings are being devalued. It is not unusual for *both* persons in a sympathetic communication to feel patronized, each by the other.

3. *In the face of difference, sympathy breeds defensiveness.* When we feel our different views of the world are ignored or devalued by others, we may take on a defensive posture to protect what we think is a successful organization of phenomena. Sympathetic strategies cannot help but ignore or devalue difference, since they are based on a strong assumption of similarity. Communication is hindered by defensiveness,[11] and sympathy appears to be a major factor contributing to that defensiveness.

4. *Sympathy helps perpetuate the assumption of similarity.* Sympathy not only implements the Golden Rule; it also perpetuates it. Our choice of communication strategy and our assumptions about the nature of people are interactive. While

sometimes we may choose a strategy that is adapted to a given reality, we may more often manipulate our assumptions about reality so that a given strategy continues to work. Insofar as we choose sympathy and the Golden Rule, we will tend to ignore difference in favor of seeing the similarity necessary to our strategy.

We have now seen how the everyday use of the Golden Rule derives from an assumption of essential similarity among human beings—an assumption that is consistent with single-reality theory. The communication strategy that implements the Golden Rule is sympathy, which involves some form of generalizing thoughts and feelings from our own frame of reference. Although sympathy may yield acceptable understanding of others in situations of actual similarity, it appears to have many disadvantages in situations where human difference is encountered.

The point which might best be derived from the preceding discussion is not that the Golden Rule and its attendant assumptions and strategies never work. In its most abstract form, the Rule might limit some of the cruelties of dehumanization. But the effectiveness of similarity-based approaches is severely limited by the existence of human diversity. Specific Golden Rule strategies don't work outside of an environment carefully controlled for actual similarity, and the world is decreasingly favorable to that circumstance.

The Assumption of Difference and Multiple-Reality

In contrast to the assumption that all people are basically similar, we could assume that each human being is essentially unique. A closer look at the apparent homogeneity of human beings reveals an underlying heterogeneity of almost unimaginable scope. It becomes clear that the categories we use for assuming universal similarity are broad generalizations that can only be made at a distance—a distance preserved by abstractions such as the Golden Rule.

If we reject the Golden Rule in favor of seeking difference, an astonishing diversity of human characteristics rapidly becomes apparent. Not only are these differences obvious in language and culture, but they are also observable on the physiological level. People differ in their fingerprints, brain-wave patterns, voice patterns, blood composition, and genetic codes. While the need to eat might appear absolute from a distance, a closer look reveals some people who do not eat for long periods without ill effect. We also find people who can exist in a normally fatal oxygen-deficient atmosphere,[12] and others who are able to start and stop their heartbeat at will.[13] Even those basic categories of similarity—male and female—are only generalizations. Physiological sexual characteristics are actually distributed along a continuum ranging from completely male to completely female.[14] Medical doctors, who are aware of these differences, know better than to treat one person's dysfunction in exactly the same way as another's.

Bracketed by language and cultural differences on one side and physiological differences on the other, people also differ individually in their psychological patterns. The process whereby individuals create unique views of the world has been explored by the psychologist George A. Kelly. In his personal-construct theory, he states the fundamental postulate that "A person's processes are psychologically channelized by the ways in which he anticipates events."[15] By this, he means that each of us is, by definition, an organizer of events, and that the particular organization which we develop constitutes our experience. This organization is considered by Kelly to be a process of construing, defined as "placing an interpretation." Events are anticipated by "construing their replications."[16] Thus, in Kelly's view, our experience is created by the way in which we construe events.

Kelly goes on to state that "persons differ from each other in their construction of events."[17] By this he means simply that we can and do construe precisely the same events in different ways. Since experience is a function of this construing, it follows that experience is not inextricably connected to events.

> Experience is made up of the successive construing of events. It is not constituted merely by the succession of events themselves. A person can be a witness to a tremendous parade of episodes and yet, if he fails to keep making something out of them...he gains little in the way of experience from having been around when they happened. It is not what happens around him that makes a man experienced; it is the successive construing and reconstruing of what happens...that enriches the experience of his life.[18]

Obviously, Kelly's view of events and experience is directly opposed to that supposed by the assumption of similarity. It follows from his assumption of difference that the encountering of similar circumstances does not in any way guarantee that two people's experience of those circumstances will be similar. And, of course, without the essential connection of circumstances and experience, the communication strategy of sympathy becomes worthless as a general technique for understanding others.

We have seen, however, that sympathy does seem to work in some situations of actual similarity. If we are as different as has been implied so far, how can these situations ever come about? Kelly addresses this question: "To the extent that one person employs a construction of experience which is similar to that employed by another, his psychological processes are similar to those of the other person."[19] So, if constructions of experience can somehow be guided into similar paths, some level of actual similarity might occur.

The major guide for constructions of reality is culture. In Kelly's view, we create culture by assuming similarity. When we observe that other people have encountered similar circumstances, we assume that they are similar to ourselves. In interaction, this assumption takes the form of expectations. Other people perceive these expectations and tend to behave in accordance with them. Thus, according to Kelly, "Cultural similarity between persons [is] essentially a similarity in what they perceive is expected of them."[20] It is, then, the *assumption* of similarity which creates the actual similarity.

This circular process of culture would seem to result in widespread actual similarity if it were not for one important factor: different people and groups assume different kinds of similarity. Japanese people, for instance, may assume a significant level of similarity among themselves, but the nature of that similarity is radically different from that assumed by mainstream Americans among themselves. Specifically, Japanese may accurately assume that they are similar among themselves in "family loyalty," and Americans may accurately assume that they are similar among themselves in "desire for individual freedom," but neither assumption applies accurately to the other group. As noted earlier, this difference in the nature of intragroup similarity also appears to characterize ethnic groups, socioeconomic strata, professions, and so on. Each group, no matter how small, has its unique set of expectations (values) which maintains the group identity. And even within groups, each individual differs from every other individual in precise expectations about how events will be construed.

The assumption of difference is consistent with theories of multiple-reality. These theories contend, as does personal-construct theory, that reality is not a given, discoverable quantity. Rather, it is a variable, created quality. In philosophy, this view is

represented by phenomenology and various neophenomenologi-
cal systems which are presently exploring the philosophical implications of modern physics. The idea of primary importance in
these theories is the relativity of frame of reference.

Relative frame of reference, although it has a rather precise
meaning in physics, can be considered generally as the change
in apparent reality that accompanies a change in observational
perspective. This idea is fundamental to the assumption of difference as it affects human interaction. When we communicate,
we are operating on the pragmatic level of apparent reality. The
pitfall of sympathy is the assumption that reality appears the same
to both participants in the situation. The alternative to this stance
is to assume a relative frame of reference, where our view of
reality may be apparent only to ourselves. As we will see, the
placing of ourselves in a relative frame of reference is conducive
to empathy.

Another philosophy that contributes to the assumption of difference is systems theory. Of particular interest is the quality of a
system called *equifinality*. This principle states that in any given
system, we may achieve the same goal by starting at different
points and by using different processes within the system.[21] Kelly
states the same idea for people: "Two people can act alike even if
they have been exposed to quite different phenomenal stimuli."[22]
Both these equifinality ideas contrast with the similarity assumption that particular experience is necessarily connected to particular circumstances. If we consider society as a system and apply
the principle of equifinality, we see that people exposed to different circumstances may have very similar experiences. Reversing
this, people encountering similar circumstances may have different experiences.

The practical implication of equifinality is that there are many
ways of skinning a cat. Although such aphorisms normally state
the obvious, it is surprising how often we seem to neglect this
simple statement of relativity. When we encourage others to take
a particular trip because it is exciting or to see a certain movie
because it is meaningful, we have failed to recognize that those
activities may not elicit the same feelings at all in other people.
Further, we may also ignore the fact that feelings of excitement
and meaningfulness may be engendered in others by quite different activities. Apparently, it is one thing to quote the aphorism
and quite another to really believe that bowling and yachting
may be experienced similarly.

In the social sciences, proponents of multiple-reality theories include Gregory Bateson,[23] Paul Watzlawick,[24] and Ronald

David Laing.[25] These and other theorists agree that the reality we experience is a variable matter of perception and communication.[26] Perception itself is highly variable, particularly in cross-cultural situations,[27] and the rules of communication seem even more mutable.[28] Considering these changing factors, we might wonder that anyone ever understands anyone else at all. That we *do* sometimes understand each other seems to be largely a function of overcoming the Golden Rule, which denies these differences in perception and communication altogether.

Empathy

The communication strategy most appropriate to multiple-reality and the assumption of difference is *empathy.* Like sympathy, this term is also used variably. In everyday usage, it is often defined as standing in another person's shoes, as intense sympathy, as sensitivity to happiness rather than to sadness, and as a direct synonym for sympathy. In the literature, empathy has been defined as objective motor mimicry; as the understanding of people who have no emotional significance to us;[29] and as "a state in which an observer reacts emotionally because he perceives another experiencing or about to experience an emotion."[30] Here I will use the definition "the imaginative intellectual and emotional participation in another person's experience."[31] This definition is most consistent with the treatments of empathy by Carl R. Rogers[32] and by Robert L. Katz.[33]

As sympathy was defined as "the imaginative placing of ourselves in another person's position," empathy can be defined in terms of two important contrasts in focus. In empathy, we "participate" rather than "place," and we are concerned with "experience" and "perspective" rather than "position." Placing ourselves in another person's position assumes, as we have seen, essential similarity of experience with the other, making it sufficient to merely change places with him or her. In contrast, participation in another's experience does not assume essential similarity. The other's experience might be quite alien, even if his or her position is similar. Thus, we need to do more than merely change places or stand in the other person's shoes. We need to get inside the head and heart of the other, to participate in his or her experience as if we were really the other person. This process may be referred to as "perspective taking."

My wife and I have discovered some differences between sympathy and empathy in our own cross-gender communication. One minor example is our experience dealing with each other during slight illnesses. When I am sick, I like to be left absolutely alone (in autonomous suffering). When my wife is sick, she likes to be grandly attended to (in relational nurturance). When we were first married, I would express my sympathy for her being sick by leaving her absolutely alone. And she, of course, would sympathize by asking me how I felt every ten minutes or so. After some years of wonderment at how cantankerous we both were when sick, we found that we had different expectations about how sick people should be treated. Now we try to empathize rather than sympathize. By imagining the other person's experience of being sick, we treat each other differently than we would like to be treated ourselves. We have, at least in this area, overcome the Golden Rule.

In interethnic communication, an empathy strategy might solve many misunderstandings that derive exclusively from a misplaced assumption of similarity. Perhaps addressing these face-to-face misunderstandings will eventually influence the larger social manifestations of the Golden Rule. One such everyday case noted by Thomas Kochman concerns black/white male fighting patterns. He observes that, contrary to some stereotypes, whites usually throw the first punch in schoolyard-type fights between blacks and whites. Apparently, when certain words are used by the black, the white imagines how he himself would feel using those words. He discovers through this sympathy that he would be about ready to strike physically. So, with this assumption of imminent violence, the white strikes first. The black may be surprised at this attack, since he was "just talking"—still a long verbal development away from an actual fight. If both people in this situation empathized rather than sympathized, they might realize that they had different experiences of the same verbal circumstances.[34]

A favorite example of intercultural empathy is the news picture of Henry Kissinger, then U.S. secretary of state, holding hands side by side with the then-president of Egypt, Anwar Sadat. Kissinger was obviously behaving in a way appropriate to Sadat's experience of male hand holding, rather than reacting to what probably is his own, culturally conditioned experience of that event.

In the above cases, empathy describes a shift in perspective away from our own to an acknowledgment of the other person's different experience. This shift in perspective is often accompanied by a willingness to participate in the other person's experience, at least to the extent of behaving in ways appropriate to that experience. And, in all cases, the empathic strategy is the opposite of that called for by the Golden Rule. If people really are different, and if we want to understand, respect, and enjoy those differences, then clearly we must begin by overcoming the Golden Rule.

Developing Empathy

So pervasive is the Golden Rule that only a concerted effort can topple its influence on our communication. The following model for the development of empathy represents a coordinated attack on the assumption of similarity and a procedure for replacing sympathy with empathy. The six steps of this procedure are a guide to the sequential development of empathic skills. The order in which the steps are undertaken is important. Each step is a necessary condition to the next; there are possible pitfalls of neglecting the prior step or of failing to move on properly. Taken completely and in order, however, this procedure reflects a workable approach to understanding difference.

Step One: Assuming Difference

This assumption is the one that has already been discussed—the assumption of difference and its attendant theory of multiple-reality. When this assumption is lacking, there simply is no motivation to empathize. As we have seen, sympathy serves the similarity and one-reality assumptions very well. Without the assumption of difference, empathy is considered unnecessary, and it may even be disvalued as "insincere." In these cases, it appears that "sincerity" is defined as "being true to yourself." This stance precludes imagining being different from our usual selves—a necessary condition for empathy to occur.

The imagination of the self as potentially alien is one of the most difficult aspects of multiple-reality thinking. But this approach is necessary to bridge the otherwise impossible separation of individuals implied by the assumption of difference. If we accept that we might be different, given different constructions and circumstances, then we are free to imagine our thoughts and feelings from that different perspective. Insofar as we can then align the imagined self-perspective with that of an actual other person, we are able to empathize.

Step Two: Knowing Self

Many of us, although eager to develop empathy, are afraid of "losing ourselves." This is, indeed, a danger in empathy if we are not properly prepared. The preparation called for is to know ourselves sufficiently well so that an easy reestablishment of individual identity is possible. If we are aware of our own cultural and individual values, assumptions, and beliefs—that is, how we define our identities—then we need not fear losing those selves. We cannot lose something that can be re-created at will. The prerequisite of self-knowledge does not eliminate the possibility of change in ourselves as a result of empathizing. It merely makes such change a chosen option rather than an uncontrollable loss.

This step may also be applied effectively to "natural empathizers" who sometimes report being uncomfortable with their inability to *not* empathize. These people are sometimes assailed by the unsought experience of feelings apparently belonging to other people. A common example of this kind of natural empathy is the experience of extreme nervousness when confronted by a nervous person. Natural empathizers cannot help "picking up" the emotional states of others in their vicinity. The key to avoiding this uncontrolled empathy is self-knowledge, because it allows us to restrict our experience to a well-defined self when necessary.

An emphasis on self-knowledge should not, however, degenerate into self-celebration. The elevation of self to reverential status is not only humorless, it also impedes the suspension of self necessary for the next step.

Step Three: Suspending Self

In this step, the identity that was clarified in Step Two is temporarily set aside. This is, of course, easier said than done. One way of thinking about this procedure is to imagine that the self, or identity, is an arbitrary boundary that we draw between ourselves and the rest of the world, including other people. The suspension of self is the temporary expansion of this boundary—the elimination of separation between self and environment.

It is possible here to see the necessary sequence of the steps. Suspension of the self-boundary is facilitated by knowing where the boundary is (self-knowledge), but *only* if one first has a self-referenced assumption of multiple-reality (assuming difference). If, for instance, the multiple-reality assumption is missing, then self-knowledge tends to impede suspension of boundaries, becoming instead egocentrism.

The focus of this step is not on suspending the "content" of identity (assumptions, values, behavior sets, and so on). Rather, it is on the ability to modify and expand boundaries. The emphasis on content in Step Two was merely a device to clarify the boundary. Once clarified, suspension of self is a matter of expanding that boundary so as to "lose" the self defined by it.

Step Four: Allowing Guided Imagination

When the self-boundary is extended, the normal distinction between internal and external (subjective and objective) is obliterated. Our awareness is free to wander among "outside" phenomena, including other people, much as we normally wander within our "inside" experience. In the extended state, we can move our attention *into* the experience of normally external events rather than turning our attention *onto* those events, as we usually do. This shifting of awareness into phenomena not normally associated with self can be called "imagination."

For accurate interpersonal empathy to occur, we must allow our imagination to be guided into the experience of a specific other person. If we try to actively guide imagination, the process becomes more like thinking. Thinking is a self-activity, and thus it is inappropriate at this stage of empathy, where self is suspended. If we are successful in *allowing* our imagination to be captured by the other person, we are in the position to imaginatively participate in that person's experience. The feeling of this shift in awareness is very similar to the imaginative participation in a play or a novel.[35] It is the same kind of surrender to the drama before us—in this case, the human drama represented by the other person.

Another parallel to guided imagination is the operation of intuition in creative problem solving. Allowing intuition specific to a problem is a very similar process to that of allowing imagination specific to another person. In both cases, we are often struck with a sudden "sense of the whole," as if we were first outside the problem or person and then suddenly inside, looking out.

Step Five: Allowing Empathic Experience

When we have allowed our imagination to be guided inside the other person, we are in the position to experience that person as if that person were ourselves. While this experience is imaginative, its intensity and "reality" are not necessarily less than that of our own normal experience. The intensity of empathic experience may even be greater, in a parallel to the sometimes larger-than-life intensity of drama.

The feeling of empathic experience is both familiar and alien. It is as if we were doing a normal activity like washing dishes, only on another planet. The familiar activity is that of experiencing, which we do constantly. The unfamiliar aspect is that the experience itself is not our own. We perceive a different set of feelings and thoughts about the world—a different construing—which seems to describe a place we have never seen. And indeed, this is true. With empathy, and only with empathy, we are privileged to live briefly in the least accessible land of all—another person's experience.

Step Six: Reestablishing Self

Although finding our way into other people's experience is important, it is equally necessary to remember the way back to our selves. In this culture, at least, the reestablishment of self is a necessary component of empathic communication. The failure to do so eventuates in a diffusion of identity, or ego-loss, that is not appropriate for much of our everyday interaction. The purpose of empathy is not life everlasting as one with the universe. Rather, interpersonal empathy allows the controlled and temporary suspension of identity for a particular purpose—the understanding of another person. When this purpose is achieved, the boundaries of self are best reinstituted. One exception to this, however, might be the maintenance of an intimate relationship in which we have committed to "being one with" another person.

Identity is reestablished by first re-creating the sense of separateness between self and other that is the normal state in this culture. When this separation is regained, the content of our own worldview automatically reemerges, and a determination of which thoughts and feelings belong to whom can be made. It may even be useful to contrast our sympathetic reaction to the other person with our empathic understanding. From this contrast can emerge a clear recognition of the difference between ourselves and the other—a recognition that reinforces the necessity for empathy.

Toward the Platinum Rule

Although empathy can be used in any communication situation, we have been concerned in this article with its utility to the understanding of difference. As suggested by the ethnocentric connotations of sympathy mentioned earlier, the use of empathy might serve to create a more sensitive and respectful climate for interracial and intercultural communication.

Approaching people as if they are different from us allows us to generate an addition to the Golden Rule. It is the Platinum

Rule, which could state, "Do unto others as they themselves would have done unto them." Through empathy, we at least can be aware of how others would like to be treated from their own perspectives. We may not want or be able to provide that treatment, but the very act of acknowledging the difference and attempting empathy is profoundly respectful and affirming of others. Of course, it is that respect for the equal (but different) humanity of others that was probably the original intent of the Golden Rule.

---

[1] Bertrand Russell, *Human Knowledge, Its Scope and Limits* (New York: Simon & Schuster, 1948).

[2] Israel Zangwill, *The Melting Pot: Drama in Four Acts* (New York: Macmillan, 1921), 33.

[3] Brewton Berry, *Race and Ethnic Relations* (Boston: Houghton Mifflin, 1965).

[4] Richard E. Porter and Larry A. Samovar, "Communicating Interculturally," in *Intercultural Communication: A Reader*, 2d ed., edited by Larry A. Samovar and Richard E. Porter (Belmont, CA: Wadsworth, 1976), 10.

[5] Jon A. Blubaugh and Dorothy L. Pennington, *Crossing Differences...Interracial Communication* (Columbus, OH: Merrill, 1976), 92.

[6] Paul Watzlawick, Janet H. Beavin, and Don D. Jackson, *Pragmatics of Human Communication* (New York: Norton, 1967), 213.

[7] Milton J. Bennett, "Empathic Perception: The Operation of Self-Awareness in Human Perception" (master's thesis, San Francisco State University, 1972), 66.

[8] Lauren G. Wispé, "Sympathy and Empathy," in *International Encyclopedia of the Social Sciences*, vol. 15, edited by David L. Sills (New York: Macmillan, 1968), 441-47.

[9] Charles Hampden-Turner, *Sane Asylum* (San Francisco: San Francisco Book Company, 1976).

[10] Donn Byrne, "Interpersonal Attraction and Attitude Similarity," *Journal of Abnormal and Social Psychology* (May 1961): 62.

[11] Dean Barnlund, "Communication: The Context of Change," in *Perspectives on Communication*, edited by Carl E. Larson and Frank E. X. Dance (Madison, WI: Helix Press, 1968), 24-40.

[12] Public Broadcasing System, "The Mind of Man," from the series *Realities* (16 November 1970).

[13] Elmer E. Green, Alyce M. Green, and E. Dale Waters, "Voluntary Control of Internal States: Psychological and Physiological," *Journal of Transpersonal Psychology*, no. 1 (1970).

[14] Michael Hendrickson, personal interview, Department of Pathology, Stanford Medical School, Palo Alto, CA (1978).

[15] George A. Kelly, *A Theory of Personality: The Psychology of Personal Constructs* (New York: Norton, 1963), 46.

[16] Ibid., 50.

[17] Ibid., 55.

[18] Ibid., 73.

[19] Ibid., 90.

[20] Ibid., 93.

21 Stephen W. Littlejohn, *Theories of Human Communication* (Columbus, OH: Merrill, 1978).

22 Kelly, *Theory of Personality*, 91.

23 Gregory Bateson, *Steps to an Ecology of Mind* (New York: Ballantine Books, 1972).

24 Paul Watzlawick, *How Real Is Real?* (New York: Random House, 1976).

25 Ronald David Laing, *The Politics of Experience* (New York: Ballantine Books, 1966), 55.

26 Milton J. Bennett, "Forming/Feeling Process: Communication of Boundaries and Perception of Patterns" (Ph.D. diss., University of Minnesota, 1977).

27 Jan B. Deregowski, "Difficulties in Pictorial Depth Perception in Africa," *The British Journal of Psychology*, no. 59 (August 1968):195-204.

28 Watzlawick et al., *Pragmatics of Human Communication*.

29 Sigmund Freud, *Group Psychology and the Analysis of the Ego,* translated by James Strachey (London: International Psychoanalytical Press, 1921).

30 Ezra Stotland, Kenneth E. Mathews Jr., Stanley E. Sherman, Robert O. Hansson, and Barbara Z. Richardson, *Empathy, Fantasy and Helping.* (London: Sage Publications, 1978),12.

31 Bennett, *Empathic Perception*.

32 Carl R. Rogers, *On Becoming a Person* (Boston: Houghton Mifflin, 1961); Carl R. Rogers, "The Interpersonal Relationship: The Core of Guidance," *Harvard Educational Review* (1962): 32.

33 Robert L. Katz, *Empathy, Its Nature and Uses* (London: Free Press of Glencoe, 1963).

34 Thomas Kochman, "Cognitive Orientations, Communicative Styles and Cultural Meaning," paper presented at the annual meeting of the Society for Intercultural Education, Training and Research, Montebello, Quebec, 1976.

35 Bennett, *Empathic Perception*.

Transition Shock:
Putting Culture Shock
in Perspective

Janet M. Bennett

One of the difficulties in considering culture shock is the tendency to treat it as an exotic ailment with origins rooted in far-away places. In fact, culture shock bears a remarkable resemblance to the tensions and anxieties we face whenever change threatens the stability of our lives. Alvin Toffler has described the phenomenon of disruptive change within a culture as "future shock."[1] Gail Sheehy has focused on the painful crises in individual life cycles, what we might term "passage shock."[2] These and other forms of "shock" (including culture shock) might be subsumed under the general category *transition shock*. This article will relate various concepts of culture shock to the general category of transition shock and will suggest how this frame of reference is useful in understanding the causes, effects, and coping mechanisms of culture shock.

The expression *culture shock* was popularized by Kalvero Oberg to refer to the "anxiety that results from losing all of our familiar signs and symbols of social intercourse."[3] Edward T. Hall suggested the added dimension of replacement of familiar cues with new, strange elements.[4] According to Peter S. Adler, "Culture shock is primarily a set of emotional reactions to the loss of perceptual reinforcements from one's own culture, to new cultural stimuli which have little or no meaning, and to the misunderstanding of new and diverse experiences."[5] LaRay M. Barna broadens the concept to include physiological aspects. She defines culture shock as "the emotional and physiological reaction of high activation that is brought about by sudden immersion in a new and different culture."[6]

I would like to go one step further and suggest that culture shock is in itself only a subcategory of transition experiences. All such experiences involve loss and change: the loss of a partner in death or divorce; change of lifestyle related to "passages"; loss of a familiar frame of reference in an intercultural encounter; or reshaping of values associated with rapid social innovation. The reaction to loss and change is frequently "shocking" in terms of grief, disorientation, and the necessity for adjustment. According to Peter Marris,

> a similar process of adjustment should work itself out whenever the familiar pattern of life has been disrupted. For once the predictability of events has been invalidated—whether from the collapse of the internal structure of purpose or of our ability to comprehend the environment—life will be unmanageable until the continuity of meaning can be restored, through a process of abstraction and redefinition.... Even changes which we scarcely think to involve loss may be analyzable in similar terms.[7]

Our adaptive processes fail to meet the needs of the moment, and we find ourselves overwhelmed by the stimuli we are forced to assimilate. Therefore, if transition shock is a state of loss and disorientation precipitated by a change in one's familiar environment that requires adjustment, then culture shock may be characterized as transition shock in the context of an alien cultural frame of reference. This experience may be linked to visiting another country, or it can occur within a subculture of one's home country.

The important factor is that culture shock, as a subcategory of transition experiences, is more recognizable, more understandable, even more tolerable, when viewed in the light of previous life experiences. We each have had some experience with the elements of culture shock. Perhaps we have not experienced all the elements, or possibly not in exactly the same form, but the similarities may provide us with confidence that we are not entirely without resources. We have all experienced life change before, if only in the form of change of residence, marriage, divorce, new employment, and so on. The mere idea that culture shock is not an alien feeling can give us the confidence that we have the ability to adapt to it comfortably.

Symptoms

Transition shock, though quite common, appears to elicit different responses from different people in different places at different times. The symptoms vary from case to case, as the virtual infinity of variables interacts to create an individualized impact. Time and space, place and person each create a unique chemistry and a personalized reaction. Some of the symptoms suggested by various authors (Kalvero Oberg,[8] Robert J. Foster,[9] Peter S. Adler[10]) include: excessive concern over cleanliness and health; feelings of helplessness and withdrawal; irritability; fear of being cheated, robbed, or injured; a glazed stare; desire for home and old friends; and physiological stress reactions. We are essentially in a state of frustration, anxiety, and paranoia induced by the unfamiliar environment in which we find ourselves. Marris neatly describes this state of ambiguity inherent in transition experiences

> as the need to reestablish continuity, to work out an interpretation of oneself and the world which preserves, despite estrangement, the thread of meaning; the ambivalence of this task as it swings between conflicting impulses; the need to articulate the stages of its resolution; and the risk of lasting disintegration if the process is not worked out.[11]

Transition shock often leads to communication problems as well. When we are anxious, lonely, and disoriented, our communication skills degenerate. Isolation and tension are exacerbated, producing barriers and defensive communication. In the intercultural context, disorientation is particularly lethal, for it only serves to further isolate us from our environment. We block out the new forms and styles of communication available to us in order to preserve the old. Culture shock is thus a major obstruction in intercultural communication.

Responses

Frequently, as a reaction to such change, culture shock takes the form of psychic withdrawal. One of the nearly universal aspects of transition experiences is *cognitive inconsistency*: what was once a coherent, internally consistent set of beliefs and values is suddenly overturned by exterior change. One of those values, self-preservation (or psychological stability), is called into serious question unless an alteration is made in our entire value system. Transition shock—and culture shock—may be viewed as defense mechanisms in reaction to cognitive inconsistency. If, as Dean Barnlund suggests, people become defensive when they perceive a threat to their worldview, then what greater situation of threat exists than immersion in an alien culture?[12] Barnlund describes the increasing level of stress which results as the threat to worldview increases: "As the perceived threat increases, they narrow their vision, resist certain kinds of information, distort details to fit their own biases, even manufacture evidence to bolster their preconceptions. The old, whether appropriate or not, is favored over the new. Anxiety is aroused when [people]...confront perceptions that are beyond [their] capacity to assimilate."[13]

This threat may be perceived as a case of cognitive inconsistency. We arrive overseas with a well-established hierarchy of assumptions, values, and beliefs. The chances are excellent that we will be in an environment where things may look familiar, but they don't operate in familiar ways. Indeed, perhaps nothing will even look familiar! In either case, worldview, including our view of ourselves, is assailed by verbal, nonverbal, physical, and psychological stimuli. If we cling to our own worldview, we may experience an untenable state of cognitive inconsistency: "Either they're crazy, or I am!" At the same time, we value our old belief system as well as adaptation to the new; we seek a way to survive within our former worldview yet recognize the necessity for a new perspective. Often two very contradictory systems vie for equal time. All we have held sacred is reflected in a distorting mirror, and the image flashed back throws us off balance, a sort of cultural fun house where previous orientations contribute little or nothing to the survival of the psyche.

We all depend to a certain extent on the norms of our environment, norms which we have cultivated carefully in our socialization process. In another culture that careful cultivation goes to seed and the neat systems of categories with which we have arranged our lives go askew. Dissonance is exacerbated by the loss of familiar cues and distortion of seemingly familiar responses. Previously high expectations of exotic overseas life have gradually been crushed, causing us to question the wisdom of our decision to embark on this adventure. In short, all that we once held as true is called into question, and daily life becomes an endless attempt to achieve balance in this incongruous world. Our first reaction is to fight for the survival of our worldview and to rescue it by reaching for our defenses. But the only defenses we have are those from our own culture, defenses which are rarely helpful in the new culture. Our sense of alienation increases as our defense mechanisms drive us further from understanding the culture. The old frame of reference doesn't help in the least, but it's all we have, so we protect it furiously. Perhaps in doing so, we prolong culture shock and delay the acquisition of a new frame of reference.

It is important to note here that it is not merely the loss of the frame of reference that causes culture shock, but the defensiveness that such a loss engenders. Not knowing what to do is difficult enough, but, not being *able* to do what one has come to value doing is even more challenging. Recognition of the inappropriateness of our responses arouses tremendous inconsistency; we choose to deal with this dissonance by defending our familiar worldview, and we find ourselves deep in the throes of culture shock.

Stages

If we can overcome the tremendous desire to flee this discomfort, we may recognize several stages which may be familiar from other transition experiences that we have survived. A number of authors deal with various phases in transition shock; here we will employ the U.S. Navy's presentation of Clyde Sergeant's model, which suggests four phases of the psychological aspects of environmental adjustment: fight, flight, filter, and flex.[14] During an exploratory phase in which the initial impact of immersing ourselves in another culture occurs, we recognize that our worldview is dissonant in a new culture. We proceed from early enthusiasm and high expectations to a *fight* stance, where self-protective mechanisms are engaged. Moving from the exploratory to the crisis phase, we become discouraged, bewildered, withdrawn, and may choose *flight* as the most effective defense mechanism available. During the recovery and adjustment phase, we resolve our incongruous perspectives, lower our defenses, and absorb new stimuli (*filter*). Finally, we reach the accommodation phase, where we give up defending our worldview and *flex* in our perspective on the new environment.

This particular flex does not imply a surrender of worldview; rather, it suggests a variety of adaptations which may be employed to reduce dissonance in the new culture. Taft's research in this area identifies three varieties of adaptation, as discussed by Juris Draguns.[15] The *monistic* adaptation will lead us to either "go native" and submerge ourselves in the host culture or cause us to retreat to the safety of people from our own country who are in residence. If we choose the *pluralistic* adaptation, we will both maintain our own culture and assimilate the host culture, becoming bicultural. Using the *interactionist* adaptation, we choose portions of both cultures and become a mixture of each.

Resolutions

The flex response is based on several personality characteristics that aid us in resolving conflicts more quickly and comfortably in our new environment. These characteristics include self-awareness, nonevaluativeness, cognitive complexity, and cultural empathy. During any transition experience, the quandary is frequently "Who am I?" The loss of continuity in one's purpose and direction must be reestablished to overcome the resulting sense of alienation. The individual who is most likely to master this situation is the one who has a firm sense of self-identity. Draguns notes, "To the degree that one's identity is crystallized and independent, many jolts from the encounters with a new, confusing social reality can be absorbed."[16]

In the culture shock experience, we must be very attuned to our own cultural values and beliefs so that the contrast culture is more understandable. If we recognize our own assumptions, then the elements of the new environment stand out in clear relief for us to examine. As Barna suggests, "[If you] become secure in your own identity...there is little chance for serious loss of self-esteem and more freedom for open investigation."[17]

However, I would suggest that a strong sense of identity can also be a hindrance, especially if we are inflexible and become threatened too quickly by conflicting stimuli. Awareness of our own culture needs to be complemented by a nonjudgmental stance in which we can easily separate what we see from our interpretation and evaluation of that event. If we enter each interaction in the host culture with evaluation as our first choice of communicative style, our culture shock will be maximal. Among the first skills we need to develop are the abilities to withhold evaluation, to refrain from cultural absolutism, and to accept rather than reject. As Conrad Arensberg and Arthur H. Niehoff describe,

> The newcomer purposefully pushes ahead and bends all efforts to understand the other system.

The new ways will become familiar and even comfortable only by coming back to them again and
again, seeking understanding without applying the
values of one's own culture.[18]

This nonevaluative characteristic is a prerequisite for the development of cultural empathy. *Empathy* may be defined as "the
use of imagination to intellectually and emotionally participate
in an alien experience."[19] Often people discuss empathy in terms
of "putting yourself in the other person's shoes." But such a simple
shift in position without an equal shift in personal perspective
merely elicits a sympathetic response. From such a view, we know
how we would feel in the situation, but not how the other person
feels. To achieve an empathic response, we must not only step
into the other person's shoes, but we must imaginatively participate in the other's worldview. We must not only shift our *position*
but also our *perspective* on the event. This is an essential difference in the cultural context, for very rarely do sympathetic responses prove insightful across cultural boundaries. We need to
briefly suspend our worldview and to participate as deeply as we
can in the view of the other culture. According to a study at the
University of Alberta, the "culturally insensitive individual, contrary to a pervasive myth, was revealed as the individual who
believed that 'people are about the same everywhere'." This sympathetic response is inadequate to bridge the culture gap, and
the study concluded that "culturally sensitive workers were those
who evidence cultural empathy."[20] As cultural empathy aids communication in intercultural transitions, empathy in general should
facilitate adaptation to all transition experiences.

The final personal correlate of successful adaptation to another culture may well be *cultural complexity*, which is defined by
Draguns as "the number of descriptive and explanatory notions
at one's disposal for the ability to make sense of and to integrate
into a preexisting cognitive structure, discrepant, incongruous
and surprising bits of information."[21] He suggests that those who
thrive on complexity and ambiguity are more likely to deal with
the confusion of the transition experience comfortably. Exposure
to a variety of cultures and worldviews helps us to tolerate differences more easily. We find the new culture stimulating and
challenging rather than threatening and anxiety producing.

Potentials

The potential for stimulation and challenge is as much a part of
culture shock and transition shock as is the potential for discom-

fort and disorientation. As Marris suggests, "Change appears as fulfillment or as loss to different people, and to the same person at different times."[22] Culture shock need not be viewed as a disease; depending on the way we direct our change processes it may yield considerable growth. While few writers deal with culture shock in terms of personal growth, Adler attempts to offer that perspective. He writes that the

> cross-cultural learning experience...is a set of intensive and evocative situations in which the individual experiences himself and other people in a new way distinct from previous situations and is consequently forced into new levels of consciousness and understanding.[23]

Just as other life-change experiences often force us to examine our identities and adaptability, culture shock can also be perceived as a highly provocative state in which we may direct our energies toward personal development. We are forced into greater self-awareness by the need for introspection. We must reexamine our ability to form relationships and our communicative skills. We are also placed in the position of trying new norms and values and of experimenting with new behaviors. During transition experiences, our analytic processes are often in high gear, drawing on an unlimited wealth of diversity for comparison and contrast.

While I have suggested earlier that self-awareness and cultural empathy are significant personal characteristics in the adaptation process, it should also be noted that those characteristics may very well be *developed* during the cross-cultural learning process. Perhaps the greatest degree of shock in the cultural transition experience can be related to the recognition of our own values and beliefs in the light of the new environment.

Summary

It is evident that the culture shock experience is not necessarily an alien one. We may have had similar transition experiences in our lives before exposure to another culture, in any number of intracultural situations. If we recognize transition shock as a defensive response to the dissonance we feel when our worldview is assaulted, we can learn to cope with the symptoms and develop methods of channeling shock—including culture shock—into personal growth. With knowledge gained from those previous transitions, plus the personal characteristics of self-awareness, nonevaluativeness, cultural empathy, and cultural complexity, we can transform our defensiveness into stimulating cross-cultural learning. How we deal with change affects our communication patterns. Perceived as disorientation, change may produce barriers and defensive communication. Perceived as challenge, change can stimulate creativity and flexible communication.

---

[1] Alvin Toffler, *Future Shock* (New York: Bantam, 1970).

[2] Gail Sheehy, *Passages: Predictable Crises of Adult Life* (New York: E. P. Dutton, 1976).

[3] Kalvero Oberg, "Cultural Shock: Adjustment to New Cultural Environments," *Practical Anthropology* 7 (1960): 177.

[4] Edward T. Hall, *The Silent Language* (1959; reprint, New York: Anchor/Doubleday, 1981), 174.

[5] Peter S. Adler, "The Transitional Experience: An Alternative View of Culture Shock," *Journal of Humanistic Psychology* 15, no. 4 (Fall 1975): 13.

[6] LaRay M. Barna, "How Culture Shock Affects Communication," *Communication—Journal of the Communication Association of the Pacific* 4, no. 3 (1976): 3.

[7] Peter Marris, *Loss and Change* (New York: Anchor/Doubleday, 1975), 45.

[8] Oberg, "Cultural Shock."

[9] Robert J. Foster, *Examples of Cross-Cultural Problems Encountered by Americans Working Overseas* (Alexandria, VA: Human Resources Research Office, May 1965).

[10] Adler, "Transitional Experience."

[11] Marris, *Loss and Change,* 46.

[12] Dean Barnlund, "Communication: The Context of Change," in *Basic Readings in Communication Theory,* edited by C. David Mortenson (New York: Harper and Row, 1973), 5-27.

[13] Ibid., 15.

[14] *U.S. Navy Overseas Diplomacy Guidelines for I.C.R. Specialists* (Washington, DC: Bureau of Naval Personnel, 1973), 42-45.

[15] Juris Draguns, "On Culture Shock, Biculturality and Cultural Complexity," paper presented at the Symposium on Culture Shock as a Social and Clinical Problem, American Psychological Association, Washington, DC, 1976, 5.

[16] Ibid., 5.

[17] Barna, "How Culture Shock Affects Communication," 16.

[18] Conrad Arensberg and Arthur H. Niehoff, *Introducing Social Change: A Manual for Community Development* (Chicago: Aldine, 1971), 237.

[19] Milton J. Bennett, "Overcoming the Golden Rule: Sympathy and Empathy," this volume.

[20] John Regan, *Culture Shock: An Exploration in Observation,* University of Alberta, Phi Delta Kappa, 1966.

[21] Draguns, "On Culture Shock," 4.

[22] Marris, *Loss and Change,* 46.

[23] Adler, "Transitional Experience."

Beyond Cultural Identity: Reflections on Multiculturalism

Peter S. Adler

Introduction

Multiculturalism[1] is an attractive and persuasive notion. It suggests a human being whose identifications and loyalties transcend the boundaries of nationalism and whose commitments are pinned to a larger vision of the global community. To be a citizen of the world, an international person, has long been an ideal toward which many strive. Unfortunately, history is also rich with examples of totalitarian societies and individuals who took it upon themselves to shape everyone else to the mold of their planetary vision. Repulsive as it was, Hitler had a vision of a world society.

Less common are examples of men and women who have striven to sustain a self-process that is inclusively international in attitude and behavior. For good reason. Nation, culture, and society exert tremendous influence on each of our lives, structuring our values, engineering our view of the world, and patterning our responses to experience. Human beings cannot hold themselves apart from some form of cultural influence. No one is culture free. Yet, the conditions of contemporary history are such that we may now be on the threshold of a new kind of person, a person who is socially and psychologically a product of the interweaving of cultures in the twentieth century.

We are reminded daily of this phenomenon. In the corner of a traditional Japanese home sits a television set tuned to a baseball game in which the visitors, an American team, are losing. A Canadian family, meanwhile, decorates their home with sculptures and paintings imported from Pakistan, India, and Ceylon. Teenagers in Singapore and Hong Kong pay unheard-of prices for used American blue jeans while high school students in England and France take courses on the making of traditional Indonesian batik. A team of Malaysian physicians inoculates a remote village against typhus while their Western counterparts study Ayurvedic medicine and acupuncture. Around the planet the streams of the world's cultures merge together to form new currents of human interaction. Though superficial and only a manifestation of the shrinking of the globe, each such vignette is a symbol of the mingling and melding of human cultures. Communication and cultural exchange are the preeminent conditions of the twentieth century.

For the first time in the history of the world, a patchwork of technology and organization has made possible simultaneous interpersonal and intercultural communication. Innovations and refinements of innovations, including modems, electronic mail, facsimile machines, digital recording, cable television, satellite dishes, and desktop publishing have brought people everywhere into potential contact. Barely a city or village exists that is more than a day or two from anyplace else; almost no town or community is without a television. Bus lines, railroads, highways, and airports have created linkages within and between local, regional, national, and international levels of human organization.

The impact is enormous. Human connections through communication have made possible the interchange of goods, products, and services as well as the more significant exchange of thoughts and ideas. Accompanying the growth of human communication has been the erosion of barriers that have, throughout history, geographically, linguistically, and culturally separated people. As Harold Lasswell once suggested, "The technological revolution as it affects mass media has reached a limit that is subject only to innovations that would substantially modify our basic perspectives of one another and of man's place in the cosmos."[2] It is possible that the emergence of the multicultural person is just such an innovation.

A New Kind of Person

A new type of person whose orientation and view of the world profoundly transcends his or her indigenous culture is developing from the complex of social, political, economic, and educational interactions of our time. The various conceptions of an "international," "transcultural," "multicultural," or "intercultural" individual have each been used with varying degrees of explanatory or descriptive utility. Essentially, they all attempt to define someone whose horizons extend significantly beyond his or her own culture. An "internationalist," for example, has been defined as a person who trusts other nations, is willing to cooperate with other countries, perceives international agencies as potential deterrents to war, and who considers international tensions reducible by mediation.[3] Others have studied the international orientation of groups by measuring their attitudes toward international issues, that is, the role of the United Nations, economic versus military aid, international alliances, and so on.[4] And at least several attempts have been made to measure the world-mindedness of individuals by exploring the degree to which persons have a broad international frame of reference rather than specific knowledge or interest in some narrower aspect of global affairs.[5]

Whatever the terminology, the definitions and metaphors allude to a person whose essential identity is inclusive of different life patterns and who has psychologically and socially come to grips with a multiplicity of realities. We can call this new type of person multicultural because he or she embodies a core process of self-verification that is grounded in both the universality of the human condition and the diversity of cultural forms. We are speaking, then, of a social-psychological style of self-process that differs from others. The multicultural person is intellectually and emotionally committed to the basic unity of all human beings while at the same time recognizing, legitimizing, accepting, and appreciating the differences that exist between people of different cultures. This new kind of person cannot be defined by the languages he or she speaks, the number of countries visited, or the number of personal international contacts made. Nor is he or she defined by profession, place of residence, or cognitive sophistication. Instead, the multicultural person is recognized by a configuration of outlooks and worldview, by how the universe as a dynamically moving process is incorporated, by the way the interconnectedness of life is reflected in thought and action, and by the way this woman or man remains open to the imminence of experience.

The multicultural person is, at once, both old and new. On the one hand, this involves being the timeless "universal" person described again and again by philosophers through the ages. He or she approaches, at least in the attributions we make, the classical ideal of a person whose lifestyle is one of knowledge and wisdom, integrity and direction, principle and fulfillment, balance and proportion. "To be a universal man," wrote John Walsh, using *man* in the traditional sense of including men and women, "means not how much a man knows but what intellectual depth and breadth he has and how he relates it to other central and universally important problems."[6] What is universal about the multicultural person is an abiding commitment to the essential similarities among people everywhere, while paradoxically maintaining an equally strong commitment to differences. The universal person, suggests Walsh, "does not at all eliminate culture differences." Rather, he or she "seeks to preserve whatever is most valid, significant, and valuable in each culture as a way of enriching and helping to form the whole."[7] In this embodiment of the universal and the particular, the multicultural person is a descendant of the great philosophers of both the East and the West.

On the other hand, what is new about this type of person, and unique to our time, is a fundamental change in the structure and process of identity. The identity of the multicultural person, far from being frozen in a social character, is more fluid and mobile, more susceptible to change, more open to variation. It is an identity based not on a "belongingness," which implies either owning or being owned by culture, but on a style of self-consciousness that is capable of negotiating ever new formations of reality. In this sense the multicultural person is a radical departure from the kinds of identities found in both traditional and mass societies. He or she is neither totally a part of nor totally apart from his or her culture; instead, he or she lives on the boundary. To live on the edge of one's thinking, one's culture, or one's ego, suggested Paul Tillich, is to live with tension and movement: "It is in truth not standing still, but rather a crossing and return, a repetition of return and crossing, back and forth—the aim of which is to create a third area beyond the bounded territories, an area where one can stand for a time without being enclosed in something tightly bounded."[8] Multiculturalism, then, is an outgrowth of the complexities of the twentieth century. As unique as this kind of person may be, the style of identity that is embodied arises from the myriad of forms that are present in this day and age. An understanding of this new kind of person must be predicated on a clear understanding of cultural identity.

The Concept of Cultural Identity:
A Psychocultural Framework

The concept of cultural identity can be used in two different ways. First, it can be employed as a reference to the collective self-awareness that a given group embodies and reflects. This is the most prevalent use of the term. "Generally," writes Stephen Bochner, "the cultural identity of a society is defined by its majority group, and this group is usually quite distinguishable from the minority subgroups with whom they share the physical environment and the territory that they inhabit."[9] With the emphasis upon the group, the concept is akin to the idea of a national or social character which describes a set of traits that members of a given community share with one another above and beyond their individual differences. Such traits almost always include a constellation of values and attitudes toward life, death, birth, family, children, god, and nature. Used in its collective sense, the concept of cultural identity includes typologies of cultural behavior, such behaviors being the appropriate and inappropriate ways of meeting basic needs and solving life's essential dilemmas. Used in its collective sense, the concept of cultural identity incorporates the shared premises, values, definitions, beliefs, and the day-to-day, largely unconscious patterning of activities.

A second, more specific use of the concept revolves around the identity of the individual in relation to his or her culture. Cultural identity, in the sense that it is a functioning aspect of individual personality, is a fundamental symbol of a person's existence. It is in reference to the individual that the concept is used in this article. In psychoanalytic literature, most notably in the writing of Erik Erikson, identity is an elemental form of psychic organization which develops in successive psychosexual phases throughout life. Erikson, who focused the greater portion of his analytic studies on identity conflicts, recognized the anchoring of the ego in a larger cultural context. Identity, he suggested, takes a variety of forms in the individual. "At one time," he wrote, "it will appear to refer to a conscious sense of individual identity; at another to an unconscious striving for a continuity of personal character; at a third, as a criterion for the silent doings of ego synthesis; and, finally, as a maintenance of an inner solidarity with a group's ideals and identity."[10] The analytic perspective, as voiced by Erikson, is only one of a variety of definitions. Almost always, however, the concept of identity is meant to imply a coherent sense of self that depends on a stability of values and a sense of wholeness and integration.

How, then, can we conceptualize the interplay of culture and personality? Culture and personality are inextricably woven together in the gestalt of each person's identity. Culture, the mass of life patterns that human beings in a given society learn from their elders and pass on to the younger generation, is imprinted in the individual as a pattern of perceptions that is accepted and expected by others in a society.[11] Cultural identity is the symbol of one's essential experience of oneself as it incorporates the worldview, value system, attitudes, and beliefs of a group with which such elements are shared. In its most manifest form, cultural identity takes the shape of names which both locate and differentiate the person. When an individual calls himself or herself an American, a Buddhist, a Democrat, a Dane, a woman, or John Jones, that person is symbolizing parts of the complex of images that are likewise recognizable by others. The deeper structure of cultural identity is a fabric of such images and perceptions embedded in the psychological posture of the individual. At the center of this matrix of images is a psychocultural fusion of biological, social, and philosophical motivations; this fusion, a synthesis of culture and personality, is the operant person.

The center, or core, of cultural identity is an image of the self and the culture intertwined in the individual's total conception of reality. This image, a patchwork of internalized roles, rules, and norms, functions as the coordinating mechanism in personal and interpersonal situations. The "mazeway," as Anthony Wallace called it, is made up of human, nonhuman, material, and abstract elements of the culture. It is the "stuff" of both personality and culture. The mazeway, suggested Wallace, is the patterned image of society and culture, personality and nature—all of which is ingrained in the person's symbolization of self. A system of culture, he writes, "depends relatively more on the ability of constituent units autonomously to perceive the system of which they are a part, to receive and transmit information, and to act in accordance with the necessities of the system...."[12] The image, or mazeway, of cultural identity is the gyroscope of the functioning individual. It mediates, arbitrates, and negotiates the life of the individual. It is within the context of this central, navigating im-

age that the fusion of biological, social, and philosophical realities forms units of integration that are important to a comparative analysis of cultural identity. The way in which these units
are knit together and contoured by the culture at large determines the parameters of the individual. This boundary of cultural identity plays a large part in determining the individual's
ability to relate to other cultural systems.

All human beings share a similar biology, universally limited
by the rhythms of life. All individuals of all races and cultures
must move through life's phases on a similar schedule: birth, infancy, adolescence, middle age, old age, and death. Similarly,
humans everywhere embody the same physiological functions
of ingestion, irritability, metabolic equilibrium, sexuality, growth,
and decay. Yet the ultimate interpretation of human biology is a
cultural phenomenon: that is, the meanings of human biological
patterns are culturally derived. It is culture which dictates the
meanings of sexuality, the ceremonials of birth, the transitions
of life, and the rituals of death. The capacity for language, for
example, is universally accepted as a biological given. Any child,
given unimpaired apparatus for hearing, vocalizing, and thinking, can learn to speak and understand any human language.
Yet the language that is learned by a child depends solely upon
the place and the manner of rearing. Clyde Kluckhohn and
Dorothea Leighton, in outlining the grammatical and phonetic
systems of the Navajo, argued that patterns of language affect
the expression of ideas and very possibly more fundamental processes of thinking.[13] Benjamin Lee Whorf further suggested that
language may not be merely an inventory of linguistic items but
rather "itself the shaper of ideas, the program and guide for the
individual's mental activity."[14]

The interaction of culture and biology provides one corner-
stone for an understanding of cultural identity. How each
individual's biological situation is given meaning becomes a psychobiological unit of integration and analysis. Humanity's essential physiological needs—food, sex, avoidance of pain, and so
on—are one part of the reality pattern of cultural identity. Another part consists of those drives that reach out to the social
order. At this psychosocial level of integration, generic needs are
channeled and organized by culture. The needs for affection,
acceptance, recognition, affiliation, status, belonging, and interaction with other human beings are enlivened and given recognizable form by culture. We can, for example, see clearly the in-
tersection of culture and the psychosocial level of integration in

comparative status responses. In the United States economic status is demonstrated by the conspicuous consumption of products, while among the Kwakiutl, status is gained by giving all
possessions away in the potlatch. In many Asian societies age
confers status, and contempt or disrespect for old people represents a serious breach of conduct demanding face-saving measures.

It is the unwritten task of every culture to organize, integrate,
and maintain the psychosocial patterns of the individual, especially in the formative years of childhood. Each culture engineers
such patterns in ways that are unique, coherent, and logical to
the conditions and predispositions that underlie the culture. This
imprinting of the forms of interconnection that are needed by
the individual for psychosocial survival, acceptance, and enrichment is a significant part of the socialization and enculturation
process. Yet of equal importance in the imprinting is the structuring of higher forms of individual consciousness. Culture gives
meaning and form to those drives and motivations that extend
toward an understanding of the cosmological ordering of the
universe. All cultures, in one manner or another, invoke the great
philosophical questions of life concerning the origin and destiny
of existence, the nature of knowledge, the meaning of reality, the
significance of the human experience. As George Peter Murdock
suggested in "Universals of Culture," some form of cosmology,
ethics, mythology, supernatural propitiation, religious ritual, and
soul concept appears in every culture known to history or ethnography.[15] How an individual raises these questions and
searches for ultimate answers is a function of the
psychophilosophical patterning of cultural identity. Ultimately, it
is the task of every individual to relate to his or her god, to deal
with the supernatural, and to incorporate for himself or herself
the mystery of life. The ways in which individuals do this, the
relationships and connections that are formed, are a function of
the psychophilosophical component of cultural identity.

A conceptualization of cultural identity, then, must include
three interrelated levels of integration and analysis. While the
cultural identity of an individual is comprised of symbols and
images that signify aspects of these levels, the psychobiological,
psychosocial, and psychophilosophical realities of an individual
are knit together by the culture, which operates through sanc-
tions and rewards, totems and taboos, prohibitions and myths.
The unity and integration of society, nature, and the cosmos are
reflected in the total image of the self and in the day-to-day aware-

ness and consciousness of the individual. This synthesis is modulated by the larger dynamics of the culture itself. In the concept of cultural identity we see a synthesis of the operant culture reflected by the deepest images held by the individual. These images, in turn, are based on universal human motivations.

Implicit in any analysis of cultural identity is a configuration of motivational needs. As the late Abraham Maslow suggested, human drives form a hierarchy in which the most prepotent motivations will monopolize consciousness and will tend, of themselves, to organize the various capacities and capabilities of the organism.[16]

In the sequence of development, the needs of infancy and childhood revolve primarily around physiological and biological necessities, that is, nourishment by food, water, and warmth. Correspondingly, psychosocial needs are most profound in adolescence and young adulthood when people engage in establishing themselves through marriage, occupation, and social and economic status. Finally, psychophilosophical drives are most strongly manifest in middle and old age when people are more prepared to occupy themselves with creative pursuits, philosophic self-actualization, and transcendental relationships. As Charles N. Cofer and Mortimer H. Appley rightly pointed out, Maslow's hierarchy of needs is not an explicit, empirical, verifiable theory of human motivation.[17] It is useful, however, in postulating a universally recognized but differently named process of individual motivation that carries the individual through the stages of life. Each level of integration and analysis in cultural identity can thus be viewed as both a part of the gridwork of one's self-image as well as a developmental road map imprinted by one's culture.

The gyroscope of cultural identity functions to orchestrate the allegiances, loyalties, and commitments of the individual by giving him or her direction and meaning. Human beings, however, differentiate themselves to some degree from their culture. Just as no one is totally free of cultural influence, no one is totally a reflection of his or her culture. Cultural identity, therefore, must be viewed as an integrated synthesis of identifications that are idiosyncratic within the parameters of culturally influenced biological, social, and philosophical motivations. Whether, in fact, such unity ever achieves sufficient integration to provide for consistency among individuals within a given culture is an empirical matter that deals with normality and modal personality. The concept of cultural identity can at best be a schema for comparative research between cultures. Although, admittedly, a fundamental rule of social science must be human variation and the unpredictability of models and theories, a schema of cultural identity and the interplay of psychological and cultural dynamics may lay a groundwork for future research and conceptualization. Particularly useful may be the *eiconic* approach proposed by Kenneth Boulding. His typology of images, which includes the spatial, temporal, relational, personal, value, affectional, conscious-unconscious, certainty-uncertainty, reality-unreality, and public-private dimensions, adds important perspectives to the comparative study of cultural identity.[18]

The Multicultural Identity

The rise of the multicultural person is a significant phenomenon and represents a new psychocultural style of self-process. The multicultural person arises amidst the metamorphoses of both traditional and mass societies in a transitional time in which humans are redefining themselves politically, socially, and economically. Multiculturalism offers a potentially different sort of human being. Three characteristics distinguish this style of personality from the traditional structure of cultural identity.

First, the multicultural person is psychoculturally adaptive; that is, he or she is situational in relationships with others. The multicultural person maintains no clear boundaries between self and the varieties of personal and cultural contexts he or she encounters. The multicultural identity is premised not on the hierarchical structuring of a single mental image, but rather on the intentional and accidental shifts that life's experiences involve. Values and attitudes, worldview and beliefs are always in reformation, dependent more on the necessities of experience than on the predispositions of a given culture. For the multicultural individual, attitudes, values, beliefs, and a worldview are relevant only to a given context (as is frequently discovered in the culture shock process) and cannot be translated from context to context. The multicultural person does not judge one situation by the terms of another and is therefore ever evolving new systems of evaluations that are relative to the context and situation.

Second, the multicultural person seems to undergo continual personal transitions. He or she is always in a state of "becoming" or "un-becoming" something different from before while yet mindful of the grounding in his or her primary cultural reality. In other words, the multicultural individual is propelled from identity to identity through a process of both cultural learning and cultural unlearning. The multicultural person, like Robert J. Lifton's concept of "protean man," is always re-creating his or her identity. He or she moves through one experience of self to another, incorporating here, discarding there, responding dynamically and situationally. This style of self-process, suggests Lifton, "is characterized by an interminable series of experiments and explorations, some shallow, some profound, each of which can readily be abandoned in favor of still new, psychological quests."[19] The multicultural person is always in flux, the configuration of loyalties and identifications changing, the overall image of self perpetually being reformulated through experience and contact with the world. Stated differently, life is an ongoing process of psychic death and rebirth.

Third, the multicultural person maintains indefinite boundaries of the self. The parameters of identity are neither fixed nor predictable, being responsive, instead, to both temporary form and openness to change. Multicultural people are capable of major shifts in their frame of reference and embody the ability to disavow a permanent character and to change in sociopsychological style. The multicultural person, in the words of Peter L. Berger, is a "homeless mind," a condition which, though allowing great flexibility, also allows for nothing permanent and unchanging to develop.[20] This homelessness is at the heart of one's motivational needs. The individual is, suggests Lifton, "starved for ideas and feelings that give coherence to his world," that give structure and form to the search for the universal and absolute, that give definition to the perpetual quest.[21] Multicultural persons, like great philosophers in any age, can never accept totally the demands of any one culture, nor are they free from the conditioning of their culture. Their psychocultural style must always be relational and in movement, enabling them to look at their own original culture from an outsider's perspective. This tension gives rise to a dynamic, passionate, and critical posture in the face of totalistic ideologies, systems, and movements.

Like the culture-bound person, the multicultural person bears within him- or herself a simultaneous image of societies, nature, personality, and culture. Yet in contrast to the structure of cultural identity, the multicultural individual is perpetually redefining his or her mazeway. No culture is capable of imprinting or ingraining the identity of a multicultural person indelibly; yet the multicultural person must rely heavily on culture to maintain his or her own relativity. Like human beings in any period of time, he or she is driven by psychobiological, psychosocial, and psychophilosophical motivations; yet the configuration of these drives is perpetually in flux and situational. The maturational hierarchy, implicit in the central image of cultural identity, is less structured and cohesive in the multicultural identity. For that reason, needs, drives, motivations, and expectations are constantly being aligned and realigned to fit the context.

The flexibility of the multicultural personality allows great variation in adaptability and adjustment. Adjustment and adaptation, however, must always be dependent on some constant, on something stable and unchanging in the fabric of life. We can attribute to the multicultural person three fundamental postulates that are incorporated and reflected in thinking and behavior. Such postulates are fundamental to success in cross-cultural adaptation.

1. Every culture or system has its own internal coherence, integrity, and logic. Every culture is an intertwined system of values and attitudes, beliefs and norms that give meaning and significance to both individual and collective identity.

2. No one culture is inherently better or worse than another. All cultural systems are equally valid as variations on the human experience.

3. All persons are, to some extent, culturally bound. Every culture provides the individual with some sense of identity, some regulation of behavior, and some sense of personal place in the scheme of things.

The multicultural person embodies these propositions and lives them on a daily basis and not just in cross-cultural situations. They are fundamentally a part of his or her interior image of the world and self.

What is uniquely new about this emerging human being is a psychocultural style of self-process that transcends the structured image a given culture may impress upon the individual in his or her youth. The navigating image at the core of the multicultural personality is premised on an assumption of many cultural realities. The multicultural person, therefore, is not simply one who is sensitive to many different cultures. Rather, this person is always in the process of becoming a part of and apart from a given cultural context. He or she is a formative being, resilient, changing, and evolutionary. There is no permanent cultural "character," but neither is he or she free from the influences of culture. In the shifts and movements of his or her identity process, the multicultural person is continually re-creating the symbol of self.

The indefinite boundaries and the constantly realigning relationships that are generated by the psychobiological, psychosocial, and psychophilosophical motivations make possible sophisticated and complex responses on the part of the individual to cultural and subcultural systems. Moreover, this psychocultural flexibility necessitates sequential changes in identity. Intentionally or accidentally, multicultural persons undergo shifts in their total psychocultural posture; their religion, personality, behavior, occupation, nationality, outlook, political persuasion, and values may, in part or completely, reformulate in the face of new experience. "It is becoming increasingly possible," wrote Michael Novak, "for men to live through several profound conversions, calling forth in themselves significantly different personalities...."[22] The relationship of multicultural persons to cultural systems is fragile and tenuous. "A man's cultural and social milieu," says Novak, "conditions his personality, values, and actions; yet the same man is able, within limits, to choose the milieus whose conditioning will affect him."[23]

Stresses and Tensions

The unprecedented dynamism of the multicultural person makes it possible to live many different lives, in sequence or simultaneously. But such psychocultural pliability gives rise to tensions and stresses unique to the conditions which allow such dynamism in the first place. The multicultural individual, by virtue of indefinite boundaries, experiences life intensely and in telescoped forms. He or she is thus subject to stresses and strains that are equally unique. At least five of these stresses bear mentioning.

First, the multicultural person is vulnerable. In maintaining no clear boundary and form, he or she is susceptible to confusing the profound and the insignificant, the important and the unimportant, the visionary and the reactionary. "Boundaries can be viewed," Lifton suggests,

> as neither permanent nor by definition false, but rather as essential.... We require images of limit and restraint, if only to help us grasp what we are transcending. We need distinctions between our biology and our history, all the more so as we seek to bring these together in a sense of ourselves....[24]

Without some form of boundary, experience itself has no shape or contour, no meaning and importance; where the individual maintains no critical edge to his or her existence, everything can become confusion. Experience, in order to be a particular experience, must take place amidst some essential polarity in which there is tension between two opposing forces. Where there is no sense of evil, there can be no sense of good; where nothing is profane, nothing can be sacred. Boundaries, however indefinite, give shape and meaning to the experience of experience; they allow us to differentiate, define, and determine who we are in relation to someone or something else.

Second, the multicultural person can easily become multiphrenic, that is, to use Erikson's terminology, come to have a "diffused identity."[25] Where the configuration of loyalties and identifications is constantly in flux and where boundaries are never secure, the multicultural person is open to any and all kinds of stimuli. In the face of messages which are confusing, contradictory, or overwhelming, the individual is thrown back on his or her own subjectivity to integrate and sort out what is indiscriminately taken in. Where incapable of doing this, the multicultural person is pulled and pushed by the winds of communication, a victim of what everyone else claims he or she is or should be. It is the task of every social and cultural group to define messages, images, and symbols into constructs that the individual can translate into his or her own existence. But where the messages and stimuli of all groups are given equal importance and validity, the individual can easily be overwhelmed by the demands of everyone else.

Third, the multicultural person can easily suffer from a loss of the sense of authenticity; that is, by virtue of being psychoculturally adaptive, the person can potentially be reduced to a variety of roles that bear little or no relationship to one another. The person can lose the sense of congruence and integrity that is implicit in the definition of identity itself. Roles, suggest psychologists, are constellations of behaviors that are expected of an individual because of one's place in particular social or cultural arrangements. Behind roles are the deeper threads of continuity, the processes of affect, perception, cognition, and value that make a whole of the parts. The multicultural personality can easily disintegrate into fragmented personalities that are unable to experience life along any dimension other than that which is institutionalized and routinized by family, friends, and society.

Fourth, and related to this, is the risk of being a dilettante. The multicultural person can very easily move from identity experience to identity experience without committing values to real-life situations. The energy and enthusiasm brought to bear on new situations can easily disintegrate into superficial fads and fancies in which the multicultural person simply avoids deeper responsibilities and involvements. The person becomes plastic. Flexibility disguises a self-process in which real human problems are avoided or given only superficial importance. Especially in societies where youth is vulnerable to the fabricated fads of contemporary world culture, the multicultural identity can give way to a dilettantism in which the individual flows, unimpaired, uncommitted, and unaffected, through the social, political, and economic manipulations of elites.

Fifth, and finally, the multicultural person may take ultimate psychological and philosophical refuge in an attitude of existential absurdity, mocking the patterns and lifestyles of others who are different, reacting at best in a detached and aloof way and at worst as a nihilist who sees negation as a salvation. Where the breakdown of boundaries creates a gulf that separates the individual from meaningful relationships with others, the individual may hide behind cynicisms that harbor apathy and insecurity. In such a condition nothing within and nothing outside of the individual is of serious consequence; the individual, in such a position, must ultimately scorn that which cannot be understood and incorporated into his or her own existence.

These stresses and strains should not be confused with the tensions and anxieties that are encountered in the process of cross-cultural adjustment. Culture shock is a more superficial constellation of problems that result from the misreading of commonly perceived and understood signs of social interaction. Nor is the delineation of these tensions meant to suggest that the multicultural person must necessarily harbor these various difficulties. The multicultural style of identity is premised on a fluid, dynamic movement of the self, an ability to move in and out of contexts, and an ability to maintain some inner coherence through varieties of situations. As for psychocultural style, the multicultural individual may just as easily be a great artist or a neurotic, each of whom is equally susceptible to the fundamental forces of our time. Any list of multicultural individuals must automatically include individuals who have achieved a high degree of accomplishment (writers, musicians, diplomats, etc.) as well as those women and men whose lives have, for one reason or another, been fractured by the circumstances they failed to negotiate. The artist and the neurotic lie close together in each of us, suggests Rollo May. "The neurotic," he writes, "and the artist—since both live out the unconscious of the race—reveal to us what is going to emerge endemically in the society later on...the neurotic is

the 'artiste Manque,' the artist who cannot transmute his conflicts into art."[26]

The multicultural individual represents a new kind of person
unfettered by the constricting limitations of culture as a total en-
tity. Yet, like women and men in any age, the multicultural person must negotiate the difficulties of cross-cultural contact. The
literature of cross-cultural psychology is rich with examples of
the kinds of problems encountered when people are intensely
exposed to other cultures. Integration and assimilation, for example, represent two different responses to a dominant culture,
integration suggesting the retention of subcultural differences, and
assimilation implying absorption into a larger cultural system. The
relationship between assimilation, integration, and identification,
according to E. Sommerlad and John W. Berry, suggests that if
people identify with their own group, they will hold favorable attitudes toward integration.[27] On the other hand, if they identify with
the host society, they should favor assimilation. Related to this
are the various negative attitudes, psychosomatic stresses, and
deviant behaviors that are expressed by individuals in psychologically risky situations. "Contrary to predictions stemming from
the theory of Marginal Man," writes Berry, "it tends to be those
persons more traditionally oriented who suffer the most psychological marginality, rather than those who wish to move on and
cannot."[28] The multicultural man or woman is, in many ways, a
stranger. The degree to which he or she can continually modify
the frame of reference and become aware of the structures and
functions of a group, while at the same time maintaining a clear
understanding of personal, ethnic, and cultural identifications,
may very well be the degree to which the multicultural person
can truly function successfully between cultures.

Although it is difficult to pinpoint the conditions under which
cultural identities will evolve into multicultural identities, such
changes in psychocultural style are most likely to occur where
the foundations of collective cultural identity have been shaken.
"Communities that have been exposed too long to exceptional
stresses from ecological or economic hardships," writes John E.
Cawte, "or from natural or man-made disasters, are apt to have
a high proportion of their members subject to mental disorders."[29]
Cawte's studies of the Aboriginal societies of Australia and Colin
M. Turnbull's studies of the Ik in Africa[30] document how major
threats to collective cultural identity produce social and psychological breakdown in individuals. Yet, potentially, multicultural
attitudes and values may develop where cultural interchange

takes place between cultures that are not totally disparate or where the rate of change is evolutionary rather than immediate. The reorganization of a culture, suggests J. L. M. Dawson, "results in the formation of in-between attitudes," which Dawson considers "to be more appropriate for the satisfactory adjustment of individuals in transitional situations."[31] The multicultural style, then, may be born and initially expressed in any society or culture that is faced with new exposures to other ways of life.

Conceptualization of a multicultural identity style in terms of personality types, behavior patterns, traits, and cultural background is at best impressionistic and anecdotal. Yet, the investigations of cross-cultural psychologists and anthropologists give increasing credence to the idea of a multicultural personality that is shaped and contoured by the stresses and strains which result from cultural interweaving at both the macro- and microcultural levels. Seemingly, a multicultural style is able to evolve when the individual is capable of negotiating the conflicts and tensions inherent in cross-cultural contacts. The multicultural person, then, may very well represent an affirmation of individual identity at a higher level of social, psychological, and cultural integration.

Just as the cultures of the world, if they are to merit survival amidst the onslaught of Western technologies, must be responsive to both tradition and change, so too must the individual identity be psychoculturally adaptive to the encounters of an imploding world. There is every reason to think that such human beings are emerging. The multicultural person, embodying sequential identities, is open to the continuous cycle of birth and death as it takes place within the framework of his or her psyche. The lifestyle of the multicultural person is a continual process of dissolution and reformation of identity; yet implicit in such a process is growth. Psychological movements into new dimensions of perception and experience tend very often to produce forms of personality disintegration; and disintegration, suggests Kazimierez Dabrowski, "is the basis for developmental thrusts upward, the creation of new evolutionary dynamics, and the movement of personality to a higher level...."[32] The seeds of each new identity of the multicultural person lie within the disintegration of previous identities. "When the human being," writes Erikson, "because of accidental or developmental shifts, loses an essential wholeness, he restructures himself and the world by taking recourse to what we may call *totalism*."[33] Such totalism, above and beyond being a mechanism of coping and adjustment, is a part of the growth of a new kind of wholeness at a higher level of integration.

Conclusions and Summary

This article does not suggest that the multicultural person is now the predominant character style of our time. Nor is it meant to suggest that multicultural persons, by virtue of their uninhibited way of relating to other cultures, are in any way "better" than those who are mono- or bicultural. Rather, this article argues that multicultural persons are not simply individuals who are sensitive to other cultures or knowledgeable about international affairs, but instead can be defined by a psychocultural pattern of identity that differs radically from the relatively stable forms of self-process found in the usual cultural identity pattern. This article argues that both cultural and multicultural identity processes can be conceptualized by the constellation of biological, social, and philosophical motivations involved and by the relative degrees of rigidity maintained in personal boundaries, and that such conceptualization lays the basis for comparative research.

Two final points might be noted about the multicultural personality. First, the multicultural person embodies attributes and characteristics that prepare him or her to serve as a facilitator and catalyst for contacts between cultures. The variations and flexibility of this identity style allow that person to relate to a variety of contexts and environments without being totally encapsulated by or totally alienated from any given culture. As Bochner suggests, a major problem in attempting to avert the loss of cultures in Asia and the Pacific "is the lack of sufficient people who can act as links between diverse cultural systems."[34] These "mediating" individuals incorporate the essential characteristics of the multicultural person. "Genuine multicultural individuals are very rare," he writes, "which is unfortunate because it is these people who are uniquely equipped to mediate the cultures of the world."[35] The multicultural person, then, embodies a pattern of self-process that potentially allows him or her to help others negotiate the cultural realities of a different system. With a self-process that is adaptational, the multicultural individual is in a unique position to understand, facilitate, and research the psychocultural dynamics of other systems.

Second, multiculturalism is an increasingly significant psychological and cultural phenomenon, enough so to merit further conceptualization and research. It is neither easy nor necessarily useful to reconcile the approaches of psychology and anthropology; nor is there any guarantee that interdisciplinary approaches bring us closer to an intelligent understanding of human beings as they exist in relation to their culture. Yet, the existence of multicultural people may prove to be a significant enough problem in understanding the process of culture learning (and culture unlearning) to force an integrated approach to studies of the individual and the group. "Psychologists," write Richard W. Brislin, Walter J. Lonner, and Robert M. Thorndike, "have the goal of incorporating the behavior of many cultures into one theory (*etic* approach), but they must also understand the behavior within each culture (*emic* approach)."[36] Empirical research based on strategies that can accurately observe, measure, and test behavior and that incorporate the "emic versus etic" distinction will be a natural next step. Such studies may very well be a springboard into the more fundamental dynamics of cross-cultural relationships.

We live in a transitional period of history, a time that of necessity demands parallel forms of psychocultural self-process. That a true international community of nations is coming into existence is still a debatable issue, but that individuals with a self-consciousness that is larger than the mental territory of their culture are emerging is no longer arguable. However, the psychocultural pattern of identity that allows such self-consciousness opens individuals to both benefits and pathologies. The interlinking of cultures and persons in the twentieth century is not always a pleasant process; modernization and economic development have taken heavy psychological tolls in both developed and Third-World countries. The changes brought on in our time have invoked revitalized needs for the preservation of collective, cultural identities. Yet, along with the disorientation and alienation which have characterized much of this century comes a new possibility in the way humans conceive of their individual identities and the identity of the human species. No one has better stated this possibility than Harold Taylor, himself an excellent example of the multicultural person:

> There is a new kind of [person] in the world, and there are more of that kind than is commonly recognized. He [or she] is a national citizen with international intuitions, conscious of the age that is past and aware of the one now in being, aware of the radical difference between the two, willing to accept the lack of precedents, willing to work on the problems of the future as a labor of love, unrewarded by governments, academies, prizes, and position. He [or she] forms part of an invisible world community of poets, writers, dancers, sci-

entists, teachers, lawyers, scholars, philosophers, students, citizens who see the world whole and feel at one with all its parts.[37]

[1] This article originally appeared in 1977 in *Culture Learning: Concepts, Applications, and Research*, edited by Richard W. Brislin and published by the East-West Center, The University Press of Hawaii, Honolulu. It has subsequently been reprinted in various other texts on intercultural communication, but it has been revised and updated specifically for this publication.

[2] Harold Lasswell, *The Future of World Communication: Quality and Style of Life* (Honolulu: East-West Center Communication Institute, 1972).

[3] D. Lutzker, "Internationalism as a Predictor of Cooperative Behavior," *Journal of Conflict Resolution* 4, no. 4 (1960): 426-30.

[4] Angus Campbell, Gerald Gurin, and Warren E. Miller, *The Voter Decides* (Evanston, IL: Row, Peterson, 1954).

[5] D. Sampson and H. Smith, "A Scale to Measure Worldminded Attitudes," *Journal of Social Psychology* 45 (1957): 99-106; K. Garrison, "Worldminded Attitudes of College Students in a Southern University," *Journal of Social Psychology* 54 (1961): 147-53; S. Paul, "Worldminded Attitudes of Punjab University Students," *Journal of Social Psychology* 69 (1969): 33-37.

[6] John Walsh, *Intercultural Education in the Communication of Man* (Honolulu: The University of Hawaii Press, 1973).

[7] Ibid.

[8] Paul Tillich, *The Future of Religions* (New York: Harper & Row, 1966).

[9] Stephen Bochner, "The Mediating Man and Cultural Diversity," *Topics in Culture Learning* 1 (1973): 23-37.

[10] Erik Erikson, "The Problem of Ego Identity," *Psychological Issues* 1, no. 1 (1959): 101-64.

[11] Marshall R. Singer, "Culture: A Perceptual Approach," in *Readings in Intercultural Communication*, edited by David Hoopes (Pittsburgh: Regional Council for International Education, 1971), 6-20.

[12] Anthony Wallace, "Revitalization Movements: Some Theoretical Considerations for Their Comparative Study," *American Anthropologist* 58 (1956): 264-81.

[13] Clyde Kluckhohn and Dorothea Leighton, "The Language of the Navajo Indians," in *Culture Shock*, edited by Philip Bock (New York: Alfred A. Knopf, 1970), 29-49.

[14] Benjamin Lee Whorf, *Language, Thought, and Reality: The Selected Writings of Benjamin Lee Whorf*, edited by John B. Carroll (Cambridge: Technology Press of MIT, 1957); a technical reference to the controversial literature examining the Sapir-Whorf Hypothesis can be found in "Psycholinguistics," by G. Miller and D. McNeill in volume 3 of the *Handbook of Social Psychology*, edited by Gardner Lindzey, Elliot Aronson, and Elmer R. Smith (Reading, MA: Addison-Wesley, 1968).

[15] George Peter Murdock, "Universals of Culture," in *Readings in Anthropology*, edited by Jesse Jennings and Edward Adamson Hoebel (New York: McGraw-Hill, 1955), 13-14.

[16] Abraham Maslow, *Toward a Psychology of Being* (Princeton: Van Nostrand, 1962).

[17] Charles N. Cofer and Mortimer H. Appley, *Motivation: Theory and Research* (New York: John Wiley & Sons, 1964).

[18] Kenneth Boulding, *The Image* (Ann Arbor: University of Michigan Press, 1956).

[19] Robert J. Lifton, *History and Human Survival* (New York: Vintage Books, 1961).

[20] Peter L. Berger, *The Homeless Mind: Modernization and Consciousness* (New York: Random House, 1973).

[21] Lifton, *History and Human Survival*.

[22] Michael Novak, *The Experience of Nothingness* (New York: Harper & Row, 1970).

[23] Ibid.

[24] Robert J. Lifton, *Boundaries* (New York: Vintage Books, 1967).

[25] Erik Erikson, *Insight and Responsibility* (New York: W. W. Norton, 1964).

[26] Rollo May, *Love and Will* (New York: Dell Publishing, 1969).

[27] E. Sommerlad and John W. Berry, "The Role of Ethnic Identification," in *The Psychology of Aboriginal Australians*, edited by G. E. Kearney, P. R. de Lacey, and G. R. Davidson (Sydney: John Wiley & Sons Australasia Pty Ltd., 1973), 236-43.

[28] John W. Berry, "Marginality, Stress and Ethnic Identification," *Journal of Cross-Cultural Psychology* 1 (1970): 239-52.

[29] John E. Cawte, "A Sick Society," in *The Psychology of Aboriginal Australians*, edited by G. E. Kearney, P. R. de Lacey, and G. R. Davidson (Sydney: John Wiley & Sons Australasia Pty Ltd., 1973), 365-79.

[30] Colin M. Turnbull, *The Mountain People* (New York: Simon and Schuster, 1972).

[31] J. L. M. Dawson, "Attitude Change and Conflict," *Australian Journal of Psychology* 21 (1969): 101-16.

[32] Kazimierez Dabrowski, *Positive Disintegration* (Boston: Little, Brown, 1964).

[33] Erikson, *Insight and Responsibility*.

[34] Bochner, "Mediating Man," 23-37.

[35] Ibid.

[36] Richard W. Brislin, Walter J. Lonner, and Robert M. Thorndike, *Cross-Cultural Research Methods* (New York: John Wiley & Sons, 1973).

[37] Harold Taylor, "Toward a World University," *Saturday Review* 24 (1969): 52.

Additional Readings

Often newcomers to the field ask for some basic background reading. The following texts, listed alphabetically by author, offer an overview of the field from a variety of perspectives.

Adler, Nancy J. *International Dimensions of Organizational Behavior*. 2d ed. Kent International Business Series. Boston: Wadsworth, 1990.

Althen, Gary, ed. *Learning across Cultures*. Washington, DC: NAFSA: Association of International Educators, 1994.

Banks, James A. *An Introduction to Multicultural Education*. Boston: Allyn and Bacon, 1994.

Banks, James A., and Cherry A. McGee Banks, eds. *Multicultural Education: Issues and Perspectives*. 3d ed. Boston: Allyn and Bacon, 1996.

Barnlund, Dean. *Communicative Styles of Japanese and Americans: Images and Realities*. Belmont, CA: Wadsworth, 1989.

Brislin, Richard W. *Cross-Cultural Encounters: Face-to-Face Interaction*. New York: Pergamon Press, 1981.

———. *Understanding Culture's Influence on Behavior*. Fort Worth, TX: Harcourt Brace Jovanovich, 1993.

Carbaugh, David, ed. *Cultural Communication and Intercultural Contact*. Hillsdale, NJ: Lawrence Erlbaum, 1990.

Carr-Ruffino, Norma. *Managing Diversity: People Skills for a Multicultural Workplace*. Albany, NY: International Thomson, 1996.

Condon, John C., and Fathi Yousef. *An Introduction to Intercultural Communication*. New York: Macmillan, 1975.

Gonzáalez, Alberto, Marsha Houston, and Victoria Chen. *Our Voices: Essays in Culture, Ethnicity, and Communication: An Intercultural Anthology*. 2d ed. Los Angeles: Roxbury, 1997.

Gudykunst, William B. *Bridging Differences: Effective Intergroup Communication*. 2d ed. Thousand Oaks, CA: Sage, 1994.

Gudykunst, William B., Stella Ting-Toomey, and Elizabeth Chua. *Culture and Interpersonal Communication*. Vol. 8. Interpersonal Communication Series. Newbury Park, CA: Sage, 1988.

Gudykunst, William B., Stella Ting-Toomey, and Tsukusa Nishida, eds. *Communication in Personal Relationships across Cultures*. Thousand Oaks, CA: Sage, 1996.

Gudykunst, William B., Stella Ting-Toomey, and Lea P. Stewart. *Building Bridges: Interpersonal Skills for a Changing World*. Boston: Houghton Mifflin, 1995.

Hall, Edward T. *The Silent Language*. 1959. Reprint, New York: Anchor/Doubleday, 1981.

———. *The Hidden Dimension*. 1966. Reprint, New York: Anchor/Doubleday, 1982.

———. *Beyond Culture*. 1976. Reprint, New York: Anchor/Doubleday, 1981.

Harris, Philip R., and Robert T. Moran. *Managing Cultural Differences*. 4th ed. Houston: Gulf, 1996.

Hofstede, Geert. *Cultures and Organizations: Software of the Mind*. London: McGraw-Hill, 1991.

Ivey, Allen E., Mary Bradford Ivey, and Lynn Simek-Morgan. *Counseling and Psychotherapy: A Multicultural Perspective*. Boston: Allyn and Bacon, 1993.

Kim, Uichol, Harry C. Triandis, Cigdem Kagitcibasi, Sang-Chin Choi, and Gene Yoon, eds. *Individualism and Collectivism: Theory, Method and Applications*. Thousand Oaks, CA: Sage, 1994.

Kochman, Thomas. *Black and White Styles in Conflict*. Chicago: University of Chicago Press, 1981.

Kohls, L. Robert. *Survival Kit for Overseas Living*. 3d ed. Yarmouth, ME: Intercultural Press, 1996.

Kohls, L. Robert, and John M. Knight. *Developing Intercultural Awareness: A Cross-Cultural Training Handbook*. 2d ed. Yarmouth, ME: Intercultural Press, 1994.

Lustig, Myron, and Jolene Koester. *Intercultural Competence: Interpersonal Communication across Cultures*. New York: HarperCollins, 1993.

Martin, Judith N., and Thomas K. Nakayama. *Intercultural Communication in Contexts*. Mountain View, CA: Mayfield, 1997.

Martin, Judith N., Thomas K. Nakayama, and Lisa A. Flores. *Readings in Cultural Contexts*. Mountain View, CA: Mayfield, 1998.

Matsumoto, David R. *Culture and Psychology*. Albany, NY: International Thomson, 1996.

Paige, R. Michael, ed. *Education for the Intercultural Experience*. 2d ed. Yarmouth, ME: Intercultural Press, 1993.

Ponterotto, Joseph P., and Paul Pedersen. *Preventing Prejudice: A Guide for Counselors and Educators*. Newbury Park, CA: Sage, 1993.

Pusch, Margaret D., ed. *Multicultural Education: A Cross Cultural Training Approach*. Yarmouth, ME: Intercultural Press, 1979.

Samovar, Larry A., and Richard Porter. *Communication between Cultures*. Belmont, CA: Wadsworth, 1991.

———, eds. *Intercultural Communication: A Reader*. 8th ed. Belmont, CA: Wadsworth, 1997.

Stewart, Edward C., and Milton J. Bennett. *American Cultural Patterns: A Cross-Cultural Perspective*. Rev. ed. Yarmouth, ME: Intercultural Press, 1991.

Sue, Derald W., Edwin H. Richardson, Rene A. Ruiz, and Elsie J. Smith. *Counseling the Culturally Different: Theory and Practice*. 2d ed. New York: John Wiley and Sons, 1990.

Tannen, Deborah. *Gender and Discourse*. New York: Oxford University Press, 1994.

———. *You Just Don't Understand: Women and Men in Conversation*. New York: Ballantine, 1990.

Ting-Toomey, Stella, ed. *The Challenge of Facework: Cross-Cultural and Interpersonal Issues*. Albany: State University of New York Press, 1994.

Triandis, Harry C. *Culture and Social Behavior*. New York: McGraw-Hill, 1994.

Trompenaars, Fons, and Charles Hampden-Turner. *Riding the Waves of Culture: Understanding Diversity in Global Business.* 2d ed. New York: McGraw, 1998.

Weaver, Gary R., ed. *Culture, Communication and Conflict: Readings in Intercultural Relations.* 2d ed. Needham Heights, MA: Ginn Press, 1998.

Author Index

A

Abrahams, Roger D., 138, 140
Adler, Peter S., 25, 215, 217, 222, 225
Anzaldúa, Gloria, 72, 73
Applebee, Arthur N., 71
Appley, Mortimer H., 233
Arensberg, Conrad, 220
Austin, Lewis, 117

B

Banks, James A., 69
Barna, LaRay M., 173, 185, 216, 220
Barnlund, Dean, 1, 35, 113, 218
Bateson, Gregory, 206
Becker, Ernest, 181
Benedict, Ruth, 48
Bennett, Janet M., 25, 215
Bennett, Milton J., 1, 179, 191
Berger, Peter L., 235
Berry, John W., 240
Blubaugh, Jon A., 196
Bochner, Stephen, 229, 242

Subject Index

░░

A

Activity modality, 159
Activity orientations, 159–60, 167
Adaptation. *See* Cultural adaptation
Affective memory, 136–37
Alienation, 218, 243
Altruism. *See* Sympathetic altruism
Ambiguity, 40, 42–43
Americanization, 195. *See also* Melting pot
Animism, 163
Anxiety/tension (stress), 105–06, 183–87, 215. *See also* Culture
    shock
    basic to culture shock, 184–86, 239
    defenses against, 183–84
    high level as block to communication, 183–87
    management of, 186–87
    physiological component, 186-87
Assimilation. *See* Cultural assimilation
Assumptions. *See* Cultural assumptions; Cultural patterns; Dif-
    ference, assumption of; Similarity, assumption of
Autonomy, 163–64

W

Weak hypothesis, 13
Whorf/Sapir hypothesis, 13, 15–16, 89–93, 98, 231
World community, 244. *See also* Global village
Worldview, 12, 29, 39–40, 162–63, 169, 218, 221, 227, 230
    changes in, 55, 212